Showtime at the Royal

About the Author

Thomas Myler is a well-known writer, historian, journalist and author of six previous books. He was show business and TV editor of the *Evening Herald* for many years and has written for newspapers and magazines at home and abroad, including the *Hollywood Reporter*. He writes regularly for *Ireland's Own* and lives in Dublin.

SHOWTIME AT THE ROYAL

The Story of Dublin's Legendary Theatre

Thomas Myler

The Liffey Press

Published by
The Liffey Press
Raheny Shopping Centre, Second Floor
Raheny, Dublin 5, Ireland
www.theliffeypress.com

A catalogue record of this book is
available from the British Library.

ISBN 978-1-908308-91-7

Printed in Spain by GraphyCems.

Contents

Foreword

Mary Kenny

Dublin is a beautiful city, and we Dubliners love its history and character. Yet there was a time, back in the 1960s and 1970s when there appeared a destructive mania for pulling down some of our capital's most historic edifaces. But for the valiant efforts of organizations like the Irish Georgian Society, as well as outstanding conservation champions like Father Michael Sweetman, and, as a young senator, Mary Robinson, more of Dublin's heritage might well have been destroyed.

As it was, much of the inner city was gutted – the picturesque tenements of Gardiner Street, in which Sean O'Casey memorably set his plays – were bulldozed. Admittedly, they were in a bad state, and probably in some cases a danger, but they could have been saved through re-structuring, had there been a will to do so.

There were a number of different motives behind this craze for the wrecking ball. Architects and builders saw new opportunities to create new dwellings. It was unfortunate that the decade of the 1960s, with its dedication to concrete 'brutalism', brought so much uglification. And modernisers thought it innovative to be rid of the old and archaic.

Some strong Irish nationalists also regarded anything from the past as colonialist, and such colonialist building could stretch from the Danish Vikings – whose archeological deposits are buried under a concrete block on Wood Quay – to the longest, Georgian vista in the world, known as the Georgian Mile, going from Merrion Square up to Leeson Street.

The ESB, the Electricity Supply Board, deliberately broke up that vista, and commissioned a modern concrete-block replacement for a terrace of the dazzling Georgian houses in Fitzwilliam Street. Many were the protests, in 1963, against this decision, but all in vain. Decades later, before he died in 2006, the ESB architect Sam Stephenson expressed his regret at what had occurred and the ESB sought to make amends by dedicating one of the neighbouring houses to a domestic museum of Dublin life in the eighteenth century. But when something historic is gone, it's gone.

And was the wonderful old Theatre Royal in Hawkins Street also a victim of that same zeitgeist? It was old and traditional. It was associated with an ancient regime – the very word royal indicated that. Wasn't it one of the favorite haunts of King Edward VII, who always attended the Royal when he visited Dublin in that Edwardian age named after him?

As with all these situations, there were economic arguments, too, for change. The Theatre Royal was a very big arena, with a capacity of nearly 4,000, and designed in the grand Victorian manner. It takes a lot of paying customers to fill such a huge venue. Show business was changing by the 1960s, and the sensational success of television was altering everything.

Even before TV was launched in Ireland in 1961, it had made a cultural impact in Britain, and consequently on performing artistes. Just as the cinema had killed off the music hall of the 1900s, so TV would undermine and eventually destroy the traditions of the variety show which had once been the staple fare at the Royal.

The theatre organ rising from the pit between acts was beginning to seem dated. And while everyone thought the Royalettes – that polished troupe of dancing girls modeled on the Broadway chorus lines – were fabulously glamorous, by the 1960s the seeds of feminism would start to suggest that this was no way to enhance female equality.

Thus the Royal seemed to belong to another age. And yet, this venue was, for many of our generation of Dubliners, our introduction to the gossamer world of performance, everything that Judy Garland alludes to when she belts out that great song *That's Entertainment*:

A clown with his pants falling down
Or the dance that's a dream of romance
Or the scene where the villain is mean
That's entertainment!

I am so grateful that I was taken to the Theatre Royal as a child in the 1950s, and up to my teens in the early 1960s. The experience stirred my imagination in a way that has never left me. All my life I'll remember seeing my favourite pantomime there over the Christmas of 1957, *Dick Whittington*, with Jimmy O'Dea and Danny Cummins, and the adorable Micheál MacLiammóir as the Lord Mayor's cat. The panto had everything, including an enduring message about persistence in the face of difficulties – 'Turn again, Whittington, and keep on the road.'

I have often talked about those days with my oldest Dublin friend, Tony Duff, who now lives in Italy. He so vividly recalls some of the childhood memories we both shared from that time. Tony says that a visit to the Royal as a child was responsible for him falling in love – with theatre, opera and spectacle.

A matinee at the Royal included a movie, a stage show and in between the two, Tommy Dando, with his introduction 'Keep Your Sunny Side Up – *Up!*' on the organ. This was extremely popular with the audience. For the stage show, the conductor Jimmy Campbell appeared, sleek as a well-groomed cat, with Clark Gable moustache – and highly disciplined. He was a consummate professional.

Then came the Royalettes – usually in gleaming white tap shoes, going thrillingly clackety-clack, who were put through their paces by the admired dance duo Alice Dalgarno and Babs de Monte. As a stylistic quirk, the last Royalette in line usually exited winking at the audience and kicking a leg backwards.

Music was central to the Royal's repertoire, and the soprano Patricia Cahill was compared, by her enthusiastic fans, to Maria Callas. The penultimate act at the Royal shows was often a grand guest artiste. I remember Lena Horne in that slot, also the epitome of glamour.

The Royal also put on high-minded productions such as Handel's *Messiah*. Tony remembers: 'The imperial Archbishop of Dublin, John Charles McQuaid, sweeping in in his crimson robes flanked by lines of acolytes – almost as good as a Royalette sequence in its low camp!'

Oh yes, the Royal thrilled our imagination. My lifelong passion for ballet started with a 1950's *Swan Lake* by a visiting ballet company.

It was so sad when it closed down, and it seemed awful for Dublin's skyline that it was replaced by a noticeably unattractive office building. But now Thomas Myler's research has thrillingly re-captured the Royal's spirit. Anyone with an association with Dublin's heritage should be grateful to Thomas for giving us this unique account, and restoring to our memories that great landmark by the Liffey.

And who knows what the future may bring? In the 1960s and 70s, we feared that all of Dublin's architectural heritage might disappear. Yet a new generation took a different view, and invested a sense of pride in conservation and restoration. Some of Dublin's Georgian heritage was restored, and modernisation took place behind the eighteenth century facade.

We have learned much better how to mix and match the old with the new. It is not beyond the realms of imagination that the Theatre Royal could once again rise from the ashes – different from what went before, and yet echoing and maintaining the continuity of the tradition. If so, it will be in no small measure due to this excellent book.

Mary Kenny is a Dublin-born writer, journalist, broadcaster and playwright.

Acknowledgements

Any work of this kind has to depend on a great many people including the many fine authors of books about the entertainment industry, whether dealing with the stage, television, radio or the cinema. This one is no exception. All books are fully credited in the bibliography but in this regard it would not be amiss to note the standard work by the late historian and author Philip B. Ryan. *The Lost Theatres of Dublin*, first published in 1998, is the definitive chronicle of the 11 Dublin theatres no longer on the landscape and of the many great artistes who performed in them. This book often refers to material in Ryan's book and is duly acknowledged. His daughter Deborah was most helpful in this regard.

Thanks too must go to the celebrated author and journalist Mary Kenny for her enthusiasm and kindness in writing the foreword. Of immense help too were artistes who helped with interviews including Patricia Cahill, the Bachelors, Val Doonican and Carmel Quinn as well as RTÉ broadcasters John Murray and Larry Gogan. Linda Doherty, daughter of crooner Frankie Blowers, kindly gave me access to the family album, as did the actor Eddie Byrne's two daughters Catherine and Susan.

This book would not have been possible without the help of sources such as *Independent News and Media* which supplied many of the photographs, as did *Photoshop*, the *Press Association* and Channel

Acknowledgements

Four's Stills Department. Some pictures are from the author's own collection.

Freelance photographer Aidan Walsh also supplied prints as did the many people who answered the request published in the *Irish Independent* and *Irish Times* for photographs as well as information, clippings and programmes. The excellent picture of Patricia Cahill with her dogs is by Zita Bolton.

Some asked to be anonymous but sincere thanks to Pat Foley, John Devitt, Therese Coffey, Andrew Crockart, Sheila O Callaghan, John Swift, Robert and Mary Hayes, Donal O Colmain, Pauline Allen, Maura Bradner, Thomas A. Menton and Nicholas Charlesworth. Also extremely helpful was the staff of *Ireland's Own*, such as Shea Tomkins, Sean O'Sullivan and Phil Murphy. Needless to remark, my family were always supportive, as usual. My one regret is that my loving and devoted wife Betty never saw the finished product. She passed away after a relatively short illness in December 2013.

Last but certainly not least, a big thank you to The Liffey Press for such a lovely job of work. In this regard, credit is due to publisher David Givens for his continued faith in the project.

Apologies to anybody who has been inadvertently left out, as many photographs sent in were uncredited. Any omissions will gladly be rectified in future editions.

Remembering Betty, for her love and devotion

Prologue

I'm part of what was Dublin in the rare old times
– Pete St John

The rare old times of 1962 seem like only yesterday. In October the world would watch in disbelief as President John F. Kennedy and his Soviet counterpart Nikita Krushchev waged a battle of nerves over what would become known as the Cuban Missile Crisis. Five months earlier, Russia had supplied missiles to Communist Cuba, and US intelligence discovered that much of the east coast was within reach of these warheads.

In August photographs of launch sites by the US spy plane U-2 were delivered to Kennedy. After considering the alternatives, he ordered a naval blockade of Cuba and warned that US armed forces would seize offensive weapons and associated material which Soviet vessels were trying to deliver to Cuba. Khrushchev backed down and the Cuban Missile Crisis was over before it really began.

In other major news of 1962, a brand new movie hero was launched in October with the first Bond film, *Dr No* starring Sean Connery, who had received his early start in the Disney movie about a leprechaun, *Darby O'Gill and the Little People*. The Beatles burst on to the music scene in February with their first single 'Love Me Do,' which made the charts at No. 15.

July saw the launching of Telstar, the first commercially developed satellite, which promised to change the broadcasting of pictures quite dramatically and make worldwide television possible for the future. In August, movie queen Marilyn Monroe was found dead in bed at her Hollywood apartment, and in August, Vatican II opened, after Pope John XXIII had announced its setting up three years earlier.

At home, the first edition of *The Late Late Show*, intended as a six-week summer filler and hosted by newcomer Gay Byrne, was screened in July by Telefís Éireann. In GAA in September, Tipperary retained the All-Ireland senior hurling title with a 3-10 to 2-11 win over Wexford, and in the football decider, Kerry beat Roscommon 1-12 to 1-6 in what were the first All-Ireland finals to be televised live on the home station.

In November, Aer Lingus hostesses wore their new 'fern green and St Patrick's blue' uniforms for the first time. The year also saw the launching of two music groups who would make a significant impact on the international stage, the Dubliners and the Chieftains.

Then there was the night of 30 June in Dublin when the big heavy curtain came down on the Theatre Royal stage for a last time, leaving the way clear for the demolition workers to move in a few days later and leave the famous old building a heap of rubble. The 12-storey Department of Health now stands on the site.

The Royal, as it was known to generations of not only Dubliners but all over the nation, played an important role in the cultural and social life of the capital for 300 years. There had been no less than three previous Royals, but this one in Hawkins Street was the most successful. It opened in 1935 and now, in 1962, sadly it was no more.

With a capacity of 3,850 and under the guidance of impresario Louis Elliman, known affectionately as 'Mr Louis', it became the premier entertainment venue in the land. It was not only the biggest theatre in Ireland but the largest in Europe, with the lone exception of one in Germany.

The Theatre Royal, Ireland's most famous showplace

Ireland had never seen anything quite like it, nothing on its scale. There were two performances a day, a stage show under the musical direction of Jimmy Campbell and his 25-piece orchestra, the latest new movie in town, and you could have a meal in the restaurant. Visits to the Royal were so popular that many people were said to have left 'lifetime' tickets to their children in their wills.

On that final night, many a tear was shed not only by the capacity attendance but by the many artistes on the last bill. It was the Palace of Dreams, giving the public the opportunity of seeing all the great stars in concert. For a few hours, one could forget their troubles and be transported into a magical world. The late 1940s, 1950s and into the 1960s saw the Royal at its magical best.

It must be remembered that in those years Ireland, with its mass emigration and high unemployment, was teetering on the brink of economic failure, though in fairness, it was not all gloom and despondency, despite what many eminent historians would have us believe. Not *all* children went around in their bare feet, a fact that this writer, born in a Liberties tenement in Patrick Street, directly opposite the cathedral, can testify to.

All the same, times were tough until they got better. Families who were born in and had lived in decaying tenements, which had once been fine old houses but gradually abandoned by the aristocracy, were moved out into the suburbs, to places like Cabra, Crumlin, Drimnagh and other locations, where their houses had front gardens for the first time.

Others moved to blocks of flats such as those in Bridgefoot Street, James's Street, Marrowbone Lane and other areas. These were small, generally with one bedroom, but still luxurious as compared to where the families had been. Nevertheless, many families resented having their roots pulled up, taken away from their neighbours they had known all their lives and bidding farewells to the familiar shops and public houses they frequented.

The many cinemas which dotted the city and suburbs were in many ways the great escape for Dubliners, as were the theatres including the Queen's, the Capitol, the Olympia and of course the 'serious' playhouses such as the Abbey and the Gate. But for so many, the Theatre Royal was the best, *the* place to visit. It was known simply as 'the Royal.'

The list of international stars who appeared on its big stage over the years reads like the index to a who's who of entertainment. It included Bob Hope, Judy Garland, Maurice Chevalier, Joan Hammond, James Cagney, Danny Kaye, Gene Autry, Roy Rogers, Tom Mix, Nat 'King' Cole, Frankie Vaughan, Paul Robeson, George Formby, Anna Neagle, the Three Stooges, Frankie Laine, Johnnie Ray, Guy Mitchell,

Allan Jones, Jimmy Durante, the Mills Brothers, Max Miller, Ramon Novarro, Rock Hudson, Barbara Rush, Robert Donat, Betty Hutton, Tommy Steele, Donald Wolfit and many more.

And if you wanted a touch of the classics, you had the likes of Margot Fonteyn, Yehudi Menuhin, Arthur Rubenstein, Sir Thomas Beecham, Jussi Bjorling and Lauritz Melchior. The visiting stars either stayed in hotels or lodgings in and around Parnell Square, and the landlords and landladies were only too happy to welcome such famous stars on their doorsteps and get their autographs, often on photos.

There were the big bands, too, including Joe Loss, Geraldo, Stan Kenton, Billy Cotton, Harry Roy, Ambrose, Mantovani, Henry Hall, Jack Jackson, Johnny Dankworth, Ray Noble, Jack Hilton and the group who ushered in the new rock 'n 'roll era, the sensational Bill Haley and His Comets with their ground-breaking hits including 'Rock Around the Clock', 'Shake Rattle and Roll' and 'See You Later, Alligator.'

What other theatre in this part of the world, outside of London perhaps, could boast such a 'cast list'. Indeed, it was said in theatrical circles that if artistes or bands did not play the Royal, then they really had not made it. The reputation of the theatre was so widespread and respected that top names in Britain and the US always insisted to their managements or agents that playing the Royal in Dublin was an essential part of their trip, a must stop-over. And the managements/agents dared not disagree.

Danny Kaye was once quoted that he had very happy memories of appearing in the Royal and noted: 'What a great loss when it was pulled down.' Judy Garland remembered: 'The Theatre Royal was a wonderful theatre and I had a very happy time there. I got a wonderful reception and the audiences were so responsive.'

There were several visits by touring circuses, and boxing tournaments always pulled in the crowds. Films of famous fights in the US and Britain were flown to Dublin and shown just days after the results in the days before television, YouTube and mobile phones. Charity events, benefits and celebrity concerts were certain to fill seats, and major movies were shown from the early 1930s, not long after talking pictures revolutionised the motion picture industry.

The Irish stars who tread the boards at the Royal included Count John McCormack, Jimmy O'Dea, Noel Purcell, Cecil Sheridan, Danny Cummins, Frankie Blowers, Josef Locke, Margaret Burke Sheridan, Ruby Murray, Peggy Dell, Mickser Reid, Eddie Byrne, the Bachelors, Val Doonican, Eamonn Andrews, Albert Sharpe, the celebrated Abbey actor and movie star F. J. McCormick and newcomers like Frank Carson, Dave Allen and Chris Casey.

Not forgetting the high-stepping line-up of showgirls, the Royalettes, who put a real touch of glamour into the shows and were equal to any chorus line in any part of the world not excluding London, New York or Paris. At one time Bob Geldof's mother worked at the Royal as a cashier.

Val Doonican, the Waterford singer and international star, got his start in the Royal as part of the Four Ramblers, a close harmony group. 'My days at the Royal are a far off memory but they are very vivid in my mind and I am very proud and privileged to be able to look back all those years with great fondness,' he would recall.

Deirdre Purcell, the best-selling author born and raised in Dublin, remembered: 'We sure got value for our admission ticket at the Royal, with a Marx Brothers, Laurel and Hardy or a Charlie Chaplin film, a variety show, which frequently included a complete one-act play, comedy sketches, Jimmy Campbell's live orchestra, an audience participation quiz with a prize of half a crown, and in the interval, many people's favourite, Tommy Dando on the Compton organ.

'The house lights came on and the curtains swished open to show a blank white screen and then, to the thunderous strains of "Keep Your Sunny Side Up, *Up*!" Tommy, chubby on the little seat attached

6

to the massive theatre organ, rose smoothly from the orchestra pit into a rainbow of light. He rode that organ as though it were an unruly yearling, pounding and pedalling to get the last ounce of power out of it.

'After "Sunny Side", we clapped, cheered and then cleared our throats because we knew what was coming. And there it was, up on the screen, the words of the next song. A flourish from Tommy and all we had to do was to follow the bounding ball as it hopped shakily from word to word.

'Sometimes it fell behind us, or sometimes it ran ahead or even disappeared but it didn't matter. We knew where we were going. We gave ourselves huge rounds of applause. We risked damage to the carpet with our stamping invitation to "come into the parlour" because we were Irish and there was a welcome for us on the mat. We swayed in our seats and even held hands with the perfect stranger in the next seat.'

Deirdre's comments evoke wonderful memories of times past. I worked in London and Birmingham for periods in the 1950s but on return visits to Dublin I always made sure that trips to the Theatre Royal were imperative. I have fond recollections of going to see many of the popular entertainers of the day, local and visiting stars.

Even if some of us did not have the price of admission, or were working late or couldn't get to the show on time or for whatever reason, we could always hang around and wait for the star to make an appearance from the dressing room window high above the stage door in Poolbeg Street where he or she would wave to the fans. And if the star were a singer, always a few bars of one of their best-known songs – and the fans were rarely if ever disappointed.

I was fortunate to have secured a job as a reporter in Dublin with the *Evening Mail* in June, 1960 and, to my great pleasure and surprise, my duties included covering the regular shows at the Royal. Those were indeed the rare old times. When the theatre sadly closed for the

The author as a reporter with the Evening Mail in 1960

last time on the night of 30 June 1962 I was there for the *Mail*, and when I look at the programme today, the memories all come flooding back, like the dam gates opening and the water gushing through.

What memories! The Dublin comedian Cecil Sheridan, who was in the big cast for the last show, would describe the Royal as a place with 'a big heart, big capacity and big audiences.' How true. So now, the house lights have slowly dimmed and there's the overture by the Jimmy Campbell Orchestra. It's curtain up again and I hope you have as good a time reading about the rise and fall of the Theatre Royal, Dublin's very own Palace of Dreams, as I had researching and writing it. As they say, there's no business like show business. Enjoy the journey.

1

The Barefooted Dublin Urchin
Who Became a Star

It all started with a cup of tea with the King of England over 350 years ago. John Ogilby, a Scottish impresario well known for his translations and skills as a cartographer, left his Dublin home for London in 1661 at the invitation of King Charles II to talk over plans for a new theatre in his adopted city. Ogilby always had a vision to provide Dublin with a proper playhouse that natives could be proud of, and to invite works by world famous playwrights with great actors appearing in them.

Ogilby had a long and pleasant chat with King Charles II, recently restored to the throne. The result was that the Scot returned to Dublin with permission from the king to raise £4,500 to build the theatre, and given the rather grandiose-sounding titles of 'Historiographer to His Majesty' and 'Master of the Revels in the Kingdom of Ireland.'

His duties as historiographer would entail keeping records, and the Revels would be a body responsible to the Lord Chamberlain for overseeing and paying for entertainments. The Revels would later be extended to the full responsibility of the stage, becoming effectively a censorship organisation as well as other duties.

Ogilby previously had a theatre in 1637 situated near Christ Church cathedral in Werburgh Street, a location probably more associated for many years and up to the present day with Burdocks'

*Seventeenth century
impresario John Ogilby*

fish and chip shop than anything else. Known as the New Theatre and built at a cost of £2,000, it was the first custom-built theatre in the city. During its brief history, however, it never managed to attract spectators in sufficient numbers to make it pay.

In a desperate effort to attract more punters, the enterprising Ogilby occasionally put on boxing matches, cudgelling, bear bating and cock fighting contests, and these evenings seemed to have been the only times that the theatre managed to attract good crowds. In particular, bear baiting and cock fighting were very popular sports, although whether they can be referred to as 'sports' is highly debatable. There were many references to both these practices in the Dublin newspapers at the time.

In 1639, Ogilby was able to dispense with the bear bating, cock fighting and the rest when he presented a long run of the play *Landgartha* by Henry Burnell, a Dublin-born playwright, politician and landowner. A tragic-comedy, and Burnell's only surviving work, the play holds the distinction of being the first by an Irish playwright produced in an Irish theatre.

In 1641, however, it was closed down by the Puritans, an activist movement within the Church of England which apparently had more powers than the Revels. Dublin was without a proper theatre for many years until Ogilby, a theatre man at heart, finally sent his famous telegram to King Charles II and set about his ambitious plan to build his new venture, the Theatre Royal in Smock Alley, a narrow street once known as Smoke Alley, alongside the River Liffey and now known as Exchange Street in the Temple Bar quarter.

Ogilby raised the necessary finance by asking the citizens of the day to support his vision, and through Dublin Castle he received a royal patent allowing it to be called the Theatre Royal.

Opened in 1662 after many delays, it turned out to be a hugely popular venue and staged mainly Shakespearean classics before full houses. There was a close affinity between the Theatre Royal/Smock Alley and the more famous Theatre Royals in London, at Drury Lane and Covent Garden. Many of the London artistes appeared in Smock Alley and vice versa. It seemed a good arrangement as Irish audiences were given opportunities to see many top performers they would not otherwise have had an occasion to watch.

Katherine Philips, the first Englishwoman to enjoy widespread public acclaim as a poet during her lifetime, came to Dublin in late 1662 to pursue her husband's claim to certain Irish estates. While there, she completed a translation of Pierre Corneille's *Pompee* and produced it with great success at Smock Alley. While other women had translated or written dramas, Katherine's translation of *Pompee* broke new ground as the first rhymed version of a French tragedy in English, and the first play written by a woman to be performed on the professional stage.

In the following years, as the theatre was built on land claimed from the River Liffey, the gallery collapsed. Three people were killed and many others injured. Effectively, there seemed to be something of a jinx on the theatre. In 1701, during disturbances there a number of people were killed. Soon after, it was burned to the ground but was rebuilt in 1735 on the same site.

The *General Evening Post* of 24 May 1735 reported: 'Yesterday was begun the building of the new Theatre Royal in Smock Alley, the foundation stone being laid in presence of the Gentlemen of Distinction. Several pieces of gold were given to the workmen to drink

Thomas Sheridan

their majesties' health and wish success to the undertaking. This house is erected pursuant to his Majesty's Royal Patent, and will be as complete a theatre as any in Europe.'

It was opened later that year and for a time was managed by the actor manager Thomas Sheridan, father of the renowned playwright and politician Richard Brinsley Sheridan. An ambitious figure with a flair for publicity and organisation skills, he made many improvements and gave Irish audiences an opportunity of seeing not only his father's plays, but those of George Farquhar and Oliver Goldsmith.

Farquhar was a Derryman who studied at Trinity College Dublin and later went to London where he gained a reputation for his contributions to Restoration comedy. He also did Shakespeare. Goldsmith was born in a tumbledown farmhouse at Pallas, a small hamlet to the east of Ballymahon in County Longford. His father was the Rev. Charles Goldsmith, curate in the local Forgney Church. Like Farquhar, Goldsmith went to Trinity College Dublin before leaving for London and gaining international fame as a poet, essayist and dramatist.

Sheridan also laid claim to introducing to Irish audiences the actress who would later become 'the Grande Dame of Tragedy on the American stage', Charlotte Melmoth. She began her illustrious career at the Theatre Royal, and always spoke well of 'her new life'. Sheridan too gave Royal audiences a chance to appreciate the acting talents of Donegal's Charles Macklin and a local star, Spranger Barry.

In 1742, Sheridan introduced to Royal patrons the English actor David Garrick, considered the greatest Shakespearean performer of his day. With him was his live-in lover Peg Woffington, an established actress from Dublin who had recently appeared with him at the Theatre Royal, Drury Lane, after starting her career in her native city.

Peg's story is a most extraordinary one, and could have come from the pages of fiction. On a cold, wet evening in October 1727 in Dublin, a barefooted urchin of about seven years of age from the slums tottered along Ormond Quay supporting a heavy earthenware jug of water from the River Liffey on her head. It was for her mother who took in washing and had tried to run a little grocery shop but failed.

The drenching rain soaked her thin frock and inadequate shawl as she watched one or two coaches rattling clip-clop over the uneven cobble-stoned street, designed so as horses could get a better grip on the surface.

A few passersby with heads bowed low and cloaks drawn tightly around them as protection against the bitter wind and sweeping rain ignored the child shivering in her wet rags and seeking shelter in a doorway, weeping in her misery.

Unaware that she had been followed by a lady who now sought the protection of the doorway, the stranger said in a soft voice: 'You look very cold, my child.' The little girl raised her eyes in surprise and replied simply: 'Yes, ma'am.'

'And what is your name, my child?' asked the stranger in a soft, foreign accent.

'Peg, ma'am,' said the urchin, wiping the rain off her face. 'Peg Woffington. Margaret is my birth name.'

Encouraged by the mysterious stranger, Peg told her story. She lived nearby in George's Court, off Dame Street, and since this was washday, she had been helping her mother by carrying jugs of water all day for the washing. She had a baby sister Polly. Their father had been a bricklayer and she learned from her mother that he hated doctors, and did not trust them.

When he fell ill with a fever, he fiercely refused to have a physician summoned. As it happened he rapidly grew better. As he was convalescing, he developed a fever again and Mrs. Woffington called the local doctor. The physician looked at Peg's father, gave him a few pills and assured him he was out of danger. The next day he died, leaving nothing for young Peg, her mother and baby sister. He was buried in a pauper's grave.

'That was about six or seven years ago, so that's my story, ma'am,' said Peg to the stranger, adding, 'I must be going now because me mother will be wondering where I am and what's been keeping me.'

'I will go with you Peg, and meet your mother. I am Madame Violante. Perhaps you have heard my name?'

'Are you Madame Violante, the same lady who dances on the tightrope in the booth in Fownes Court, with a live baby hanging from each foot?'

'That's me. Now how would you like to dance on the rope yourself.'

'Oh, ma'am, I'd be delighted.'

'Very well then. I will teach you and someday you will be able to do it and be very successful at it. But first we must talk it over with your mother. Let's go and see her.'

As they walked together, Peg could imagine herself balanced on a tightrope high above the heads of applauding crowds and wearing beautiful dresses with spangles and a dazzling silver star on her forehead.

Continuing with her story, she told Madame Violante how the family had become impoverished when her father died and how she helped her mother with the washing all day long. It was very hard work but she did it without complaining. She said she also sold oranges at the Theatre Royal in Smock Alley to help the family make ends meet, and often got the odd penny by selling watercress from a basket outside Trinity College.

Peg directed her new friend to a dimly-lit George's Court and her mother welcomed the stranger in the mistaken belief that she was another customer who wanted her clothes washed in the tub.

'Mother, this is the lady who dances on the tight rope in Fownes Court and she was looking forward to meeting you,' said Peg.

Madame Violante explained she had been struck by the natural beauty and grace of Mrs.Woffington's little daughter. 'I am convinced she has a great future on the stage,' she said. She was impressed with Peg's seemingly natural creamy complexion, perfect white teeth, dark expressive eyes and thick black hair – perhaps the young Elizabeth Taylor of her day. Madame Violante was offering to take Peg on as an apprentice and teach her the act of tightrope dancing.

'It's a good opportunity for Peg,' she said. 'I've been in the business for a long time and there are good openings for newcomers to learn the tricks of the trade. She would earn a good salary in a short time and I will dress and support her in the meantime. What do you think?'

Mrs. Woffington had been silent as she listened to the stranger. When Madame Violante finished, she said in a highly sceptical tone: 'Thank you for your interest, miss, but I don't think it's a good idea. Nobody in the family down the years has ever been in your business in any shape or form and I don't think Peg is going to be the first.

'I will look after Peg and her sister with the work I do, taking in the washing and we can manage, thank you.'

The two women parted with a handshake but not before Madame Violante asked Mrs Woffington to consider her proposition and that they would keep in touch. Peg's mother did think hard about it and came to the realisation that if this new plan brought in a little extra money, what was wrong with that.

So it came to pass that a week or so later Peg made her debut in the booth in Fownes Court by dancing and skipping about the stage. As the weeks went on, she got to sing some songs Madame Violante taught her, much to the delight of the audiences who tossed pennies on to the stage which she duly gave to her mother.

But with public taste being notoriously fickle, especially in the entertainment world, customers began to tire of Madame Violante's tightrope act, as outstanding as it was and that it had never been seen in Dublin before. Gradually, attendances fell away and the show closed.

Madame Violante, however, was an enterprising woman. She became aware of a recent London production which had caused tremendous excitement called *The Beggar's Opera*, written by the poet John Gay, with music arranged by Johann Christoph Pepuschted. A ballad opera in three acts, it had premiered at the Lincoln's Inns Fields Theatre in January 1728 and ran for 62 consecutive performances, the longest run in theatre history up to that time.

She formed a company of children, which included 10-year-old Peg, and cast them in the parts of the juvenile opera which she presented in a new and more commodious booth in George's Court. The principal role of Polly Peachum was given to Peg Woffington. It was an immediate success and the booth was packed for the opening performance.

Peg was a natural. Her vivacity, wit and humour, amazing memory and adaptability were apparent not long after she made her appearance on stage. She would admit during the interval that her voice was not particularly strong, but Madame Violante assured her that her range and projection were fine. She herself had gone down to the back of the booth and could hear her perfectly. It is worth remembering that this was the age before microphones.

Wrote a contemporary reviewer: 'Peg's old friends and admirers from Trinity College, who, when this lovely girl with the blue, black hair and the liquid eyes came forward, received her with an ovation that sent her nervousness to flight.'

Looking back in later years, Madame Violante told friends: 'Peg was a genuine trouper and never missed an opportunity of trying to improve herself. She was never really satisfied with her performance, which I suppose is the mark of the true performer.'

Among those impressed with Peg's performance was the Irish playwright and composer Charles Coffey, who came to see her. He had written a ballad opera *The Beggar's Wedding*, obviously on the strength of John Gay's *The Beggar's Opera*, and it met with some success on London stages. Coffey felt a Dublin production would go down well and when he suggested this to Madame Violante and her protégé, the response was very enthusiastic.

It was performed in the George's Court booth and turned out to be sensational. Audiences and critics literally fell over themselves to heap praise on the young Dublin girl.

'You have a fine actress there in Peg Woffington, Miss Violante,' said Coffey. 'Much is going to be heard from her, I can assure you.'

Coffey's words were prophetic. After Coffey gave her the lead in his comedy *The Devil to Pay*, which was another big success, Peg was sought after by Dublin nobility who seemed honoured to be in her company. Being very impressionable but clever, she quickly found herself fitting in well with her newly found friends and acquaintances.

Peg's mode of speech improved, as did her manners, just as she had learned singing and stage presentation from Coffey and her knowledge of French from Madame Violante. For some time after that, Peg returned to small parts and sang ballads under Miss Violante's management until the latter found herself in financial difficulties and had to let her go from the booth.

Not all the new tenants wanted to present plays and operas, and gradually the booth closed down. Luckily for Peg, she had already earned her reputation as a fine performer and actress. John

Elrington, manager of the Theatre Royal in Smock Alley, had seen her perform in George's Court and gave her parts in operas and farces, as well as dance routines. Though very beautiful, she often played old or disfigured characters.

On 17 February 1737, Peg was offered her first important role at the Royal, and purely by accident. The play was *Hamlet, Prince of Denmark* and 48 hours before the performance, the lady who was cast in the role of Ophelia fell ill. Suddenly at the loss of such an important member of the cast, Erlington wanted to cancel the production but was persuaded by some of his associates to look for another actress.

'Where can I find one at such short notice?' he asked. When somebody suggested Peg Woffington, he said that while he thought she was a fine performer, he doubted if she was good enough for such a demanding role as Ophelia in what was arguably Shakespeare's finest tragedy.

It was suggested that he give her an audition, with the result that he was totally impressed and had her name announced in the playbills to play the part of the tragic heroine. When the curtain went up on her first night before a full house, Peg was naturally nervous, always a sign of producing a fine performance, and predictably she performed flawlessly.

When the curtain fell, the applause was warm and enthusiastic. The production was saved and, more importantly, Peg was a star – at the age of 19. She had successfully tackled the difficult role of the young noblewoman of Denmark, one of only two female characters in the play.

Contemporary reports said that 'Peg held her audience as if by a spell,' and had scored 'a major theatrical triumph.' She was now an actress of considerable stature with great promise for the future. From this date on she no longer sang ballads in minor roles or danced

between acts. Only big parts. Peg Woffington was on her way to becoming a
real star.

Peg's next important role, again at
the Royal, was that of Phyllis in *The
Conscious Lovers* by the Dublin playwright Sir Richard Steele. The play had
been a big success in London earlier,
packing out the Theatre Royal, Drury
Lane, and there was no reason to doubt
that it would do the same in Dublin.
It did not disappoint, receiving glowing reviews, notably in the *Manchester
Guardian*, which would become simply

*Derry-born dramatist
George Farquhar*

the *Guardian* in 1959 and said to be co-founded by Steele himself,
although this claim has been denied.

The newspaper described the play as 'a departure from the popular comedies of the day, and impressed on the audience the primacy
and morality over lewd jokes and licentious behaviour.'

For two seasons Peg played many leading roles, both here, Paris
and London, notably in *The Constant Couple*, a comedy by the Derry
dramatist George Farquhar and which would become a mainstay
of her repertoire for the next two decades. With a tricky plot about
cross-purposes and cross-dressing, and in which she appeared as a
woman fully attired as a man, Peg played Sir Harry Wildair to great
acclaim, a well-bred rake of quality. She caused quite a stir in this part
by wearing breeches.

Peg would, in fact, be setting a trend in breeches roles, which
would become very fashionable stage wear in later years, and the
vogue for ladies to take on male roles in pantomimes as the principal
boy in such productions as *Dick Whittington, Aladdin* and *Jack the
Giant Killer*. It's a trend that still exists today so Peg Woffington, the

eldest daughter of a destitute Dublin washerwoman, was setting a new fashion over 300 years ago. She succeeded in changing around trends, moving away from the somewhat stodgy, dull, tightly-corseted style of the Victorian era and into the rather liberated 1770s.

Meanwhile, around this time in her fledging career Peg fell in love with Nicholas Taaffe, an Irish peer, in Dublin. The feeling was mutual and they were considered a happy couple on the streets of the capital. They planned to marry, and Taaffe persuaded her to leave the stage for a while and settle down. They travelled to London and took up residence in York Street, Covent Garden. All went well with the happy couple in the first few months as they enjoyed the many attractions of the big city, and attended theatres and art galleries, although as yet, there was no indication that Taaffe planned to marry Peg.

Gradually, however, Taaffe seemed to grow distant from her and whenever she asked him what was wrong, he would dismiss it with a wave of his hand. 'I'll be all right, my love. I suffer from pangs of depression now and again,' he assured her. Eventually, Taaffe would disappear for days on end, sometimes even weeks. When Peg would ask him where he was, he would tell her he had property interests in Ireland.

One day he told her he would have to spend about three weeks in Ireland as there had been problems with his property. He had gone scarcely a week when Peg learned that he had been unfaithful. She discovered that he had been seeing 'a young lady of quality and fortune' named Miss Dallaway, an alleged heiress, and that they planned to marry when he returned to London.

Shocked but undaunted by events, Peg challenged Taaffe on his return to explain his alleged actions. He admitted that yes, he had an affair but it had been a mistake and that he had broken off the relationship with Miss Dallaway. However, Peg was unconvinced but let the matter lie for the moment. Secretly, though, she resolved to get her revenge on Taaffe and his lover, and expose him for what he really was, a cheat. After all, his family had said that he was always something of a rake and attempted to disassociate themselves from him. Peg had heard this but felt she could change him.

But it was now too late, far too late. Drastic action was needed. What was it the poet William Congreve said: 'Heaven has no rage like love to hatred turned, Nor hell a fury like a woman scorned.' Here was a chance to put it into practice.

Peg knew that Miss Dallaway frequented the fashionable Vauxhall Gardens, but she knew she herself would not be admitted unaccompanied as a single female. Remembering how successful she had been in the role of Sir Harry Wildair on the stage, she dressed up as a young man in fashionable attire.

As Peg's biographer J. Fitzgerald Molloy put it so eloquently in his book *The Life and Adventures of Peg Woffington*, published in 1884: 'Attired in silken hose and satin breeches with broidered waistcoat and wide flapped coat, powered, painted and bewigged, Peg met her rival discreetly and informed her that Taaffe had made love to her for purely mercenary motives while conducting an affair with an actress whom he had brought to London from Ireland.

'The letters she produced, some of recent date, bearing Taaffe's seal and addressed to Peg Woffington, spoke of love and faithfulness for the actress. The horrified Miss Dallaway terminated her association with her deceitful lover, and Peg, a woman scorned, had her revenge in a fantastically unusual way.'

Now to put that failed affair behind her and resume her career. The Theatre Royal management in Dublin wanted Peg back but there were demands from the London stage too. She promised Dublin she would not forget them when time and circumstances allowed.

Soon the impresario and man-of-many-trades and professions John Rich entered the picture. At one time actor-manager of the Duke's Company at Lincoln's Inns Fields Theatre in London, in 1728 he commissioned *The Beggar's Opera* from John Gay. The success of

Impresario John Rich

this venture provided him with the capital to build the Covent Garden Theatre, designed by Edward Shepherd at the site of an ancient convent garden and church. The theatre is now the Royal Opera House. A Royal Charter created a fruit and vegetable market in the area, hence the name Covent Garden. The market survived in that location until 1974.

On 7 December 1732, Rich was carried by his actors in processional triumph into the theatre for its opening production of William Congreve's *The Way of the World.*

Peg had come across Rich's name in reviews and decided to seek an interview with him with the object of getting into one of his productions. When she called at his home in Bloomsbury Square, Rich, a notorious eccentric, refused to see her because she had not sent in her name in advance. She returned and handed her name on a piece of paper to his butler, but Rich still refused, saying he was 'too busy and come back another time.'

Peg called again and told the servant to announce that 'Miss Peg Woffington requested to meet the master of the house.' He came out, apologised for the long delay in arranging a meeting, and told the washerwoman's daughter that he knew all about her and her magnificent achievements on the stage in London and in Dublin. Yes, he would be delighted to have her perform at his theatre.

'My first meeting with Rich never ceased to amaze me,' Peg told friends later. 'Entering his lavish room, I found him lounging on a sofa, book in one hand, a china cup from which he eventually sipped tea in the other. Around him were 20 or 30 cats engaged in the various occupations of staring fixedly at him, and frisking round his shoulders and about his person. It was incredible, and I had never seen anything like it.'

Rich offered her a salary of nine pounds per week, with the contract stipulating that she should make her first appearance before the British public before the end of the year as Sylvia in George Farquhar's comedy *The Recruiting Officer* at Covent Garden. The production opened on the evening of 6 November 1740 before a full house and attended by the Prince of Wales. It was indeed an auspicious occasion.

The play was a resounding success and got excellent reviews, with Peg's fine acting being the central point. She was soon the talk of the coffee houses and people in the street began to point her out. The production was repeated for three consecutive nights. There is no record of a romance between Rich and Peg and it seems they were merely acquaintances.

Later in the season she appeared successfully in two comedies by English playwrights, as Lady Sadlife in *The Double Gallant*, subtitled *The Sick Lady's Cure*, by the poet laureate Colley Cibber, and as Aura in *The Country Lasses*, subtitled *The Custom of the Manor*, by the sometime tavern keeper Charles Johnson.

Peg would also repeat her earlier success as Sir Harry Wildair in *The Constant Couple*, which she had performed at the Theatre Royal in Dublin to great acclaim. 'So infinitely did she surpass expectations,' wrote the Shakespearean actor Tate Wilkinson in his memoirs, 'that the applause she received from her London audience was beyond any at that time ever known.'

Attendances were so good that the play was repeated for 20 consecutive nights. One night, after a performance, she was in the dressing room and told a reviewer of her acquaintance: 'You know, I've played this part so often that half the town believes me to be a man.'

'Aye, Miss Woffington,' retorted the critic, 'but I can assure you that the other half *knows* you to be a woman!'

It seemed audiences loved Peg, and the feeling was mutual. She continued her London success with performances in *Spanish Fryar, The Double Falsehood, Old Bachelor, Love's Last Shift* and the role she had played at the Theatre Royal in Dublin, Phyllis in Richard Steele's *Conscious Lovers*. She knew the script backwards but she still practiced it again and again before each performance. Always, too, Peg make sure her make-up was done with great care and attention, and made certain she got into the character she was playing. Always the perfectionist.

Poets wrote sonnets to her and artists painted her portrait. She was at the height of her success. However, in May 1741, she had a disagreement with John Rich at Covent Garden – 'He was difficult to get along with', she was quoted as saying – and threatened to leave.

Rich himself was also having rows with his partners over financial matters and salaries, with the result that an actors' revolt was organised and executed. Finally, Rich was sacked and a new manager came in, Charles Fleetwood. The new man had his own personal issues, notably a serious gambling problem, but he kept the theatre going.

Four months after leaving Rich and Covent Garden, Peg moved to the Theatre Royal, Drury Lane and starred in a revival of her greatest success, *The Constant Couple*. She enjoyed her new location and soon settled in. The Royal, commonly referred to simply as Drury Lane, is built on the oldest theatrical site in London, dating back to 1663. The same building is the fourth Theatre Royal in Drury Lane and has been called one of the world's most haunted theatres.

Legend has it that the appearance of almost any one of the handful of ghosts that are said to frequent the theatre has the power to send out good luck signals for an actor or production, a story related by several present-day Irish actors who have played Drury Lane. The most famous ghost is the Man in Grey, who appears dressed as a nobleman of the late eighteenth century: powdered hair beneath a tricorne hat, a dress jacket and cloak or cape, riding boots and a sword. Legend also has it that the Man in Grey is the ghost of a man stabbed with a knife and whose skeletal remains were found within a walled-up side passage in 1848.

Peg Woffington, the street urchin who became the first great Irish actress and a popular Royal performer

The ghosts of the Donegal-born actor Charles Macklin and the English clown Joseph Grimaldi are also supposed to haunt the theatre. The Macklin ghost is said to appear backstage, wandering the corridor which now stands in the spot where, in 1735, he killed fellow actor Thomas Hallam in an argument over a wig. 'Goddamn, you are a blackguard, scrub, rascal!' he shouted, thrusting a cane into Hallam's face and piercing his left eye. He never fully recovered from the attack and died soon afterwards.

Grimaldi is reported to be a helpful apparition, purportedly guiding nervous actors skilfully about the stage on more than one occasion. The English comedian Stanley Lupino claimed to have seen the ghost of Dan Leno, famous for his dame roles in pantomime at Drury Lane, in a dressing room.

Whatever about the ghostly figures, the Irish were always well represented at Drury Lane by actors, actresses, dramatists, managers and patentees, indeed anyone connected to the theatre. Drury Lane had a proud tradition and was described by one playwright as 'the greatest theatre in the Empire.' Very often, too, Irish artistes working there would return to Dublin with their English counterparts and play at the Theatre Royal in Smock Alley before all returned to London.

Peg often sat in the stalls at Drury Lane when time permitted and enjoyed the productions. She knew the theatre's strong Irish connections. *The Bohemian Girl*, the opera composed by Dublin-born

William Balfe and who has a street named after him in his native city, was first produced at Drury Lane in November 1843.

It ran for more than 100 nights and enjoyed many revivals worldwide including New York and Philadelphia in 1844 and Madrid in 1845. Dubliners saw it at the Theatre Royal in Smock Alley in 1844. Several versions around Europe, notably in Germany, Italy and France, were also elaborately mounted, an indication of the opera's universal popularity and appeal.

With her contract now ended at Covent Garden, Peg thought it would be nice to work at Drury Lane. She made enquiries and found that the theatre was managed by a Charles Fleetwood, an English gentleman with a deep interest in the stage. During his tenure there, he had introduced a number of reforms including the abolition of the Footman's Gallery. This gallery was provided for the servants and lackeys of the ladies and gentlemen in the audience and generally it was noisy and disorderly. When the gallery was abolished in 1737, riots broke out in the theatre.

Fleetwood's management was artistically noteworthy but eventually it was a financial disaster due to his gambling. Nevertheless, he was essentially a man with a love for the theatre and he presented several plays with Peg prominently in the cast. Peg also began to notice that an Irishman in the company named John Delane was showing her particular attention.

Delane said his father had hoped he would be destined for the church but instead opted for the stage. He remembered Peg when he was a student at Trinity College in Dublin and how she sold oranges and cress, and entertained customers with her wit. Peg liked his gentlemanly behaviour and admired his good looks. The romance might have blossomed had it not been for the arrival on the scene of one David Garrick.

2

Love at First Sight

A handsome young man, well attired and groomed, David Garrick was the greatest male actor of his day, capable of winning over audiences in any role, any production, any place, any time. Born into a family with French Huguenot roots in Hereford, an idyllic town in the English West Midlands, Garrick was also a theatre manager and producer who influenced nearly all aspects of stage practice throughout the eighteenth century.

A close friend and pupil of Dr Samuel Johnson, Garrick developed a very natural style of delivery in contrast to the more strutting, ranting method of acting which pertained up to then. In a productive career, Garrick would add two new roles to his repertoire, Abel Drugger in Ben Johnson's *The Alchemist*, a part that earned him much acclaim, and Captain Plume in Farquhar's *The Recruiting Officer*.

Some of his success could be attributed to one of his earliest fans, John Boyle, the fifth Earl of Cork, who wrote letters to many noblemen and gentlemen recommending Garrick's acting. Boyle's writings led Garrick to exclaim that it must have been the reason he was 'more caressed' in Dublin. Garrick liked Dublin and would make several appearances on stage at the Theatre Royal.

When he first met Peg Woffington, however, he was a struggling young actor. Coming from a very respectable family, his father wanted him to become a wine merchant like himself, but David privately

David Garrick by Thomas Gainsborough

thought it was 'a very boring occupation' and yearned for a more exciting profession – like the stage. He risked the ire of his family by going secretly to Ipswich, a town in Suffolk, to test his talents with a strolling theatrical company.

Garrick would enjoy the experience and back in London he obliged an actor friend by standing in for him at the unlicensed Goodman's Fields Theatre, Whitechapel, in London's East End. The part happened to be the lead role in *The Life and Death of Richard*

III and he was announced on stage as 'a young actor who has never appeared on any stage,' even though he'd had that brief sojourn with the strolling players.

The young man was a revelation in what was virtually the first demonstration of natural, realistic acting in place of the bombastic style theatregoers had become used to. Garrick was bringing something different to the stage and that was always very welcome. Besides, as well as being a fine actor with a resonant voice, as far as the ladies were concerned he was also dashing and handsome.

Crowds came to see him in a somewhat deprived area which was considered out of bounds by many, and their patronage hit the box offices of the other theatres. In April 1742, Garrick accepted an offer to appear in a benefit concert at Drury Lane. Afterwards in the Green Room he chanced to see Peg with a couple of friends. 'Excuse me intervening like this,' said Garrick, always the gentleman, 'but aren't you Peg Woffington, the Dublin girl who is such a big hit here in London?'

Peg nodded modestly and accepted David's invitation to the bar for a drink. In a long conversation, he told the Dublin girl how his friends were raving about her and that he would have to go and see her on stage at the first opportunity. She said she knew all about him and admired his acting ability. It was love at first sight for both – the wispy, beautiful girl and the handsome, dashing man of the world.

'As it happens, I've been offered a summer season, June, July and August, in Dublin though nothing definite has been arranged as far as particular plays are concerned,' he said. 'Why don't we try to appear on the Dublin stage, not necessarily in the same play, but maybe that could be arranged. What do you say?'

Peg agreed with enthusiasm, saying that while she enjoyed performing in London, particularly in such a famous theatre at Drury Lane, it would be nice to go back to her roots for a while. Final arrangements were made with Francis Du Val, manager of the Theatre

Royal, Smock Alley and the announcement caused great excitement in the city.

The little theatre was packed every night. Playing the first week was the comedy *The Constant Couple*, with Peg, without David, reprising her cross-dressing role as Sir Harry Wildair. 'The audience remembered her beauty, and cheer after cheer greeted her entrance in response to which, with tears streaming down her face, she bowed again and again,' said a contemporary critic. Garrick was in the wings and when she came off stage, he whispered in her ear: 'My love, my Peg, you are the queen of all hearts. The audience loves you and so do I.'

For the second week, *Hamlet* was the presentation, with both Peg and David in the starring roles. Peg had already appeared in the Shakespeare classic five years earlier in Dublin when she got her first big break playing Ophelia so she was familiar with the tricky dialogue.

With Garrick, it was all new but he studied the script day after day and in the end was satisfied that all would be well on the night. It was a resounding success, and there were several standing ovations at the finish. The third week reverted to *The Constant Couple* and then back to *Hamlet* for the fourth week, with the productions alternating until the end of August.

With the huge success of Dublin behind them, Peg and David returned to London to prepare for their season at Drury Lane starting in September. However, not before a heated controversy arose over what many people were calling 'their illicit relationship.'

Certainly there were many raised eyebrows over the love match, although the affair had not affected attendances at Smock Alley. The general feeling was that they should have married and made the whole thing legal. Papers and correspondence at the time would indicate that Peg was anxious to marry Garrick, but for his own personal reasons he kept delaying it.

In any event, it was no secret in theatrical circles that he was something of a womaniser, an eighteenth century playboy. Some historians believe that Peg knew all about his affairs but preferred to look the other way for the sake of her career. It should not be forgotten that she and Garrick were big attractions together on the stage, a fact very apparent to both of them, so why break it up?

Their relationship would in many ways be a forerunner of the twentieth century torrid love affairs of movie stars Laurence Olivier and Vivien Leigh, and later on, Richard Burton and Elizabeth Taylor, both of which scandalised society.

Mind you, not that Peg herself was a one-man woman. During her lifetime her love affairs, besides Garrick, included liaisons with several other actors as well as the Welsh MP and satirist Charles Hanbury Williams, and Edward Bligh, the Meath-born Second Earl of Darnley, a noted cricketer. It will be gathered that Peg had an eye for the men of power and influence.

Meanwhile, back in London, Peg and David returned to Drury Lane where lines of carriages blocked up the area when the two favourites appeared together. The loving couple set up house in nearby Bow Street, where another tenant was the Donegal-born actor Charles Macklin, a big favourite on the London stage. Besides being a fine performer with a very natural style, whether in tragedy or comedy in a long career, he gained his greatest fame in the demanding role of Shylock in *The Merchant of Venice*.

Macklin always claimed he learned his acting style from his friend David Garrick whom he admired greatly and received many tips in presentation. He was also a somewhat eccentric character. Macklin's real name was Cathal McLaughlin but as he explained: 'I invented the name Charles Macklin because I wanted to get rid of that damned Irish name which nobody can either spell or pronounce properly anyway.'

Peg and David later moved to Southampton Street and agreed to share the living expenses equally, but Garrick, for all his gentlemanly conduct and manners, was extraordinarily mean. It was usually Peg who picked up the bills, despite the fact that he was earning three times as much as she was. He also made her take turns in the monthly upkeep of the house.

It became a standing joke among the celebrities they entertained, including the writer and essayist Dr Samuel Johnson, the author and traveller James Boswell and the novelist Henry Fielding, that the hospitality was much more lavish when it was Peg's turn to pay.

Garrick claimed that Peg was 'far too extravagant and impetuous.' He also maintained that she was too wasteful with her tea-making, brewing it so strong that it was 'as red as blood.' Whatever about his claims, there is little doubt that she was generous to a fault. She loaned her costumes to struggling young actresses and gave lavishly to charitable causes. She also supported her mother and younger sister Polly back in Dublin and would later pay for Polly's education in a French convent.

Nevertheless, it was always assumed that they would marry as, despite their personal differences, they did feel deeply for each other. It was now 1745 and they had been together for four years. Close friends claimed that Garrick once admitted trying a wedding ring on her finger. Other friends insisted that they really had nothing in common except their love for the stage. The feeling among their close circle, too, was that Garrick knew her attraction to other men would not make her an ideal wife, even though he himself was no saint.

Towards the end of the year he wrote Peg a love poem in which he expressed doubts about what he called her 'wavering heart.' Sometime later he made what she claimed was 'a very half-hearted proposal' which Peg refused, saying: 'Either you want to marry me or you don't.' They had an argument and Peg left the house. She returned after he had gone out and left for him a parcel containing all the many presents he had given her, and with it a letter requesting that he might care to return those she had given him. This he did, with the exception of a pair of silver shoe buckles which she never saw again.

Peg moved out and went to live in Udley Hall, Teddington, some 13 miles upriver from London 'to get my life back together again' and sent for her sister in France to join her. When Garrick became joint patentee of Drury Lane in 1747 he invited Peg to return as he had some interesting roles coming up for her. She did so and they appeared together several times but their old love affair never returned. At this stage it was simply a job for Peg.

Meanwhile, when Peg's younger sister Polly returned from her convent education in France, paid for by Peg, the sibling came to live with her. Peg always had social ambitions for her sister and introduced her to an aristocratic gentleman, the Honourable Captain Robert Cholmondeley.

It was Peg's undoing because Polly went on to become a very successful hostess in English high society, and more or less cut herself off from her elder sister who had always looked after her since their childhood in Dublin besides paying for her expensive education. 'Polly became an out-and-out snob who looked down on the big sister to whom she owed everything,' noted Marian Broderick in her book *Wild Irish Women*.

Peg settled in well at her new 'stage home' in Covent Garden, but found that competition in the theatre for women's roles had become very competitive and a sense of bitchiness began to seep in among actresses. London rivals would refer slightingly to her as 'that Irish actress' and point out 'her funny brogue.'

Normally an even-tempered woman, Peg often lost her temper with other actresses and had a tendency to throw tantrums, once coming to blows with some of them at Drury Lane. She finally left the company and returned to the Covent Garden Theatre, still under the management of the eccentric John Rich.

George Anne Bellamy

If things had been bad at Drury Lane, they became progressively worse at Covent Garden. One of the actresses there was George Anne Bellamy, the bastard Dublin-born daughter of an Irish peer and at least ten years younger than Peg, a fact she never failed to mention whenever they had a row, which was often. George Anne got her name when the clergyman at the christening, who was hard of hearing, did not quite get the name 'Georgina' when her mother said it and he announced the baby as 'George Anne,' so the girl had a boy's name! By all accounts George Anne was a nasty piece of work and had conveniently forgotten that it was Peg who had got her started on the London stage. On one occasion backstage, her taunting was so bad that Peg picked up a nearby knife, a prop, and attempted to stab her. George Anne quickly ran off and hid behind a curtain, prompting her to remark to friends: 'Honestly, I preferred to run away out of sight, and live to fight another day.'

Peg and George Anne were direct opposites. Although both were very popular on the stages of Dublin and London, Peg was conscientious and very reliable, always making sure she knew her lines thoroughly, while George Anne, known in theatrical circles as Blue-eyed Bellamy, was inclined to be lazy, vain, impulsive and extremely extravagant.

Peg and George Anne were bitter rivals on and off the stage. 'They simply hated each other,' a contemporary fellow actor was quoted as saying. Despite earnings from her six-volume memoirs, *Apology*, published in 1785 and dealing mainly with her shameless love life, George Anne died in extreme poverty in London three years later.

Peg received an attractive offer in the late summer of 1751 to leave London and return to Dublin for a season at Smock Alley. 'It'll be nice to get back to the Theatre Royal, and I'm really looking forward to it,' she said. The offer came from the manager, Thomas Sheridan, as noted earlier the father of future playwright and politician Richard Brinsley Sheridan, who was offering her a weekly salary of £400, good money in the mid-eighteenth century as can be imagined.

She looked forward to working under Sheridan, who would, co-incidentally, run the Theatre Royal, Drury Lane for many years. In any event, Peg had yearned to perform in her native city again. 'To be honest, I was always a bit homesick for Dublin whenever I was in London,' she admitted to a friend.

Peg lived in a house in Capel Street, across the river from the theatre, and opened her season on 5 October in *The Provoked Husband* and the packed attendance gave her a very warm welcome, with several curtain calls. She followed that with *The Distressed Mother*, performing alternatively as Andromache and Hermione.

After that, it was Sylvia in *The Recruiting Officer*, Calista in *The Fair Penitent* and then her own personal favourite, Sir Harry Wildair in *The Constant Couple*. This was followed by Maria in *The Nonjuror*, always with full houses. It seemed that Dublin audiences could not get enough of their returning heroine.

When Sheridan announced that he and Peg would be on the same stage together in six plays by Shakespeare, there was great delight by Dubliners. They knew that Sheridan was a fine actor himself, and to see him paired with Peg was a delight they could hardly miss. The bills announced that the plays would be *Richard III, Hamlet, Macbeth, The Merchant of Venice, As You Like it* and perhaps one of the least known of his plays, *King John*. Sheridan also announced that the theatre would be illuminated with wax lights.

All were hugely popular and both performers got standing ovations nightly. Peg found that at the end of the season her appeal had increased in all her old roles and several new ones. The run had made a lot of money for Sheridan, and when he offered her a second season, this time at £800 per week, she was flattered. 'The public want you, Peg, that's plain to see,' he told her.

In the following season, 1752, her appearances included Lady Betty Modish in *The Constant Husband*, Belvidera in *Venus Preserved*, as well as roles in *Julius Caesar, Ulysses* and several comedies by the English playwright and poet William Congreve. Peg Woffington, the bedraggled washerwoman's daughter, had truly conquered Dublin.

In her spare time she associated with the cream of society, as she had in London. Soon she was elected president of a society known as the Beefstake Club, a social gathering for the Dublin Castle set and run by Thomas Sheridan. Peg was the only female ever admitted to the club, regarded as the pinnacle of social achievement for a woman of her deprived background.

Now it is no secret that a common trait of the Irish is to often resent one of their own getting above their station, especially if they adopt newly-found airs and graces. 'Who do they think they are?' would be a common modern expression. So it was with Peg, although it did not detract from her ability as a fine actress. It was just personal.

There were many harmless high jinks that took place at the club, but some that were not so harmless. It was bad enough that Peg was entertaining William Cavendish, the third Duke of Devonshire and Lord Lieutenant of Ireland, but stories filtered out about anti-Irish toasts being drunk by the oppressors and uncomplimentary jokes being used.

There were also stories that Peg, a devoted Catholic all her life, was converting to Protestantism. Some of her friends denied this but

Peg herself said the rumours were true, and felt she had good reasons for transferring to her 'new religion,' as she put it. The Penal Laws forbade Catholics from inheriting property but an old actor and theatrical agent named Owen Swiney wanted to leave his property to Peg. Ever the pragmatist, she simply threw off her religion like an old cloak and converted so as to claim the inheritance.

'What else could I do,' she told a close friend. 'The opportunity was too good to let pass.' All this was too much for the Irish public, with that old jealously again rearing its ugly head. Questions were asked: 'What has come over Peg, one of our own?' 'Does she not remember where she came from, the bedraggled little Dublin girl who used to take in washing for her mother and carried a jug of water on her head?'

Peg entertained William Cavendish, Lord Lieutenant of Ireland

When Sheridan got her to perform in *Mahomet*, a five-act tragedy by the controversial French playwright and philosopher Francois-Marie Arouet, known by his *nom de plume* as Voltaire, there was trouble ahead. His study of religious fanaticism and strong criticism of the Christian church both placed him under the strict censorship laws of the time. Voltaire's advocacy was freedom of religion, freedom of expression and separation of church and state.

Mahomet contained incendiary passages about very touchy subjects such as court favouritism and tyranny, and there was strong criticism as to why Sheridan agreed to put on the play in such an established theatre as the Royal in the first place. On the opening night, sections of the crowd grew restless and soon became outraged at what they perceived as Peg's treacherous behaviour. Inflamed by Voltaire's contentious text, they started booing and shouting obscenities.

A crowd outside the theatre quickly realised what was going on and smashed through the doors, stormed the theatre and demanded to take the play off. Peg ran off the stage screaming and an equally terrified Sheridan cancelled all further performances.

Peg vowed never to appear on any stage again after her traumatic experience and announced her retirement, having enough money to live on in Dublin. She also spent some time in Paris and generally took things easy. Peg may well have stayed in retirement had it not been for a request from one of her former lovers, David Garrick, to return to London and appear at Covent Garden, which he was now managing.

Garrick was now happily married to the German operatic dancer Eva Marie Veigel, whom he called 'the best of women and wives.' Their marriage lasted 21 years until his death in 1770 at the age of 61. Garrick was given a lavish public funeral at Westminster Abbey, where he was laid to rest in Poet's Corner.

Peg returned to the footlights in October 1754 after a three-year absence and found her popularity was as strong as ever. She appeared in a variety of roles, from Shakespeare plays to contemporary comedies, and got standing ovations. Peg had never lost her old magic. Garrick complimented her from the beginning, saying to her once: 'Covent Garden is yours, Peg.'

Sadly, just when it appeared that Peg was attaining the position of grande dame of the theatre, her career was nearing its end. After one particular performance at the close of 1756, Garrick noticed that she looked tired and maybe needed a break. The Dubliner insisted she was fine and could carry on. After all, she would insist, the theatre was her life. There were overtures from Dublin to return to the Royal but she had a contract at Covent Garden and fully intended to honour it.

In May 1757, at the end of her fourth successful season at the London theatre, she was playing her old role of Rosalind in Shakespeare's *As You Like It*. It was a benefit performance for two minor actors. The boxes were filled with beautiful women, only too pleased too show off their fashionable refinery, and the pit was overflowing with its usual complement of critics, elegant dilettanti and gentlemen about town. This was the night when London came out in style.

The first four acts of the play went well, though it was obvious to those backstage that Peg was not herself. She was fluffing the occasional line and complained of serious indispositions – her eyes wearing a somewhat haggard look and her cheeks appearing blanched under her make-up.

When she left the stage in the last scene to change her dress, she spoke again of being unwell but insisted like a true professional of finishing the play. She was very conscious of the fact that her sudden non-appearance would make things difficult for the other actors. Speaking the epilogue, Peg's voice faltered.

She clasped her hands to her side and cried out in a voice mingled with pain and terror, 'Oh God! Oh God!' Tottering to the wings, she was caught by a fellow actor to break her fall before the curtain came down. Peg had had a massive stroke.

Everybody thought she would die but she lingered along for another three years. In any event, her performing days were over. She became a virtual cripple although her mind was still sharp. 'When I find that I can no longer bound to the boards with elastic step,' she once said, 'and when the enthusiasm of the public begins to show symptoms of change, that night will be the last public appearance of Peg Woffington.' That fateful, final night had come.

Peg kept to her word, residing quietly at her home in Udley Hall, Teddington Lock, Middlesex, which she had purchased in the 1740s.

During those last three years, she was visited by old friends, though many of her fellow performers were either dead or retired. Her last lover, an army man named Colonel Julius Caesar, took care of her and made sure she was comfortable and always had enough to eat.

Having converted to Protestantism some years earlier, Peg changed back to Catholicism even though she had never been very religious anyway. Today she would be described as 'a luke warm Catholic.' She died in hospital in Queen Square, Westminster and her remains were laid in a vault beneath Teddington Church near her home. The inscription on a tablet reads: 'Near this monument lies the body of Margaret Woffington, spinster, born October 18th, 1720 who departed this life March 26th, 1760 aged 39 years.'

3

Riot and the Night of the Big Fire

The Theatre Royal eventually closed in 1787 when it was decided to build a new and better one in Hawkins Street in the city centre. Meanwhile, the old Royal became a grain store before the building came into the hands of a local priest, Father Michael Blake. With some associates, the good priest set about turning it into a Catholic church. For purely financial reasons, as money was scarce, much of the old building as possible was retained.

The pit became the crypt of the church and much of the walls survived with old openings being blocked up and new openings being inserted. Father Blake now amalgamated other parishes and named it the Parish of St Michael and John. When the bell tolled in 1811, just 18 years before Catholic Emancipation, the first Catholic bell to ring in Dublin in nearly 300 years was heard.

Remarkably, the church survived the ravages of time but by 1989 it was failing into disrepair, and coupled with falling attendances it was deconsecrated. Two years later the old building was sold to a business consortium. On discovering this development, the theatre historian Seamus de Burca protested in a letter to the *Sunday Independent* in April 1991.

'I am saddened and shocked to notice that Dublin's SS. Michael and John's Church is to be sold,' he wrote. 'May I remind the reader that the church is built on the actual site of the Smock Alley Thea-

Smock Alley, site of the original Theatre Royal, is a cultural centre today

tre, possibly the finest permanent theatre in Dublin. I loved the church where the crypt was built on the theatre pit and in the balcony the acoustics were so perfect I was reminded of a theatre.'

There were several other letters in a similar vein in the following weeks, one calling for the government to intervene but nothing came of the issue. Subsequently, the building was redeveloped and housed the Viking Adventure as part of the Temple Bar Rejuvenation Scheme but closed down in 2002. In 2012, it was completely renovated, with the facade boasting its ornate stained glass windows as well as the original ceiling plasterwork remaining as a witness of its time.

Under its original name Smock Alley in honour of the first Theatre Royal, it is now a cultural venue with a 800-seating capacity and home to events such as the Dublin Writers' Festival and the Dublin Dance Festival. Well-known writers also give readings and engage in public conversation from the stage. The venue is also the headquarters of the Gaiety School of Acting, where budding actors and actresses receive their coaching and early theatrical education.

So in a strange way, the building that started as a theatre over 350 years earlier and after a number of re-incarnations was back again in modern Ireland as a vehicle once more for the stage. It is a fascinating link with the past and present.

Meanwhile, and not long after the original Theatre Royal was built in Smock Alley in 1735, there were reports that a rival theatre was to be erected in nearby Fishamble Street, named after a medieval fish market on the site. This came to pass in 1741. Known as the Fishamble Street Musick Hall, and under the management of a Dublin actor, Spranger Barry, George Frederic Handel's *Messiah* had its first performance there on 13 April 1742.

While the oratorio by the German-born, British Baroque composer received a modest reception here, it subsequently gained in popularity in England, eventually becoming one of the best-known and most frequently performed choral works in western culture. A link with today is that the George Frederic Handel hotel can be located in nearby Temple Bar.

Barry and his partners later succeeded in obtaining official recognition for the Musick Hall to be called the Theatre Royal. It closed in 1777, and after being reopened as a playhouse called the Gentleman's Theatre, it finally ceased production in 1793.

In 1820 Henry Harris, a London businessman, paid £50,000 for a site which was originally a meat market near the River Liffey in Hawkins Street, Dublin and built what was to become officially the second Theatre Royal. Designed by the English architect Samuel Beazley, the venue had 2,000 seats and was originally named the New Albany Theatre. It opened with a flourish in January 1821 with the nobility and gentry of the city in attendance.

It is important to recognise at this stage that in the early days of the nineteenth century, Dublin was entering a Renaissance in an architectural way, with new buildings and structures springing up, a makeover in a modern sense. The Royal College of Surgeons opened its splendid new building on the west side of St Stephen's Green in 1806, thus giving the least fashionable side of the Green a building of distinction.

In Sackville Street, now O'Connell Street, the Dublin architect Francis Johnston started building the new General Post Office in 1814, completing it in 1818, and which dominates the street today.

Johnston was also responsible for Nelson's Pillar in 1808, an iconic 121-foot structure for more than a century and a half before it was blown up. Another city icon, the Ha'penny Bridge, dates from 1816.

In 1820, a more substantial memorial to the Iron Duke, who was a Dubliner named Arthur Wellesley, was the Wellington Monument in the Phoenix Park, a popular playground for youngsters like myself in those far off days. Rising to 203 feet, Dubliners boasted, because of its sheer bulk, that it was the largest monument not only in Ireland but in Europe.

With all these structures giving Dublin a new look, it seemed appropriate that the new Theatre Royal, the most famous venue for entertainment in the capital, should become part of the city landscape. Unfortunately as it happened, the building, including the auditorium, was far from finished on the opening night in the first month of 1821.

A number of unsold seats in the side boxes were boarded up. Moreover, the staircases and lobbies presented such a dangerous appearance that many of the celebrity guests were alarmed for their safety. One was reportedly saying that the whole structure was 'wobbly' and another claiming that 'the whole thing was looking liable to collapse.'

It could well be said, too, that there was an overflowing audience in more senses than one, as those seeking entry through the pit doors found themselves up to their ankles in water, with many slipping and promising never to attend again. Moreover, all the doors had not been fitted to the pit entrance, which resulted in a very cold January breeze sweeping through the stalls.

Many patrons complained that Harris should have at least disposed of piles of builders' rubble and rubbish scattered throughout the theatre as the elegant ladies and their properly attired gentlemen escorts made their way to their seats. 'This is just disgraceful,' one lady was heard to say.

The following August, George IV attended a performance of Thomas Sheridan's play *St Patrick's Day*. As a result, a licence was granted to allow the name of the theatre to be changed to the Theatre Royal to reflect its status as a patent theatre. It would be the first of three to be built on the Hawkins Street site.

Although the theatre attracted a number of famous performers including Niccolo Paganini, the celebrated violin virtuoso, Jenny Lind, billed as the Swedish Nightingale and actor Tyrone Power Senior, father of the Hollywood star of the 1940s and 1950s, it was losing money. Harris himself claimed this was due to the high cost of performers' salaries but the general feeling was that he was not looking after the theatre properly because of other interests.

Nor did conduct in the exclusive boxes on either side of the theatre escape attention. Criticism was expressed, in deference to the ladies who occasionally graced the theatre by their presence, and the custom of mixing whiskey in the lobby behind the boxes, was deplored. The suggestion was made by the management that if gentlemen could not enjoy a feast without washing it down with hot whiskeys, then they were advised to repair for that purpose to a nearby tavern kept by a veteran actor Tom Lee who would welcome them with open arms and a big smile.

The 1820s saw the Royal start its tradition of pantomimes, the first one being *Dick Whittington and His Cat*. In the following years *Cinderella* was a big success as was *Ali Baba and the 40 Thieves*, but there were other less well-known ones at the time including *Gulliver's Travels*, written by the Dublin essayist Jonathan Swift, who was born in Hoey's Court adjoining Werburgh Street and who later became dean of St Patrick's Cathedral in the Liberties area of the city.

Despite the successes of the pantomimes and other productions, Harris had his critics who claimed he had basically no real interest in the theatre and in particular, less interest in improving public taste. He insisted for example of presenting incomplete versions of operas, and transforming the works of Shakespeare into musical farces by introducing songs and laughter into the proceedings.

This was effectively reducing the role of the theatre manager into almost a bystander. It should be pointed out too that highly respected actors had been known to sing sea shanties and dance a hornpipe into one of the more harrowing scenes in a Shakespearean tragedy. One particular actor, Luke Plunkett, upon receiving an encore for his death scene in *Richard III*, responded with a lively rendition of 'Scots Wha Hae.'

On another occasion, when Charles Keen, a respected Shakespearean actor, was playing in *Richard III*, his fearful grimaces in character, much to his amusement, almost paralysed some of the other actors with fright. On one occasion, a late substitute actor was called upon to take the role of the sentinel who awoke Richard. When asked: 'Who is there?' he was scripted to say: 'Tis I my lord, the early village cock hath twice done salutation to the morn.'

Keen, however, was making such fearful grimaces, and scowling at him, that the poor fellow completely lost his concentration, forgot his lines and could only stammer: 'Tis I my l-l-lord, tis I my l-l-lord, – the village c-c-cock!' By this time there were roars of laughter all over the theatre as Keen growled: 'Okay then, but why the hell don't you c-c-crow, you damn fool' before storming off the stage, red-faced. As one newspaper critic remarked the next morning: 'Believe you me, Shakespeare himself would never have wanted it to be like this.'

There was a much nastier experience at the theatre on the evening of 14 December, 1822 when a performance of Oliver Goldsmith's *She Stoops to Conquer* was staged. It would become known as 'the Bottle Row' and resulted in four men being charged with attempted murder. Among those in attendance was Richard Colley Wellesley, or to give him his official title, the Lord Lieutenant Marquis Wellesley, the eldest brother of Arthur, the Duke of Wellington.

The Lord Lieutenant was quite unpopular at the time among Orange Order members in the city because of his role in preventing an annual ceremony at the bronze statue of King William of Orange, commonly known as King Billy, and on his horse, in College Green in the city centre, from going ahead. He was also the first Lord Lieutenant to be openly favourable to Catholic Emancipation.

Lord Lieutenant Marquis Wellesley

As it happened, Henry Goulburn, a well-known anti-Emancipationist, was appointed as Chief Secretary. Goulburn was said to have accepted the position because of the imminent return to the administration of the future British Prime Minister Robert Peel, a close friend and fellow anti-Emancipationist.

It does not take much imagination to realise that the somewhat uneasy Wellesley-Goldburn administration in Ireland attempted, by its policy and its composition, to steer what must have been an almost neutral course between the Orange Order on one side and the nationalists on the other.

The statue was the location for annual rituals organised by loyalist elements in Dublin, with special events in July to mark the Battle of the Boyne and in November to honour the birthday of King William. It was common at the ceremonies to decorate the statue with orange sashes and shamrock strewn under the feet of the king's horse 'to symbolise William's victory over Catholics,' as the historian Shunsuke Katsuta put it. Both dates were sensitive flashpoints on the Dublin calendar and the police had to be vigilant to prevent any disturbances. Heavily criticised by many nationalists, including Daniel

O'Connell, who campaigned for Catholic Emancipation, such as the right for Catholics to sit in Westminster denied for 100 years, Dublin Castle would always ensure to distance themselves from the ceremonies. But it was the eventual banning and outlawing of the November ceremony which infuriated the Orange Order and set off the trouble that was sure to follow.

On 9 December an announcement appeared in the *Freeman's Journal*. Under the heading The Lord Lieutenant's first visit to the Theatre Royal, it read:

'His Excellency the Marquis Wellesley has been pleased to command a play, and signify his intention of going in state to the Theatre Royal on Saturday next. This is the first public visit of his Excellency to the theatre, and on that account, as well as the Lord Lieutenant's popularity, it is supposed that every person of rank, fashion and consideration in the city and neighbourhood will be present. We have reason to believe that this visit may be regarded as a sort of prelude to a very gay and hospitable season. The play is *She Stoops to Conquer*.'

This announcement was read with more than a little interest by the Orange Order, and six men met in the Shakespeare Tavern at the end of a grimy little alley known as Leinster Market, opposite the canopied state entrance of the theatre, to devise a plot, known only to themselves and each sworn to secrecy.

The six Orangemen – John and George Atkinson, George and William Graham, Matthew Handwith and James Forbes – managed to get their hands on 100 tickets for the play as they planned to recruit others to join in the protest.

Their aim was to embarrass the Lord Lieutenant, who had described himself as 'being placed on the throne by the favour of a beloved sovereign, surrounded by the attributes of majesty and royal power and entrusted with the sword of justice and mercy for the good government of Ireland.' The men were also demonstrating against the

Lord Mayor of Dublin, John Fleming, who had banned the practice of 'dressing up' the statue of King William in the future.

As the anonymous reviewer of the *Theatrical Observer* wrote the following Monday: 'His Excellency the Lord Lieutenant honoured the theatre with his presence on Saturday night, when the rank and file of the metropolis crowded to meet him. Upon his arrival, he was cheered with the most ardent and enthusiastic plaudits, which continued uninterrupted throughout for several minutes.

'But soon, a serpent's hiss, poisoning the atmosphere of the house, became the signal to some sanguinary confederation of satanic monsters and rebellious cowards to mar the harmony of the evening and kindle within the theatre the torch of political discord and rebellious fanaticism.'

What happened was that before the curtain went up, several of the protesters tossed pamphlets towards the stage area with the slogan 'No Popery' on them. There were cries, too, of 'No Popish Lord Lieutenant' from the six leading troublemakers. When the curtain went up, they started booing at first, then hissing and calling on the crowd to sing 'God Save the King.'

After that, copper pipes, sticks, a steel blade, oranges and a wide selection of empty glass bottles rained down on the stage, causing the terrified performers to scramble to the wings for safety, and the performance suspended, at least for the moment. Mob rule in Dublin was now at its nasty height. A bottle smashed near the Lord Lieutenant's vice regal box but he was not injured.

Outside there were skirmishes too, with several sections of the crowd armed with a variety of missiles, stones, eggs and firecrackers, and pelted everyone in sight, including the Dublin Metropolitan Police who had quickly arrived on the scene. The police drew their batons and sabres and charged through the unruly mob, trampling some of the crowd, before forcing their way into the theatre.

Several in the crowd also received cuts and bruises and were rushed to hospital, as were some members of the police, as the shouting and hissing continued, though the missiles had stopped. Eventually some semblance of order was restored.

At least half a dozen men, all with addresses in Hawkins Street and admitting membership of the Orange Order, would appear before the courts on two separate occasions, first being tried on the grounds of conspiracy to murder, and the attempted murder of, the Lord Lieutenant, and later of conspiracy to riot and looting. The riot caused much anger in the city.

Much to the huge disappointment of the authorities, not to mention fervent nationalists, all the men walked free. Wellesley naturally took the whole incident very seriously and attempted unsuccessfully to have the perpetrators convicted on a more serious charge of conspiracy, which the grand jury refused to do.

Chief Justice Charles Kendal Bushe had remarked to the jury in his summation that 'an audience may cry down a play, or hiss or boo an actor, but that riotous behaviour was not permitted.' Dismissing the case, Bushe issued a warning that the men would have to watch their behaviour in future.

One positive effect of 'the Bottle Row' was the outlawing of the Orange Order in the city centre, and which led to the Unlawful Societies Act of 1825 being introduced. Meanwhile, the statue, installed in 1701, remained in College Green, though it was the subject of many vicissitudes. Over the years it was constantly the target of vandals, being mutilated, daubed with paint and spat at until the IRA finally placed explosives under the horse in 1929 and blew everything to pieces.

Whatever about riots in the city, the Royal steered free of any similar incidents from then on, although the noisy presence of some of the audience in the 'gods' on many occasions caused considerable discomfort to other patrons and gave rise to repeated complaints.

The *Dramatic Argus* reported in 1824: 'There is no matter in the whole course of our theatrical experience which has given us so much pain as the truly disgraceful conduct of a portion of our Dublin audience, and the still more shameful apathy of that part of it which should act as a corrective.

'Why, we ask, does our audience, and we mean the better educated part of it, permit a nightly display of the grossest and most indecorous and often ruffian conduct? We were not a little surprised on perceiving by a morning paper on Saturday that the person who threw an orange at one of the female performers was discharged by the magistrate without any punishment whatsoever. Now, this is most lamentable in the extreme.'

There were criticisms too that the theatre proprietor, Henry Harris, was fostering the stage Irishman a little too much with his productions, although one play by Thomas Sheridan called *Captain O'Blunder* presented the stage Irishman in an unexpectedly favourable light. However, many works were unflattering and enraged the public and the critics.

By 1830 Harris seemingly had had enough, resigned and John Calcraft came in as manager. Calcraft is also mentioned in contemporary newspaper reports under different Christian names but it is one and the same person.

Calcraft also ran the rival Adelphi Theatre in Brunswick Street, now Pearse Street. He would later rename his new venue the Queen's Theatre but not before he realised that the Adelphi was a serious rival to the Royal. He shut down the Adelphi and kept it closed to concentrate on the former.

Nevertheless, by 1851 the Royal was losing money and looking shabbier by the day. A new man came in named John Harris and put on successful productions including a play by the celebrated Irish playwright, actor and producer Dion Boucicault called *The Colleen Bawn*, also known as *The Brides of Garryowen*, in April 1861.

Dion Boucicault

Boucicault was a Dubliner from Gardiner Street in the inner city and is believed to been given his name by his mother following an affair with a foreign lodger at a time when she was separated from her husband. Boucicault had already established himself abroad, particularly in the US, before returning to the Royal with his wife and performing in the play, which ran for four weeks and was hailed by the critics.

It would have had a longer run but for the fact that they had other engagements. They returned in November 1864 to present for the first time on any stage *Arrah na Pogue,* with the playwright himself as Sean the Post and his wife as Arrah. Boucicault was greeted as a returning hero and was cheered in the streets, both for the play and his portrayal of the character.

The critics, however, considered the play too long and claimed that this made it tedious in parts. Nevertheless, it was successful and had a good run. Four years later Boucicault revived it at the Royal, this time 'judiciously curtailed and altered' as he put and it too had a good run. Boucicault, interestingly, was a good friend of Oscar Wilde, and he defended the playwright when Wilde was ostracised by the English establishment following his arrest for 'gross indecency with other men.'

Meanwhile, in 1857 the managements of the Royal and the Queen's amalgamated in order to block the granting of a licence for a third theatre in the city, the Gaiety, in South King Street. The patent was finally granted in 1871 to the brothers John and Michael Gunn to open their new theatre.

Despite several changes to nearby buildings and new department stores, the Gaiety is still in the same location and retains its old Victorian charm. Dublin's longest established and continuously productive theatre, it stages plays, reviews and shows, with *Riverdance* returning regularly by popular demand.

The annual Christmas pantomime, formerly starring Jimmy O'Dea and Maureen Potter, and latterly with Maureen following the death of O'Dea, would remain one of the highlights. The author has fond memories of being brought to the Gaiety pantos annually with the parents and enjoying the fun.

There is something inherent about the combination of singing, slapstick and slagging that seems to particularly suit the Irish temperament. English pantos are invariably slick but a lot of the humour is inclined to go over the heads of the children and keeps the elders laughing. In homegrown pantos one is just as likely to hear a quip about the reigning Taoiseach as a toilet. That's how it was at the Royal and the Gaiety in those far-off days, and which continues today in modern Ireland.

On the evening on Monday, 9 February 1880, during the final weeks of the Royal pantomime *Ali Baba and the 40 Thieves*, a fire burned the theatre to the ground. Two days earlier there had been a special command performance attended by the Duke and Duke of Marlborough. On the day of the fire, there was another command performance planned, the proceeds to go to the Dublin Charities Fund. The nobility and gentry of the day were on their way to Hawkins Street when news spread that the theatre was ablaze.

The curtain was ready to go up for the matinee performance of the panto at 2.00. It was now 1.00 and the doors had not yet opened. Twenty minutes later, with the doors set to open at 1.30, the building was burning. It has never been fully determined how the actual outbreak occurred, but it was generally believed at the time that a small boy had been given the task of lighting the gas chandeliers in the boxes. The chandeliers had some years earlier been installed in the theatre to replace the old oil lamps.

As the boy was lighting one of them in the Vice Regal box, the flame accidentally caught one of the plush red drapes alongside and the box was soon enveloped in flames. The blaze caught on quickly and suddenly there was a loud explosion. It was ascertained later that a careless plumber had unscrewed a gas bracket and forgot to close a pipe.

Frances Egerton, the business manager, was quickly on the scene after alerting the staff who called the fire brigade. With the aid of the assistant manager John Hyland, Egerton brought a fire hose to the stage area, and shouted for help, but the blaze was by now out of control. Efforts were made to adjust the hose but the fire attacked the stage. The curtains quickly caught fire, in the days long before safety curtains, and there seemed no hope to save the old theatre, which was by now a raging inferno.

Despite pleas by members of the staff to abandon his dangerous efforts and leave it to the firemen, Egerton stuck to his task heroically but valiantly as the auditorium was filled with smoke. All the doors, with the exception of those at the main entrance were locked, and there was only one way to get out – through the stalls and out to the front. However, the dense smoke was preventing visibility.

Nothing more was seen of Egerton from the time he was engaged in running the hose to the stage. The building was now fully ablaze and the roof collapsed. Egerton's body was not found until workmen had succeeded in removing most of the debris four weeks later.

On the morning of 10 February, *The Irish Times* quoted one of the firemen involved and who described how the flames 'galloped along the muslin draperies and soon enveloped the area. The destruction of the drapery and curtains was the work of a moment and the wings, scenery and the general accessories followed. The woodwork burned like tinder, and the flames licked everything in sight, moving along rapidly and relentlessly. I had never seen anything quite like it.'

An *Irish Times* reporter wrote: 'As the blaze raged, with the building now an inferno, huge crowds gathered in the streets in and around Hawkins Street, and the police and fire brigade had great difficulty in controlling them. So close did they press to the scene that when, later in the evening, one of the walls in Poolbeg Street alongside the building collapsed, resulting in a score of people injured, five of them seriously.'

There were reports later in the week that six people had died in the fire, but this proved incorrect. There were also stories that many stage hands were trapped in the building and unsuccessful bids were made to rescue them. There were reports too of a scene painter who had been hanging high above the stage floor and failed to be saved, as well as two youths who had been hired to play the front and hind legs on the donkey in the *Ali Baba* show and had also met their deaths. All these stories proved to be untrue. With the exception of Egerton, everybody in the theatre managed to get out safely.

There were nevertheless several gallant rescues, among them the barmaid in charge of the pit bar and who was locked inside, and John Farrar, a technician who had been putting the finishing touches to some scenery.

Farrar managed to break down the door of the bar with an axe, brought the barmaid to the second floor and lowered her by ropes to the street. Meanwhile Farrar managed to roll down the aisle, clasping the axe, and smashed down the front door into Hawkins Street and to safety.

A fund was soon started by a number of prominent citizens for the dependents of Egerton and benefit performances were given in other Dublin theatres as well as some in Belfast and in Britain.

Philip B. Ryan, the theatre historian and author, would write in his book *The Lost Theatres of Dublin*: 'Egerton is another example of theatre folk who regard their theatre as something special to them, a second home, an extension of themselves, and to very many, the theatre was regarded as holy ground.'

The day after the fire was a wet, cold and miserable one but thousands assembled to watch 'the dear old Royal', which they had grown to love, finally reduced to a heap of smouldering ashes. Later in the afternoon the seventh Duke of Marlborough, then Viceroy of Ireland, arrived accompanied by Lord Muskerry and a small group of dignitaries and were shown the results of the tragic blaze by Captain Ingram of the Dublin Fire Brigade.

'Terrible, terrible', said the Duke. One of the people in the official group was the Duke's grandson, a very young Winston Churchill, the future British Prime Minister.

The theatre library, as with everything else, was destroyed. It had contained valuable old manuscripts of plays, material relating to the history of the theatre, an artiste's salary book and photographs, including many autographed by the many famous performers who appeared on the Royal stage over the years.

Ryan recorded in his book that one item which did survive the fire was the bell which used to belong to the old Carmelite Abbey, formerly St Mary's Abbey off Capel Street and was a fixture in the Royal. It was said that the tones were reportedly often heard from the Royal stage calling mourners to the grave of the fair Ophelia.

The bell was subsequently recast and taken to the Gaiety Theatre. Successive Gaiety managers have failed to shed any light on the bell's present whereabouts, but some historians believe it may have been taken from the Gaiety premises by some long forgotten auctioneer.

All that remained of the second Theatre Royal was the statue of Hibernia which from 1876 had stood impressively over the front entrance. It was later placed over the entrance to the Grand enclosure in the showyard of the Royal Dublin Society, the RDS, in Ballsbridge, venue for the annual Dublin Horse Show, a traditional event dating back over 150 years.

4

Red Faces for the Diva and the Tenor

When the Theatre Royal was destroyed, Michael Gunn did not seek to renew his patent. He wanted a completely new venue and following consultations with the London architect C.J. Phillips decided to build what he called 'a new music hall' on the site of the old theatre.

Music hall was a type of theatrical entertainment growing in popularity in Britain around that time. It involved a mixture of popular song, comedy, speciality acts and entertainment generally. The term is derived from a type of theatre or venue in which such entertainment took place. While British music hall was similar to American vaudeville featuring rousing songs and comic acts, the term vaudeville referred to more working-class types of entertainment that would have been termed burlesque in America.

Originating across-channel in saloon bars within public houses in the 1830s, music hall entertainment became increasingly popular with audiences, so much so that during the 1850s, the public houses were demolished and music hall theatres developed in their place. These theatres were designed chiefly to facilitate people who could consume food and alcohol and smoke tobacco in the auditorium while the entertainment took place. This differed somewhat from the conventional type of theatre, which until then seated the audience in stalls with a separate bar room.

By the mid-nineteenth century, the halls created a demand for new and catchy popular songs. As a result, professional songwriters were enlisted to provide the music for a plethora of star performers including the likes of Marie Lloyd, Dan Leno, Little Tich, George Leybourne and others. Music hall did not adopt its own unique style. Instead all forms of entertainment were performed – male and female impersonators, mime artists, impressionists, trampoline acts, and comic pianists

Gradually music hall entertainment died out by the early years of the twentieth century, particularly after World War I with the arrival of jazz, swing and big bands. Music hall in London particularly was mainly confined to charity events in aid of the war effort. Nor did an important industrial conflict in 1907 help. This was between artistes and stage hands on the one hand and theatre managers on the other, which ended in a strike.

Licensing restrictions had also changed, and drinking was banned from the auditorium. A new type of entertainment had arrived, in the form of variety, and many music hall performers failed to make the transition. Deemed old fashioned and with the closure of many halls, music hall entertainment ceased and the modern day variety began.

Back in 1886, however, music hall was getting into full swing and Michael Gunn was confident he could attract big names to his new venue. Rather than call it the Theatre Royal, he opted for the Leinster Hall. It had its gala opening on 2 November which was attended by many civic and civil authorities.

Instead of going for a lighter form of entertainment befitting the term 'music hall', Gunn opted for a more serious form and used his theatre for recitals and operas. The Arthur Rousbey Opera Company regularly attracted full houses for their six-week season.

Dame Nellie Melba, the first Australian to achieve international recognition as a classical musician and of the most famous singers of the Victorian era, gave two very successful concerts at the hall in

1893. One newspaper critic observed: 'Those who attended her two concerts cannot forget the pleasurable sensation they experienced in listening to her.

'Her rendition of Tosti's 'Goodbye' was one of the most divinely dramatic things I ever listened to, and the higher she sings the sweeter and more bird-like her voice becomes. Her 'costume recital' of the 'mad scene' from Lucia de Lammermoor with its wealth of florid passages was a vocal treat to rave about.'

The old problem of money, or lack of it, would soon reappear, however, and with serious competition from the Round Room of the Rotunda at the top of O'Connell Street, something needed to be done.

The Rotunda, part of the maternity hospital, specialised in somewhat lighter entertainment, and while they presented concerts and musical evenings, circuses and exhibitions were not unfamiliar. The spectacular *Buffalo Bill's Wild West Show* was also very popular, although there is no evidence to suggest that the legendary sharpshooter Annie Oakley was in the cast.

In any event Gunn needed some money to invest in the Gaiety which he closed for a short period in 1896 for some necessary reconstruction and redecoration in preparation for its upcoming silver jubilee. He subsequently sold the Leinster Hall to a syndicate, which closed it down. A little later it was completely demolished and there were rumours that a new Theatre Royal, the third, was to be built on the site.

They turned out to be true. In the closing weeks of the year a group of businessmen sat down over lunch in a Dublin hotel to discuss plans for a new theatre and aimed for it to be built on the site of the old Leinster Hall in Hawkins Street. Present at the meeting was Frederick Mouillot, an ambitious 34-year-old actor-manager and son of a Dublin businessman.

Mouillot envisaged the most modern theatre of its kind up to then and he would call it, naturally, the Theatre Royal. Mouillot, whose memory is perpetuated by an impressive bust which can be seen in the Gaiety Theatre, was a man of vision. His partners in the project would be those in attendance at the meeting, H. H. Morell, a successful businessman, David Telford, an accountant, and the four sons of David Allen, the theatrical printer whose giant posters could be seen on hoardings all over the city.

Mouillot convinced his partners that the theatre would be of the highest quality, and they agreed that Frank Matcham would be the architect. Matcham is considered one of the most prolific and successful theatre architects in history. Born in Newton Abbot in Devonshire in 1854, he had flair and imagination, and is credited with the design of over 150 theatres across Britain, most of which, sadly, have been pulled down to make way for shopping centres and office blocks.

John Earl, a director of the Theatres Trust, an advisory body founded in the UK in 1976 to assist with the promotion and preservation of theatre buildings, wrote of Matcham, who died of blood poisoning in 1920: 'Say the words "theatre architect" and a surprising number of people claiming no particular knowledge of art history will respond immediately with "Frank Matcham".

'He is seen as the master for all the best of all reasons. In present day terms his theatres are thoroughly efficient and they generate an atmosphere and excitement which few designers have ever equalled and none have excelled.

'In every one of his theatres, Matcham demonstrated his complete mastery of the art of providing every member of the audience with a good view of the stage and excellent audibility for the performance. He also created an astonishing diversity of interior decorations to seduce the eye and generate expectation. His magical interiors delight audiences as much today as when they were built.'

Author and historian Philip B. Ryan remembered: 'Some examples of Matcham's work may still be seen today in the UK, such as the London Coliseum, the London Palladium, the Lyric Hammersmith, the Victoria Palace and the Hackney Empire. The Grand Theatre in Blackpool, built in 1894, is credited with being one of his finest creations and is now a Grade 11 listed building.

'Nearer home, the Grand Opera House in Belfast, which he designed in 1895, is reputed to be the best surviving example in these islands of the Oriental style of theatre architecture. When Matcham's Theatre Royal was replaced in 1935, Dubliners spoke nostalgically for decades of "the old Theatre Royal".

Matcham agreed to take on the project, with the result that the third Royal opened on 13 December, 1897. Officially known at first as the Theatre Royal Hippodrome, it subsequently was called simply the Theatre Royal. It had 2,011 seats and an outstanding feature was its impressive and much admired marble staircase, one of Matcham's finest works.

The third Theatre Royal, known as the Hippodrome,
opened in 1897 and was pulled down in 1935

The staircase, which is still in use today in the Marks & Spencer department store in Grafton Street, gave access from the dress circle down to the Winter Gardens, an area next door where the audience could partake of tea and sandwiches amid the potted palms and fountains to the gentle sound of a tinkling piano.

In the early years the theatre wrestled with problems such as influenza epidemics which diminished crowds and required positive advertising such as 'this theatre is fully disinfected' to restore the confidence of audiences. Equally important too was that the public health authorities had to be fully satisfied with conditions.

The third Royal also introduced in 1898 a system of queuing in consultation between the directors, Mouillot, Telford, S. C. Allen and the resident manager, Arthur Armstrong. It had recently been tried very successfully in London and came as a welcome innovation to Dublin audiences who were accustomed to an undignified and un-

The author walks down the Royal's original marble staircase,
now in the Marks & Spencer store in Grafton Street

controlled melee when the doors opened at city theatres, often with members the Dublin Metropolitan Police, the DMP, being called in.

The façade of the building bore the inscriptions Theatre Royal and Opera House, but later when variety shows were introduced it was also known as the Theatre Royal Hippodrome, as mentioned earlier. There was also a Winter Garden beside the building. However, the theatre had its critics, with many saying that it was not really suitable for light musical shows as was the Gaiety.

They felt that the thinly orchestrated music, while catchy, and the small light voices of the singers were quite lost and seemed, as one put it, 'poverty stricken in such a big theatre.' One critic felt that the Royal should forget about 'all these light shows and give the public what they really want, serious material, and leave the lighter stuff to other theatres.'

This critic had a point. Besides the Gaiety, there was the newly opened Grand Lyric Hall, later renamed the Tivoli Variety Theatre, on Burgh Quay, where the *Irish Press* newspaper offices would later stand. The Lyric presented variety shows including singers, dancers, comedians, acrobats and so on.

There was also the Empire Palace, subsequently re-named the Olympia Theatre in Dame Street and still standing, and the Queens in what was then Great Brunswick Street, now Pearse Street. The Queen's was pulled down in 1969. These theatres presented similar variety shows. It made sense to Mouillot and his directors to change direction.

Bowing to the critics and more importantly public taste Mouillot then decided to change format, and in consultation with his fellow directors, planned to put on grand opera and serious plays, including Shakespeare, which it was felt would be more suited to the Royal stage.

His first production was the Edwardian musical comedy with a Japanese background in two acts, *The Geisha*, which had been first presented at Daly's Theatre, London a few short years earlier to great acclaim. With music by Sidney Jones, the production was so successful that it was revived some years later.

Mouillot would succeed in attracting some of the greatest theatrical stars and companies to the Royal and met with a great deal of success. These included the Frank R. Benson Shakespearean and Old Comedy Company and a production of *Cyrano de Bergerac* with the British actor Charles Wyndham playing the disgraced French swordsman-poet.

Wyndham was the son of a Liverpool doctor and studied at the College of Surgeons and the Peter Street Anatomical School in Dublin with the intention of entering the medical profession. However, having taken part in amateur drama, his taste for the stage proved too strong and in 1862 he made his professional debut on the boards in London.

When further stage work was not immediately forthcoming he returned to medicine. On discovering that there was a shortage of surgeons in the United States, which was in the throes of the Civil War, he volunteered to become brigade surgeon in the Union Army and served at the battles of Fredericksburg, Chancellorsville and Gettysburg.

In November 1864 he resigned his contract with the army and returned to the stage with considerable success. Some Dublin critics felt that his performance on the Theatre Royal stage in *Cyrano de Bergerac* was much inferior to that of the French actor Benoit-Constant Coquelin, who had appeared in the role at the Gaiety, but generally the response was favourable and positive.

The same could not be said of the popular Moody-Manners Opera Company with a production on one occasion of *Faust*. A note in the programme informed patrons: 'Owing to Miss Margaret McIntyre being engaged at short notice, it was impossible for her to learn the English version of the opera. She will therefore sing in Italian.' This resulted in the audience, having heard other members sing in English, straining their ears to fully hear Miss McIntyre, with the result that they did not understand a word that came from her lips.

Philip B. Ryan, the historian, aptly put it like this: 'The Moody-Manners Company always attracted a very knowledgeable and vocal type of opera buff to the lofty heights of the "gods" where the enthusiasts sat on long bench-like seating arranged in tiers like steps of stairs with the result that patrons were conscious of the boots of the person seated directly behind digging into the small of their back.

'During the intervals certain members of this closely knit clientele rose from their uncomfortable seats and regaled other patrons with arias from the opera being performed on that evening in a feast of communal enjoyment.'

Patrons in 'the gods', from where the performers almost looked like midgets, were notorious for registering their displeasure with performers on the stage, a fact that this writer can attest to, having being up there on many occasions, not only at the Royal but other theatres. Around 1870 there appears to have been a locally imposed censorship so as not to upset the sensibilities of theatregoers, and heckling would certainly come into that category.

In Britain, the Lord Chamberlain seemingly vetted all scripts intended for public performances but his powers did not officially extend to Ireland. It appears that on one occasion at the Royal in the 1890s, one particular patron roared down to a well-known soprano on the stage: 'Terrible. Tell me, who did you sleep with last night?' The shocked diva gazed scornfully up at the top of the theatre. 'Have manners, you oaf,' she hissed, 'and please let us get on with the performance!'

On another occasion, a prominent tenor was in the middle of an aria when a dissatisfied patron shouted down from the back of 'the gods': 'Where did you learn to sing like that? In a back alley?' The shocked tenor, now quite red-faced, ignored the taunt and carried on with his performance, if more than a little shaken.

Then there were the supposedly 'immodest' gestures by some performers. One critic noted during a performance by the noted English actress Irene Vanbrugh, the daughter of a clergyman and who was playing Sophy Fullgarney in *The Gay Lord Quex*, that 'at the end of act one, Miss Vanbrugh indulged in gestures which puzzled many, to judge by their remarks, but were simply intended to see if her garters were all right.'

The action by Miss Vanbrugh, who has a theatre named in honour of her and her sister Violet in London and who was later a Dame, was certainly not approved by the *Irish Playgoer* whose critic took the high moral ground.

'Some productions cannot be recommended to every class of theatregoer,' he wrote. 'Our playhouses are public buildings. Thirty years ago denunciations were hurled at the head of Dion Boucicault for putting a courtesan on the stage. Our stomachs have grown stronger since then. Board school education has more children more precocious.

'The rapid advance of female labour, the contact of women with men in the commercial jostle of the world; the increased freedom of tone and manner in the discussion of general topics have, it would appear, make the young folk of today less sensitive than formerly.

'Old fashioned parents will adhere to the belief, honoured in many centuries of practice, that the knowledge of wickedness must obtrude itself on children quite soon enough. There is no necessity to go halfway to meet it, or to go to the theatre to search for it. But to say these things is only to echo the voice of one crying in the wilderness.

'Theatrical managers, though it is their custom to air a few feeble platitudes about art, are, in the main, traders seeking monetary success. Their "noble sentiments" vanish before the chink of their treasury returns. Spiced and seasoned to the appetite, *The Gay Lord Quex* and *The Degenerates*, and other writings of the same class found that fortune awaited them.'

It is doubtful in any event if children then could find easy access to the Royal much less find the price of admission, considering the dire poverty that existed in the city, but that was how the insular, narrow-minded arguments of moral watchdogs as the 1890s melted into the 1900s.

When the French comic opera *La Poupee*, or *The Doll*, was produced at the Royal, a large crowd was in attendance as the production had come from London where it received excellent reviews. The audience was naturally expecting the same production as in London, or one on similar lines.

Instead, the management considered the London presentation a little too risqué as monks were freely introduced so these characters were changed to Huguenots vowed to celibacy so as not to upset the religious community. Dublin critics, as well as the audiences, found this a little too complicated and the whole plot was lost. 'Those who came away expecting dangerous situations were sadly disappointed,' wrote one Dublin reviewer.

This kind of thing seemed to be putting Royal customers off. They felt they were being cheated and not seeing the real thing. The result was that attendances were down. Even when the Dublin Orchestra Society presented an afternoon concert which received good advance publicity, there was a poor house.

The orchestra was in fine form, performing many popular melodies, and certainly deserved much better support. The few people in the front row of the gallery, a sprinkling in the upper circle and a practically empty parterre was sadly a sign of the times.

It was only when Mouillot brought in the likes of concert artistes of the calibre of the Italian tenor Enrico Caruso or the Australian operatic soprano Nellie Melba, probably the only singer to have a tornado named after her, that crowds turned out in great numbers.

Count John McCormack

Nevertheless, they were not adverse to one of their own such as Count John McCormack or Margaret Burke Sheridan.

McCormack is considered Ireland's greatest tenor. Celebrated for his performances of operatic and popular song repertoires, and renowned worldwide for his diction and breath control, he could 'sing just about anything,' in the words of a contemporary artiste. He was equally at home with ballads like 'I Hear You Calling Me' and World War I songs such as 'It's a Long Way to Tipperary' and 'Keep the Home Fires Burning' as he was with Mozart's compositions or the work of Handel.

Always always a popular performer at the Royal and other Dublin theatres whenever his busy international schedule permitted it, he memorably performed on the gala opening night of the fourth and final Theatre Royal in September 1935. 'The Royal was my favourite, though,' he used to say. 'A magnificent theatre.'

Born in Athlone, County Westmeath, and not at Drumsna, County Leitrim as some claim, he was popularly known as Count John McCormack, having received the title of Papal Count from Pope Pius XI in 1928 in recognition of his work for various Catholic charities.

A close friend of James Joyce, who once had singing ambitions before going on to conquer the literary world, McCormack encouraged the Dublin author in stage presentation. They both appeared in a concert at the Antient Concert Rooms in Brunswick Street, now Pearse Street, in 1904, but there is no record of Joyce having played the Royal. Joyce is reputed to have said to McCormack around that time: 'You keep up with the singing John, I'll hang on to the writing.'

Interestingly, the Antient Concert Rooms would later become a popular cinema and was originally known as the Palace in 1920, the Forum in 1950 when Cinemascope facilities were installed and finally the Academy in 1965. After it closed in 1981, it was subsequently used as an occasional cinema and theatre until it was largely destroyed by fire in 1981. The author has happy memories of seeing some good movies as well as shows there, with the Dublin comedian Tony Kenny Senior in good form with his funny quips and stories. It is currently an office block.

McCormack appeared in several movies including the classic *Citizen Kane* and was on friendly terms with stars such as Charles Boyer, Will Rogers, John Barrymore, Janet Gaynor, Basil Rathbone and others when he lived in Hollywood in the 1930s. Already a wealthy man, ill health forced him to retire permanently in 1943 and he died in Dublin in September 1945 following a series of infectious diseases including influenza and pneumonia. Happily, his magnificent voice can still be recaptured today on CDs.

A contemporary of McCormack, and another Royal favourite, was the soprano Margaret Burke Sheridan, whom McCormack greatly admired. As a very nervous 19-year-old from Castlebar, County Mayo, she was very well received for a Thomas Moore memorial concert in the Royal in 1908. It was a similar situation a year later when, before an overflow attendance, a benefit concert was organised in the Royal on her behalf to enable her to finance her training at the Royal Academy of Music in London. Such was her popularity that the audience gave her a standing ovation.

Known as Maggie from Mayo, Sheridan is best remembered for Moore's melodies and her rendition of Balfe's 'I Dreamt I Dwelt in Marble Halls.' For 12 years she performed at La Scala in Milan and

Margaret Burke Sheridan

London's Covent Garden where she enthralled even the most discerning operagoers.

Giacomo Puccini, the celebrated Italian operatic composer, was spellbound by her moving interpretation of his *Madame Butterfly* and described her as being 'full of charismatic intensity and childlike appeal', and when the Italian tenor Beniamino Gigli was making his debut in Covent Garden, he chose her as his leading lady. Micheál MacLiammóir, the London-born actor/producer/poet who adopted Ireland as his native country, described her as 'a tropical bird blown back by the winds of war.'

Sheridan was a star on the world stage, but sadly, and unlike McCormack, her personal life did not flourish. She fell in love with Eustace Blois, the managing director of the Royal Opera House, Covent Garden. But he was married and while he was in love with Margaret, too, her moral conscience, not to mention her Catholic upbringing, would not allow herself to consummate the relationship.

Sheridan had a great many admirers. Brid Mahon recalled in her book *While Green Grass Grows* that it was widely rumoured an Italian whose overtures she had rejected had blown his brains out in a box while she was on stage in La Scala and that after the tragedy she was never the same again.

In any event, while in London for the BBC, her voice cracked on a high note, causing her to lose confidence. She came back to live in Dublin and thanks to the generosity of patrons she stayed in the Shelbourne Hotel and later had a flat in Fitzwilliam Street. It was a long and lonely retirement but she made the best of it.

Hilton Edwards, the London-born Irish-based actor/producer and co-founder of Dublin's Gate Theatre, once witnessed people laughing at her as she tiptoed down Grafton Street in her little platform shoes from Milan, long out of fashion, flamboyantly made up, with her stage make-up still on. 'She was still acting,' he recalled later, 'but she had not known that the curtain had come down.' A victim of cancer, she died in relative obscurity in April 1958.

While Sheridan and McCormack were always welcome artistes at the Royal, musicals rather than orchestral concerts were more popular. Mouillot wanted to forget that poorly attended afternoon concert by the Dublin Orchestral Society which lost money.

One particularly successful concert was in April, 1904 with a state performance by command of King Edward VII which he attended with Queen Alexandra. The specially arranged programme included excerpts from plays such as *King Richard II*, *The Last of the Dandies* and *Trilby*, all starring Beerbohm Tree, the actor-theatre manager who had helped fund the rebuilding of His Majesty's Theatre in London, of which he was manager.

A grandfather of the actor Oliver Reed, Beerbohm put on adventurous and lavish productions at Her Majesty's and often played leading roles, as happened at the Royal.

Such visits by British royalty were quite a novelty then, although the customers in the 'gods' would look down on the patrons in the dearer seats below with some envy. The historian Philip B. Ryan described it well by remembering: 'After the performance, those in the more salubrious parts of the theatre would go on to a fashionable soirée or salon and other forms of extravagant and costly entertainments and dining.'

Visits by royalty, however, did not meet with full approval, with some boos around the theatre. There was still very much resentment with the government in London over the delay of the 'Irish question' and the failure of Charles Stewart Parnell's Home Rule Bill for Ireland which would have restored the domestic autonomy of an Irish parliament.

Even less acceptable to visits of royalty was the introduction of what was known in theatrical circles as jingoism. Jingo songs were first introduced into the Victorian English music hall in 1877 by one of the biggest stars of the day, Gilbert Hastings MacDermott, who was known as the Great MacDermott.

A Londoner by birth, he was the son of an Irish bricklayer and his launderess wife and was best known for his rousing rendition of a war song he bought from a friend for one guinea in an effort to arouse public opposition to the Russians in the Near East. Known not surprisingly as 'The War Song,' its chorus was 'We don't want to fight but by jingo if we do, we've got the ships, we've got the men, and got the money too! We've fought the bear before, and while we're Britons true, the Russians shall not have Constantinople.'

The song introduced the word jingoism into the English language. It became hugely popular in 1878, so much so that the Prince of Wales, the future King Edward VII had MacDermott sing it for him at a private audience. 'The War Song' was brought back several times by other artistes and was sung in an altered version during World War I.

Not surprisingly, while it went down well with some of the Royal audience who were a mixture of loyal and rebel sentiment, many felt it distasteful and there was a riot in the theatre, with hisses and mobs chanting 'By jingo, if we do.' The police had to be called to quell the disturbances and several were arrested for breaches of the peace. Some were taken to hospital.

The Royal management, with Mouillot still at the helm, was naturally cautious of further disturbances and they instructed artistes to be careful about what they said and sang. Some of them regarded this as an early form of censorship and accused the management of downgrading their presentations but Mouillot stood firm.

When a Mrs Charles Sugden, who specialised in reciting poems, announced in the press that she would give two special readings of popular war poems called *The Moment of Britain* and *Fighting Bobs*, there was a poor attendance at the theatre. Undoubtedly, patrons feared another riot. After that, Mouillot simply banned the reading of such plays. Instead, he put on 'safe' productions with a wider appeal, mainly musicals.

As it happened, many of the musicals, for some unaccountable reason, and by a remarkable coincidence, had the word 'girl' in the title. It has never been established if this was to titillate audiences who were perhaps becoming a little tired of the more serious material. However, in the early years of the twentieth century, and in the space of a few years, Mouillot produced and presented a string of popular musicals enjoyed by appreciative audiences.

They included *My Girl, The Shop Girl, The Runaway Girl, The Country Girl, The Earl and the Girl, The Circus Girl, The School Girl, The Girl from Kay's, The Gipsy Girl, The Golden Girl* and *The Girl from Biarritz*. They seemed, for all intents and purposes, like a forerunner of the big Hollywood musicals which lit up movie screens in the 1930s and produced lines and lines of beautiful chorus girls in formation, arranged by the innovative choreographer and producer Busby Berkeley.

Mouillot's main intention was to give Royal audiences what they wanted – and they clearly wanted musicals, judging by attendances. He presented other musicals with slight variations in the titles such *An Artist's Belle of Mayfair, The Model, The Dairy Maids* and the most popular of all, *The Belle of New York*, later made into a movie.

In 1907 Mouillot brought in the American theatrical producer Charles Frohman to present *Peter Pan*, the classic story by the Scottish author and playwright J. M. Barrie about the mischievous boy who can fly and never ages. Frohman had been producing plays since 1889 and had acquired his first Broadway theatre by 1892.

He discovered and promoted many stars of the American theatre and would grow to exert monopoly control over the industry on the far side of the Atlantic for nearly two decades. Sadly, at the height of his illustrious career, he would lose his life in the 1915 sinking of the *Lusitania* by a German U-boat off the Old Head of Kinsale in County Cork.

When Frohman came to Dublin in 1907 he had been leasing the Duke of York Theatre in London, from where he brought *Peter Pan* following its Broadway run. At the Royal it was produced under the direction of Dion Boucicault, with the beautiful American actress and goddaughter of Barrie, 22-year-old Pauline Chase, in the title role, flying gracefully with Kirby's Flying Ballet.

Chase was known as the Pocket Venus of New York. Interestingly, one of the character roles was played by a curly-haired lad named Alfred Willmore, destined in later years to become famous as an Irish theatrical great, Micheál MacLiammóir.

Micheál MacLiammóir

MacLiammóir was a larger than life character – actor, dramatist, impresario, writer, poet and painter. However, he was not born in Ireland despite a common belief but into a Protestant family in the Kensal Green district of London. A member of an acting company which included Noel Coward, he travelled extensively in his twenties and, while visiting Ireland, fell in love with Irish culture to such an extent that he learned to speak and write in the language.

Presenting himself as a descendant of Cork Catholics and

changing his name to Micheál MacLiammóir, he would dominate the Irish theatrical scene for over 50 years. 'I love and adore the theatre, always have,' he would say in that lovely sonorous voice. 'It's my whole life.'

With his partner Hilton Edwards, MacLiammóir founded the Gate Theatre in Dublin's Parnell Square in 1928 and it quickly became recognised as one of Europe's most outstanding theatrical companies, with movie stars such as Orson Welles and James Mason being two of his earliest players. MacLiammóir's costume designs as well as the sets were considered key elements in the success of the theatre, which is still going strong nearly 90 years on.

In a productive life MacLiammóir toured the world with his one-man show *The Importance Of Being Oscar*. Based on the life and work of Oscar Wilde, it received great acclaim. He also toured with *I Must Be Talking to My Friends*, a production about Irish writing and writers, as well as *Talking About Yeats*, another one-man show. MacLiammóir often talked to friends about his part in *Peter Pan* at the Royal in 1907 and it remained one of his happiest memories up to his death in March 1978 at the age of 78.

In many ways *Peter Pan* was a welcome break for Royal audiences who had become used to seeing what was described as music hall shows rather than musical comedy. Although many of the artistes were of very inferior quality as far as discerning Irish audiences were concerned, especially as their brand of humour were aimed mainly at their own audiences in London and elsewhere, there were some notable exceptions.

For instance, back on 2 July 1906, in a supporting act on a variety show, there was a group billed as Eight Lancashire Lads, described in the programme as 'The smartest combination of singers and dancers extant.' One member of the group was a 17-year-old London lad named Charlie Chaplin, who would achieve world fame in Hollywood, first in silent pictures.

*Charlie Chaplin, seen here in The Gold Rush,
got his early start at the Royal in 1906*

Chaplin would recall his visit to the Royal with fondness in his retirement years. 'Yes, happy memories,' he said on one of his visits to Waterville, County Kerry where he holidayed for over 10 years. 'The Theatre Royal in dear old Dublin, and the Eight Lancashire Lads, what memories.' On being told that it had since been pulled down, he shook his head sadly and lamented: 'Yet another fine theatre gone. Where will it all end?'

5

Jabs and Uppercuts Replace
Song and Dance

Frederick Mouillot made a New Year resolution on 31 December 1907 to bring something completely different to the Royal on occasions. Following a meeting with his fellow directors in early January, they tossed around ideas without coming to any definite decision.

Their problem was solved when they heard that Tommy Burns, the world heavyweight boxing champion from Canada, was on a world tour and had expressed an interest in fighting the top contenders any country wanted to put forward, including Ireland. 'I'm a fighting champion,' he was quoted in a London newspaper as saying, 'and I'll take on all comers. Just bring them on.'

Mouillot put a syndicate together and contacted Burns' management team to work out a deal for the champion to defend his title at the Theatre Royal on St Patrick's Day 1908. His opponent would be the County Wexford blacksmith Jem Roche.

Certainly the fight caught the imagination of the nation, and further afield. There were 1,374 applications for press accreditation from Britain, France, the US, Canada and of course Ireland. Because of restrictions in space at ringside, only 16 press passes could be allocated.

For the biggest fight of his career, Roche trained in the St Iberius Club in Wexford. Barrels of fresh sea water were taken up from the harbour for his showers. Money for training, even for towels, was scarce. Then, less than a week before the big fight, he caught a heavy cold.

Jem's doctor diagnosed it as bronchial trouble and prescribed a powder to be inhaled, while keeping the incident a secret lest the fight, Roche's golden opportunity, might be called off. While the powder improved his breathing, it brought on a dazed effect, but his doctor reassured the press and the promoters that everything would be fine on the night and that they had nothing to worry about.

Certainly, Roche looked very impressive in training, with the *Irish Independent* reporting: 'The Wexford man's physique is magnificent. You must see Jem punch that bag. The thunder of it not only shivers the frame from which the bag is suspended but sends a tremor through the whole building. A member of the audience was so carried away that he shouted aloud "Heaven have mercy on poor Burns". With head bowed, guarded by his left, Roche advances on his adversary with his right, and quickly puts him on the defensive.'

Roche's manager and trainer Nick Tennant told reporters: 'Jem is just the sort to make a world's champion – strong, fast, clever, cool and determined. He can give and take more than his share of punishment and this makes him a tall order for any living fighter. I fail to see how Jem can lose. Fans at the Royal can look forward to a great fight. They have been used to watching tenors and sopranos and actors and comedians and the like. Now they are going to be hailing the first ever world heavyweight boxing champion from Ireland, Jem Roche himself.'

Certainly Roche was the new national hero. Even people with little interest in boxing became instant fans. Jem's train journey from Wexford to Dublin was like a royal procession. Cheering crowds lined the platforms at every station and whenever the train stopped, which was often, he had to get out and make a speech and shake hands with scores of well-wishers.

Roche was looking out the window, amazed by all the attention, as the train finally pulled in at Westland Row station where he was greeted by more cheering crowds and a pipe and drum band. There were shouts of 'Give it to him, Jem,' 'Let him have it good,' and 'Bring home the title, son.' Shaking scores of outstretched hands, he told reporters: 'I am confident but not overconfident. Anyway, Burns is going to get his comeuppance, that's for sure. I'll be the new heavyweight champion of the world.'

Roche was then whisked in a waiting car to Prussia Street where his training quarters were set up, with all his outdoor training being arranged for the spacious Phoenix Park. On one occasion, running up a slope alongside Dan Kelly, a former Irish lightweight boxing champion who would be in his corner, he found an old horseshoe, an item he was well used to from his days as a blacksmith.

There were six nails in the shoe and he felt this would be a lucky omen, as he was a notoriously superstitious individual. He told Kelly he would knock out Burns in six rounds. When one of the nails fell out, he changed his forecast to five rounds.

The next day, with just 24 hours to go before the fight, Roche attended 11.00 o'clock Mass at the Aughrim Street church accompanied by his handlers. Afterwards, they went for a stroll in the Phoenix Park, driving to and from the gates so as to avoid the crowds who were sure to turn up. In the evening he did light workouts at his training quarters in Prussia Street before going on to his headquarters, the International Hotel in College Green, to take things easy and read the many telegrams awaiting him.

Burns arrived by sea at Kingstown, now Dun Laoghaire, and was taken straight by car to the Dolphin Hotel in Essex Street, having completed his training in England. A big crowd gathered outside the swanky red-bricked hotel, where he had rented a suite of rooms. Later on, when he appeared at the window of the hotel, which is still standing but now used as office space for the Irish courts service, he tossed coins to the crowd below.

Asked by an *Irish Independent* reporter later if he was afraid of losing, he replied, as though shocked by the impertinence of the question: 'If I were, there would be no point in coming here, would there? I understand that the opinion here prevails that Roche will win. Well, if he beats me, I will be the first man to shake his hand.'

The fight was scheduled for 20 rounds, the regulation distance. It got massive publicity in the newspapers at home and abroad. For weeks leading up to the big night, pubs were full, and the main topic of conversation was Roche v. Burns. Prices were set at £15 15s for boxes which would hold seven, £5 5s for seats on the stage close to the ring and £2 2s for the parterre. Seats in the dress circle were £3 3s.

On fight night, all the adjoining streets around the Royal were packed with fans, either going in or those unable to procure tickets. All 2,012 tickets were quickly snapped up since the 17 March date had been first announced in January.

All was set for the action, and the city centre was thronged with enthusiastic fans. The police formed a cordon 30 yards from the entrance to the theatre and nobody was allowed in without a ticket. Hawkins Street itself was simply impassable and cars had to do a detour to reach the theatre.

Roche had great difficulty in reaching the stage door in Poolbeg Street as supporters, many waiting there for over two hours, heaved and pushed in an effort to shake the Wexfordman's hand and wish him luck. One, wearing a green flag wrapped around his shoulders, was happily singing the ditty 'The Wearing of the Green', keeping the crowd in good humour.

Burns, too, was besieged as he tried to reach the door. 'This is incredible,' the world champion remarked to one of his team. 'In all my years in the game, I've never experienced anything like this before.'

Programme for the Tommy Burns–Jem Roche fight

Burns' biographer Dan McCaffrey, a prolific Canadian author, noted: 'Hordes of people with excited features howled at the doors. There were strange sounds in many voices. One could only catch some words clearly. They were "Good luck, Tommy Burns" and "Do your best, Jem boy," repeated again and again with eager vehemence. Wexford versus America. Ireland versus the world! It was the night of nights.'

The crowd outside, estimated to run into several thousand and without tickets, waited patiently for the signal in lights specifically set up to indicate how the rounds were going. There would be a red glow if Burns won a particular round, or a green light for Roche if it went his way. As it happened, and something the crowd was not aware of, the lights system broke down before the programme commenced.

Inside the theatre, the atmosphere was full of excitement as spectators babbled away during the preliminary bouts, swapping opinions on the likely outcome of the main fight. Although Burns would enter the ring as favourite, there was still a lot of money on Roche to become Ireland's first world heavyweight champion in what would be the only title fight among the big boys to be staged in this country.

It was reported that a number of farmers put their land on the outcome, including two in Wexford, two in Cork and one in Monaghan, so confident were they that Roche would leave the ring as winner and new champion.

It was 10.15 when Roche left his dressing room and made his way to the ring and the sounds of 'The Boys of Wexford' from the orchestra pit. The big crowd joined in the singing. When he climbed into the ring, wearing a bright red jumper and green trunks with a green and white sash, he was soon accompanied by his team. Suddenly there was a last-minute flurry when it was discovered that he had forgotten his hand bandages. A messenger was despatched to the dressing room and returned, not with bandages but with a package of lint.

Burns, who had been watching the preliminary bouts from the back of the theatre, strolled down the aisle to the strains of 'Yankee Doodle Dandy'. This was not a geographical insult to Burns. Rather, the orchestra did not have the music sheets for the Canadian national anthem and, not inclined to play 'God Save the King', they opted for 'Yankee Doodle'.

In any event, Burns did not regard himself as a true son of Canada, the land of his birth, but an American. He was a US citizen, and wore red trunks with stars and stripes down the side, together with a sash around his waist.

When he climbed into the ring, he glared at Roche, trying to make eye contact. He had told a newspaper reporter earlier in the week that he could hypnotise opponents and he was going to do the same with Roche. He continued to stare at the challenger as referee Robert Watson issued the final instructions, with the Wexford man meeting him eye to eye. Both men looked the same height but in fact, Roche, at 5 feet 8 inches, was fractionally taller. He weighed 12 stone nine pounds. Burns was six pounds lighter.

There were cries of 'Go to it, Jem,' and 'Give him the old one-two, Jem' from the excited audience who were hoping to witness a thriller, with an Irish win naturally at the end. The *Evening Herald* planned a stop-press edition, and one of Roche's handlers spotted Victor Breyer, a well-known scribe for the Parisian newspaper *L'Auto,* among the press crew at ringside. Bookmakers' cries could be heard all over the theatre, 'seven to two on Burns,' 'three to one on Roche.' The black market trade was brisk.

A contemporary artist's impression of the Burns–Roche fight

The attendance included political figures, civic representatives, business people, members of the entertainment industry and notables from the world of sport. There were also scatterings of a few churchmen visible, including nuns holding Rosary beads, no doubt saying silent prayers that the Irish champion would come to no harm, let alone emerge victorious.

It was all over in 88 seconds, one of the shortest world heavyweight championship fights in boxing history when Burns landed his vaunted right and Roche was counted out. It ended so quick that one man had just taken off his coat, turned to drape it over his seat, and when he turned around the fight was over. Other latecomers, delayed by the big crowds outside, arrived to see Roche being counted out.

World heavyweight boxing champion Tommy Burns of Canada knocked out Wexford's Jem Roche in 88 seconds at the Royal on St Patrick's Day, 1908

Burns was first to leave, going out by the stage door in Poolbeg Street, and though the crowd had already begun to disperse in gossiping groups, there were no cheers for the victor. Stepping into his cab, he was driven back to his quarters at the Dolphin Hotel.

Burns had felt so confident of victory that when his car left him at the stage door at 9.45 pm, he gave instructions to the driver to call around for him punctually at 10.45 and drive straight back at the Dolphin Hotel where dinner would be awaiting him.

It was not until 11.45 that Roche, looking totally dejected, emerged from the front of the theatre. While there were only a few fans left by this time, they gave him a parting cheer, some shouting; 'Better luck next time, Jem,' as he stepped into his car with some of his handlers and was taken back to the International Hotel for a meal.

The ironic aftermath was that while the syndicate made a nice little profit on the gate receipts, and Burns increased his bank balance with his £10,000 purse and pocketing the £500 side bets as well as betting on himself, Roche came out a loser. He had not made a single a penny for the biggest fight of his career, having agreed to a winner-take-all arrangement.

One punter who did turn out a winner was the quick-thinking individual who ran out of the Royal just seconds after Roche had been counted out, waving his ticket above his head. 'I can't bear it any longer,' he shouted to anxious fans outside waiting for news. 'Roche is murdering him. There's blood all over the place. Is there anyone here who could bear to witness the horrid spectacle? He can buy my ticket for £2?'

After a mad scramble for the precious ticket, the seller got his money and disappeared into the night. The delighted purchaser made his way into the theatre, only to be met by a surge of disappointed and angry customers pushing their way out yelling: 'It's all over,' 'Roche lasted only one round,' 'Jem had no chance.'

The Royal subsequently hosted a number of amateur international boxing tournaments involving teams from the USA, Germany, Britain and Belgium from the early 1930s, before the National Boxing Stadium was built on Dublin's South Circular Road in 1939.

Professional shows were also held at the Royal throughout the 1930s, 1940s and 1950s.

6

When Suffragettes Tried to
Burn Down the Royal

Aparty made up of four members of the English suffragette movement, an activist organisation seeking voting rights for women,
arrived unannounced in Dublin on the morning of 19 July 1912. The
four – Mary Leigh, Gladys Evans, Jennie Barnes and Mabel Capper
– had one purpose in mind: to disrupt the official visit to the city by
the British Liberal Prime Minister Herbert Asquith who was due to
deliver a lecture on the Home Rule issue at the Theatre Royal that
night. He planned to give a further speech on the same subject the
following night, again at the theatre.

'If it means going further than merely disrupting the visit, then
come what may,' Leigh told an *Irish Independent* reporter who spotted her wearing the sash. She did not elaborate on what she meant by
'come what may.'

The Irish suffragette movement, set up by the nationalist Hannah
Sheehy Skeffington, was apparently unaware of the British group in
Dublin. However, it was agreed that if they did come into contact
with them, they would let the visitors get on with it with no interfer-
ence. In any event, the Irish suffragettes were not as militant as their
counterparts in Britain, where they chained themselves to railings,
set fire to mailbox contents, smashed windows and detonated bombs.

Indeed, in 1913 one member, Emily Davison, would be seriously injured and die four days later after running out on the racecourse during Derby Day at Epsom trying to seize the reins of the King's horse Anmer and attempting to pin a 'vote for women' banner on it.

The prime minister's visit caused great excitement in the city. As well as Irish and British newspapers covering the event, the *New York Times* correspondent was in town. Big crowds lined the quays as the PM's carriage made its way from the Phoenix Park and into the city centre.

As the carriage passed over O'Connell Bridge, Leigh threw a hatchet, with the handle tightly wrapped in cloth, towards the carriage. The hatchet, with a note reading 'This symbol of the extinction of the Liberal Party for evermore' narrowly missed the Prime Minister.

It struck the Irish Nationalist leader and Home Ruler advocate John Redmond, who was also in the carriage, on the left shoulder. By the time the police converged on the carriage, the women had dispersed into the crowd. There were reports from members of the public that one of the suffragettes had been thrown off O'Connell Bridge into the Liffey, but such was not the case.

There were more crowds in Hawkins Street and surrounding areas. On alighting from the carriage, Asquith was pelted with eggs by Evans as officials presented Mrs Asquith with a bouquet of flowers. As the party made their way into the theatre, the audience broke into song, first with 'A Nation Once Again' followed by 'God Save Ireland.' As Asquith walked out on the stage, which was draped in green cloth on which showed an Irish harp in gold, with ivory twined around it, the crowd sang 'For He's a Jolly Good Fellow.'

In his speech, Asquith invited suggestions for possible incorporation into the draft of the Home Rule Bill. He was repeatedly interrupted, however, by calls of 'Votes for women' and 'We want the right to vote and be heard' from the suffragettes, who by now had the support of other members of the audience.

At the conclusion, as the patrons made their way to the exits, there was the sound of an explosion, later reported as being caused by a device in a handbag. A burning chair was thrown from a balcony into the orchestra pit by one of the women, and flammable liquid was spread around the projection box by another. When an attempt was made to set it alight, it suddenly caught fire and exploded once but was quickly extinguished.

By this time there was panic in the theatre before the police came and tried to restore some kind of order. Asquith's second speech the following night went ahead but under stricter supervision, with all patrons searched before entering the theatre. There was no trouble.

All four women were brought before Green Street Special Criminal Court on 12 August charged with 'having committed serious outrages at the time of the visit of the British Prime Minister Herbert Asquith, conspiracy to commit grievous bodily harm and malicious damage and to cause an explosion at the Theatre Royal.'

The trial lasted several days during which the police came under fire for initially refusing to allow admittance to women. Sergeant Durban Cooper of the Connaught Rangers, who was in the theatre with his wife, gave evidence of going to the dress circle and finding the carpet saturated with oil and ablaze. With the help of a colleague, Sergeant Shea, they managed to beat out the fire with their coats. Soon after there was an explosion under a seat and the entire dress circle was filled with smoke.

Just then, Shea said he noticed a young woman standing near the projection box, and lighting matches. Opening the door of the box she threw in a lighted match on the back seat and soon it was ablaze. As the two policemen were making their best efforts to beat out the blaze, she tried to escape but Cooper restrained her. 'There will be a few more explosions in the future,' she shouted. 'This is only the start of it.' Cooper told the court she was very defiant.

C. A. O'Connor, the Attorney General for Ireland, conducted the prosecution and the case was presided over by Judge Madden. It was clear that the authorities were at great pains to quell the burgeoning suffragette movement, and so set out to brand the women as highly dangerous provocateurs.

O'Connor spoke of the horrors the fire in the theatre could have caused, and Judge Madden, upon passing sentence, rendered it his 'imperative duty to pronounce a sentence that is calculated to have a deterrent effect.'

Leigh and Evans each received five years penal servitude, and Baines, who called herself Lizzie Baker, got seven months hard labour. Capper was remanded in prison during the trial but the charges against her were ultimately dropped. The *Evening Post* reported that large crowds had gathered inside and outside the court for their sentencing, and 'applause rang out around a largely hostile room.'

*   *   *

Frank Mouillot had died suddenly in Brighton in 1911. Two years earlier, as manager of the Royal, he entered negotiations with his fellow directors to go into partnership with the Gaiety Theatre run by the widow of the former owner Michael Gunn. The outcome was that the Royal directors formed the Gaiety Theatre (Dublin) Co Ltd, with Mouillot as overall managing director and David Telford as chairman.

There were separate boards of management for the Gaiety who would run their own affairs and book their own performers. On Mouillot's death, Telford took overall control while allowing Mrs Gunn to look after the Gaiety. Telford promised to maintain the Royal's high standard of productions. 'This is what the public would at least expect,' he told a reporter.

While all profits from both theatres were going into Gaiety Theatre (Dublin) Co Ltd, the Royal and the Gaiety were effectively in opposition to each other, an odd situation. George Edwardes, the

Impresario George Edwardes

London impresario who was related to the Gunn family and now released from any long-standing obligations and loyalty, transferred his companies to the Royal because he felt the Hawkins Street venue presented a much lighter form of entertainment and appealed to a wider audience.

Asked by a newspaper reporter if he felt he was being disloyal to Gaiety audiences, he said: 'Goodness no. Not by any means. We will still play the Gaiety when opportunities arise from time to time, but for the forseeable future, our allegiance is to the Theatre Royal.'

Edwardes had already introduced a new era in musical theatre to the London stage and beyond. Starting out in theatre management in his late teens, he was soon working at a number of West End theatres. By the age of twenty, he was managing theatres for Richard D'Oyly Carte, the talent agent and composer who would later establish his famous opera company.

Edwardes ruled a theatrical empire across channel including the Gaiety, Daly's, the Adelphi and others, sending touring companies around Britain and Ireland. In the early 1890s, while still in his thirties, he recognized the changing tastes of musical theatre audiences and led the movement away from burlesque and comic opera to Edwardian musical comedy. The directors on the Theatre Royal side of the board felt he was the right man in the right place at the right time to bring quality productions to Hawkins Street.

Richard D'Oyly Carte, however, refused to break his allegiance to the Gaiety, and continued to present very successful, if periodic, productions at the South King Street theatre. Sir Henry Lytton, a leading member of the D'Oyly Carte company and the only person ever knighted for achievements as a Gilbert and Sullivan performer, said of Dublin audiences: 'Nowhere are there truer lovers of Gilbert and Sullivan than in Dublin. Maybe Gilbert's fantastic wit is the one they understand, and maybe too their hearts are warmed by the plaintive song of their fellow countryman, Sullivan. Whatever the cause, we had no better reception anywhere.'

Musical comedy nevertheless was starting to lose favour with audiences all over, and the Royal increasingly featured music hall productions. One of the most popular entertainers to play the Royal around this time was the English ventriloquist Fred Russell, who was known as 'the father of modern ventriloquism,' or more affectionately as 'Uncle Fred.'

Born Thomas Frederick Parnell in London, he officially changed his name to Fred Russell because of the extremely sensitive political connection to the Irish leader at the time. Growing up, Russell's hobby was ventriloquism and his career took off when he was offered a spot on a bill at London's Palace Theatre. His act, based on the cheeky-boy dummy Coster Joe, saw him break away from the prevailing format of a family of dummies. Russell established a precedent for future ventriloquists, notably the American entertainer Edgar Bergen with his Charlie McCarthy and Mortimer Snerd dummies.

Russell was also active in promoting the variety show genre and was a leading member of the entertainment industry charity, the Grand Order of Water Rats, and a founder member of the Variety Artistes Federation. One of his sons was Val Parnell, the theatrical impresario who reverted to his father's birth name and is probably best known for his television show, *Val Parnell's Sunday Night at the London Palladium*. He is credited with giving a 12-year-old Julie Andrews her first break on the English stage.

Many famous performers appeared at the Royal and were enjoyed by full houses. 'The performers were the equivalent of film stars and pop idols of their time, with magnetic personalities and songs which still live on in folk memory,' said the historian Philip B. Ryan. 'Unfortunately, it is now a matter of the song and not the singer.

'There are many enthusiastic students of the old time music hall, which disappeared after World War I to be replaced by a faster moving entertainment called variety, and these collectors of memorabilia such as old posters, programmes, sheet music and early gramophone records can unfailingly match the singer to the song. Otherwise, all that is remembered is the song, and the general public rarely recognise the once famous name associated with it.'

The song 'Daisy Bell' became very popular over the years, and is less known than its composer Katie Lawrence, who did very well financially out of it throughout the US, Britain and Ireland. Charles Coborn is another forgotten entertainer whose songs were more famous than himself. Coborn was an English music hall singer and comedian, and bought 'The Man Who Broke the Bank at Monte Carlo' from its composer Fred Gilbert outright for £10.

Gilbert confirmed that his inspiration was the gambler and confidence trickster Charles Wells, who won over a million francs at the Monte Carlo casino in Monaco, using the profits from previous fraud and who would die penniless. Gilbert is said to have seen a newspaper placard with the wording 'Man Breaks Bank at Monte Carlo', went home and composed the song. While it was unsuccessful at first, it became enormously popular when Coborn launched it at the Oxford Music Hall, repeatedly singing chorus after chorus. He eventually sold the rights for £100.

Coborn's real name was Charles Whitton McCallum but adopted his stage name from his locality, Coborn Road in London. In a long career on stage, Coborn also sang the comic ditty 'Two Lovely Black Eyes,' which he adapted from an original song, but he was best known for 'The Man Who Broke the Bank at Monte Carlo'. He estimated that he had sung it 250,000 times in the course of his career, and could sing it in 14 languages. He performed it both in English and French in the 1934 movie *Say It with Flowers.*

Billed in Royal programmes as Dublin's favourite comedian, Coborn nevertheless was never fully accepted by the music hall establishment across the water, probably because of his somewhat snobbish demeanour. Complete with his monocle, he was known as 'a literate man of high principles' and wore a top hat on stage.

At the same time he had a huge following and Dublin audiences, whether he appeared at the Royal or the Olympia in Dame Street, unfailingly accorded him a warm reception. He always said that Irish audiences were warmer than their English counterparts, and that he enjoyed playing Dublin.

Charles Coborn sang 'The Man Who Broke the Bank at Monte Carlo' 250,000 times

Coborn often sang the chorus of 'The Man Who Broke the Bank at Monte Carlo' ten times 'because the customers seemed to like it so much,' he would claim. Coborn was singing his two hit songs up to the time of his death in 1945, when he was coming up to 93.

'The Man Who Broke the Bank at Monte Carlo,' regarded today as possibly the most famous music hall song of all time, would enjoy something of a modest revival in the 1962 film *Lawrence of Arabia* when Lawrence, played by Peter O'Toole, sings the tune while riding across the desert to the camp of Prince Faisal – proving that old songs, like old soldiers, never die, but merely fade away.

Meanwhile, with a successful 1912 season at the Theatre Royal behind him, new manager David Telford had every reason to be

optimistic of repeating the tried and trusted formula in the New Year
– good productions professionally presented and, where possible,
big names. This trend happily continued into 1913 until the summer when bigger events began to take centre stage. In a Dublin filled
with slums and beset by poverty, James Larkin had founded the Irish
Transport and General Workers Union.

As the union, known as the ITGWU, pursued a course of political and industrial action aimed at securing workers' rights and fair
wages, some 400 of the capital's largest employers banded together to
put them down. Union members who refused to sign a pledge reject-
ing the ITGWU were summarily suspended or dismissed, embracing
nearly every business in the city.

Some 1,500 workers found themselves locked out in total. Un-
deterred, on 31 August, Larkin gave a public address on O'Connell
Street, then called Sackville Street. The event was declared illegal by
police who baton charged the crowd, claiming three lives.

By May 1914, the lockout had collapsed, with the employers claiming victory as a greater issue loomed, World War I, with the 1916 Re-
bellion close behind. However, the ITGWU survived and provided the
foundation stone for the labour movement to create a more equal, and
relatively prosperous, society.

The Royal continued through these difficult times, with many performers called up for war duty. Many acts, too, contracted to appear
could not honour their engagements. Nevertheless, management
was ever mindful of the age-old tradition that the show must go on.

Though the 1916 Rising was quelled within a week, the harshness
of the British response greatly increased support for the nationalist
party Sinn Féin, founded in 1905 and which won 73 of the 105 seats
in the 1918 general election.

The first Irish parliament, the Dáil, was formed in January 1919
and reaffirmed the 1916 proclamation with the Declaration of Independence and that 'a state of war existed between Ireland and

England.' There were even calls from the public that 'English artistes should be banned from appearing in Irish theatres,' an edict that happily never came to pass.

During the War of Independence in 1920 and 1921 and the Civil War from 1922 to 1923, the Royal managed to keep the doors open. Margaret Burke Sheridan, who was now a big star on the stages of London and Milan, remembered how she got her early break in Hawkins Street as a nervous 19-year-old from Mayo in 1908 and returned to the Royal in November 1922 for a sell-out concert. 'It's always nice to come back to this lovely theatre,' she told reporters at a reception.

Sheridan shared the bill with the American baritone Walter McNally, who would move to Dublin permanently, get married and settle down. Accompanied by her former teacher Dr Vincent O'Brien, Sheridan performed popular arias, much to the delight of an appreciative audience. The management was so pleased with the reception she received that she was asked back for a second concert, and was only too happy to oblige.

Around this time, the early 1920s, a new theatrical concept was gradually creeping into the theatrical world and replacing the old style music hall. The new form was called variety, which had made a big impact on the American stage. In Britain, too, audiences seemed to be looking for something new, as indicated by falling attendances. The old style music halls had gone through a lean period during World War I, with most of them staging charity events.

They continued after the war ended in 1918 but were becoming less popular due to the emergence of the upcoming era of jazz, swing and big band dance music acts. Theatre managements were now realising that a completely new type of music hall entertainment had arrived – variety.

It was similar as to what would happen when silent films gave way to talkies at the end of the 1920s, and the somewhat sedate music scene would make way for the faster tempo of rock 'n' roll in the

1950s. Big changes in entertainment were taking place. Many music hall performers, even the most prominent ones, failed to make the transition. Deemed old fashioned and with less opportunities to work due to the closure of many halls, music hall entertainment simply died out and the modern day variety era began.

Variety was essentially a faster, slicker type of entertainment, with artistes given less time on the bill. Sketches were introduced, as were cross-talk comedians with lively patter, a practice which originated in China where it is part of the country's culture.

Bob Hope, a future performer on the Royal, was among more than 20,000 artistes working on the American stage when variety was beginning to reach its highest popularity in the 1920s. Many of these performers were, like London-born Hope, recent immigrants to America who saw a career in variety as one of the few ways to succeed as a 'foreigner' in the US.

With the music halls in decline, a great many artistes, like some of the silent movie stars who found their speaking voices were unsuitable to the new medium of sound, discovered themselves unwanted after a lifetime at their profession. The old English music hall entertainers were now considered old fashioned. Out of work and with little chance of finding employment, many finished up in terrible, often tragic, circumstances.

Leo Dryden, a music hall singer and comedian known for his patriotic songs and parodies, saw his marriage break up and was reduced to busking in the streets. He died several months before the outbreak of World War II in 1939, penniless and forgotten.

T. E. Dunville, a star comedian in the 1920s, saw his popularity fade with the fickle public craving for new faces, and when he failed to get work, he began suffering fits of depression. In early 1924, his second wife, Dora, described him as a bundle of nerves. 'The slightest thing seemed to worry him,' she said, though admitting that his failure to secure engagements took a heavy toll on him. One day he left her a note that read in part: 'I feel I cannot bear it any longer. There is nothing really left to live for. I am deeply sorry.' Dunville's body was later found in the River Thames. He was 56.

Even years earlier, some music hall artistes saw the danger signs in their profession. Mark Sheridan, the comedian and singer popular on Irish stages and famous for rousing songs like 'I Do Like to Be Beside the Seaside', 'Belgium Put the Kibosh on the Kaiser' and 'I'd Like to Shake Shakespeare', shot himself in a fit of depression in a public park in 1918.

Harry Fragson, a big star best known for his rendition of 'Hello, Hello, Who's Your Lady Friend' and very popular with Royal audiences, was shot dead in 1913 by his mentally ill father Victor who suspected that his son was having an affair with his mistress. Victor himself died six weeks later in an asylum.

The artistes themselves knew only too well that they were regarded socially as the lowest of the low, merely rogues and vagabonds. Derided by the so-called legitimate theatre and scorned by both the upper and middle classes as 'a collection of painted women and vulgar men', it does not require too much imagination to realise that they had a powerful and lingering inferiority complex.

In place of the old style of individual comedians, new performers were mixing dialogue with songs. This led to the arrival on the scene of stand-up comics such as Max Miller, a big favourite at the Royal in later years, and double-acts including the likes of Flanagan and Allen in Britain and George Burns and Gracie Allen in America.

Double acts, of course, would find greater fame in Hollywood, notably Laurel and Hardy. Who can ever forget Laurel's crying while scratching his head and Hardy's downtrodden glances to the camera whenever something went wrong? The great duo never played the Royal but they did appear at the Olympia in Dame Street in the early 1950s to great acclaim.

7

King and Queen of Panto

In the 1920s following the War of Independence and the Civil War a sense of normality was beginning to return to the city and the Theatre Royal resumed with regular concerts and shows. Christmas pantomimes continued to be extremely popular, too, and were considered ideal family entertainment.

The Royal management was always aware that any shows which included songs, slapstick comedy and dancing, employing gender-crossing performers, and combining topical humour with a story loosely based on a well-known fairy tale such as the panto, was a recipe for success. With the audience invited to sing along with certain parts of the music and shout out phrases to the performers, the panto season, beginning before Christmas and running into the New Year, often as late as February, was considered a winner.

It is agreed, without any arguments, that the king and queen of Irish pantos were Jimmy O'Dea and Maureen Potter, particularly in the 1940s and 1950s. While both entertainers are generally associated with the Gaiety, they were very popular performers whenever they appeared on the Royal stage.

'Ah sure, I loved playing the Royal, a grand theatre,' O'Dea used to say. A true Dub, as he called himself, and one of eight children, 11 if some sources are to be believed, Jimmy was born in Lower Bridge

Street, down near the River Liffey, and not far from the site of the Ford of the Hurdles, Dublin's original settlement.

Jimmy's mother Martha ran a wholesale toy shop in the street while his father James was an ironmonger and had a shop in Capel Street, on the opposite side of the Liffey. As a youngster Jimmy was interested in taking to the stage as two of his classmates at St Mary's College in Rathmines, the Gogan brothers, Paddy and Tommy, were filling his mind about a life in the theatre, which they themselves would aspire to. One of the Gogan family, Larry, would become one of RTÉ radio's most popular DJs in future years.

Jimmy's father, however, would not entertain any thoughts of a theatrical career. 'No son of mine, or daughter for that matter, will ever be involved in a business that's full of rogues and vagabonds,' he used to say. 'I'd rather see them in their coffin first.' He sent young Jimmy to Edinburgh where he was apprenticed to an optician. After qualifying, Jimmy returned to Dublin to set up his own business, which he would later hand over to his sister Rita, and subsequently went into the theatrical world full-time, despite his father's objections. He started off in amateur productions of Ibsen, Chekhov and Shaw.

When O'Dea senior realised that young Jimmy only seemed happiest on the stage and did not want to do anything else, he gave the boy his full blessing and support. Jimmy's father would live to see Jimmy become an established performer on the stage. Shortly before his death, the senior O'Dea told a family member: 'I'm very glad indeed I never stood in Jimmy's way. He would have hated me for the rest of my life. I'm sure he would have gone on the stage in any event but it's nice to think he knew his dad was always behind him.'

Jimmy O'Dea would later establish himself on the cinema screen, notably when Walt Disney selected him to play the king of the leprechauns in *Darby O'Gill and the Little People*, released in 1959. Later on he would make his mark on Telefís Éireann in the comedy

Jimmy O'Dea, the panto king

series *O'Dea's Yer Man* alongside David Kelly.

To generations of Dubliners, though, he was the panto king in the Gaiety where his most famous character was Biddy Mulligan, the Pride of the Coombe, the representation of a working-class Dublin street-seller created for him by his scriptwriter, Harry O'Donovan.

As the playwright and author Hugh Leonard put it: 'In those days, our year held two great treats – Christmas and Jimmy O'Dea. In the Dublin of that time, he was not simply a comic, he *was* comedy. As with the greatest of his kind, his eyes held an ineffable sadness, and the more mournful he became, the funnier he was.'

Maureen Potter was in the spotlight from the time she became the junior Irish dancing champion at the age of seven until ill health forced her into retirement two years before her death in 2004. She too had happy memories of appearing on the Royal stage.

'What can you say about the Royal?' she commented when asked in a newspaper interview. 'It was sheer magic. When you walked out on that big, expansive stage, you always knew instinctively that you would get a warm reception from the appreciative audience. It was indeed a real tragedy when the theatre was pulled down. They should have managed to keep it open, somehow – a government intervention perhaps. I personally will always miss it, and I'm quite certain that this sentiment would go for all its regular patrons.'

Born in the northside Dublin suburb of Fairview, Maureen was discovered performing in local clubs by Jimmy O'Dea, who put her in one of his pantomimes when she was 10. In her early days, billed as the Pocket Mimic, Maureen toured Britain as a Shirley Temple impersonator with Jack Hylton's band in the 1930s, and played the London Palladium.

In 1938 she performed in front of Hitler in Berlin. Enchanted by her performance, he sent her a handwritten note, which she proudly showed to her mother, who promptly threw it in the waste bin. Potter stood just under five feet in height, but there was nothing small about her personality and voice. Years of loneliness touring as a child, having borrowed a birth certificate because she was officially too young to work, made Maureen appreciate her own fireside in Dublin, and she spent almost all her career in the Irish capital, in spite of many overseas offers.

After World War II, she resumed a professional association with O'Dea which was to last for 30 years. Each epitomised the archetypal Dubliner – impoverished but resilient and proud, contemptuous of authority, and quick with the smart answer and the withering put-down.

'They worked together brilliantly,' recalled the playwright and author James Plunkett, best known for his classic novel *Strumpet City*. 'I could never imagine one without the other. Potter began as O'Dea's "feed", but, by the time of his death in 1965, the public saw Maureen as her mentor's equal.

'She became the queen of pantomime at the Gaiety, most notably working with comedian and dancer Danny Cummins, and starred in a comedy show, *Gaels of Laughter*, that ran for 15 summers. She was a fine singer and tap-dancer, but what captivated the public were her comic characters, like the exasperated mother of the 14-year-old Christy, and the Dublin "auld wan", a version of the duologues she had performed with O'Dea as Dolores and Rose.'

For generations of Irish children, Potter was an introduction to the magical world of theatre. In her pantomimes, she made a point of

Although mainly associated with the Gaiety, Maureen Potter and Jimmy O'Dea were Royal stars as well

memorising the names of birthday children during the interval, then reeling them off in the second half without a prompt card. 'My record was 67,' she once estimated. 'Then after the show, I would entertain them, drinking milk of course to set a good example, though with a tot of whiskey in it, would you believe,' she added with a twinkle in her eye.

A woman of great sharpness, dignity and humility, Potter treated everyone she met – from the Taoiseach to Dublin street traders – with warmth and respect. Even the poet Patrick Kavanagh, considered by many as the grumpiest man in Dublin, once walked up to her and said: 'Do you know what? You're not a bad little woman at all.'

However, years of pratfalls and tap-dancing took a toll on Potter's health, at a time when traditional variety was anyway in decline. So, with the adaptability of an old pro, she changed direction and became a straight actor. She appeared, to much acclaim, in several plays, notably at the Gate as Maisie Madigan in Sean O'Casey's *Juno and the Paycock* in 1986, a production that also had a New York run, and as Mrs Henderson in *Shadow of a Gunman* in 1996. The versatile Maureen also wrote a series of children's books.

The Royal pantos in the 1920s and earlier featured many big names popular on the international stage, as well as well as promising newcomers who would later become very well established

Nobody in Ireland had ever heard of Paul Cinquevalli, a German juggler, when he was listed down the bill as 'a speciality act' when he played the Royal. In a few short years he was acclaimed worldwide, particularly at the Folies Bergère in Paris, as one of the world's leading performers, juggling with everyday objects such as bottles, plates, glasses and umbrellas. Many called him 'king of the jugglers', and in the view of contemporary observers, it was a title well earned and fully justified.

George Wood was another. Better known as Wee Georgie Wood because of his 4 feet, 9 inches stature, the Englishman appeared in panto at the Royal long before he became famous as one of the legendary stage entertainers. Wee Georgie spent most of his professional career in the guise of a child and usually appeared with his 'stage mother', Dolly Harmer.

Gracie Fields, the Lassie from Lancashire and one of the great stars in the entertainment industry as a singer and comedienne, made one of her earliest appearance on the Royal stage at the age of 14 and would return as a major star in her later years. Another Lancastrian who got one of his early breaks on the Royal was George Formby, complete with his ukulele. He too would return to great acclaim later in his career. There will be more on Fields and Formby subsequently.

By the 1930s, the old Royal had fallen somewhat into disrepair and it was decided to pull it down it and build a completely new structure on the site, a combined theatre and cinema built to modern standards of which Dubliners could be proud. The theatre now became part of the Theatre Royal Co. Ltd, of which J. E. Pearce was chairman and managing director.

Pearce was a prominent businessman from Killiney, County Dublin, and was associated through accountancy with earlier ventures into cinema

Gracie Fields, the Lassie from Lancashire

and amusements projects. He was the man behind the success stories of the Savoy cinemas in Dublin, Cork and Limerick.

The old Theatre Royal officially closed its doors for the last time on 6 May 1934. There was no show that night, just a movie, *Dinner at Eight*, a vintage MGM production with a star cast headed by John and Lionel Barrymore, Wallace Beery, Jean Harlow and Marie Dressler.

The concept of cine-variety, sometimes referred to as hybrid entertainment, was testimony to the rapid social change and revolution in entertainment since the end of World War I in 1918. The idea of combining a stage show with a movie was a package put together initially in Britain in those pre-television times by the owners of new entertainment venues, increasingly cinemas, to woo fickle audiences and maximise box-office revenue. A stage show and a film were included in the one ticket price.

While Pearce promised that a new cine-variety Theatre Royal would go up in its place, there were those who doubted his words. 'It's the end of the Theatre Royal as we know it,' wrote one correspondent to the *Irish Press*. 'There won't be another one.' Any pessimism turned out to be unfounded, however. A demolition crew soon moved in.

Another chapter of the Theatre Royal had ended and a new one, the fourth and what would be the last, was about to begin. The new Royal would surpass anything that went before, with state-of-the art décor and all modern equipment. It would provide a platform in Dublin for the best local artistes and international variety entertainers including Hollywood movie stars.

A provisional opening date was set for the autumn of 1935. Dubliners, not to mention those outside the city and county but particularly regular Royalgoers, looked forward with eagerness and anticipation to their 'new look' theatre.

On 6 May 1934 a special benefit concert was given at the Gaiety Theatre for the staff of the old Royal. The bill was headed by Jimmy

O'Dea. Also featured was the Carl Rosa Opera Company, an English touring company dedicated to making quality light opera accessible to a wider audience in the English-speaking world who could not otherwise be able to experience it. Their music proved very popular with Royal fans. Today, some 80 years on, the company is happily still going strong.

F. J. McCormick, the celebrated Abbey Theatre actor from Skerries, County Dublin, best-known for his role as the carpenter Fluther Good in Sean O'Casey's *The Plough and the Stars*, was on the bill too, as was Cora Goffin, one of Britain's most famous pantomime principal boys and musical comedy stars. Cora, a real trouper with the stage in her blood, was 102 when she died in 2004.

When O'Dea was interviewed by a reporter after the concert, he said: 'It was a fitting climax for the old Royal, and we the performers were delighted to have played a part in it. I hope the audience had a good time, and I'm sure they had. I believe the Royal tradition of continuing to present theatrical productions will continue with the new Royal and I wish everybody the very best of luck with the undertaking.'

All that survived from the old Royal was the impressive marble staircase, briefly referred to in Chapter 4, which was stored away and partly installed in the adjoining Regal Rooms restaurant when it became a cinema in 1938. The complete staircase, designed with meticulous care by Frank Matcham, was subsequently purchased by the upmarket retail store Brown Thomas in Grafton Street. It was used to provide access to the basement sales area.

When Brown Thomas amalgamated with another up-market store, Switzers, in 1995, they moved their business across the street into Switzers' premises and sold their building to Marks & Spencer. During the refurbishment of their new department store, M&S decided to feature the staircase and moved it to a prominent position on the ground floor opposite the main entrance, and leading up from the ground floor to the first floor.

As the historian Des Kerins observed: 'Hundreds of customers daily use this staircase in the course of their shopping and it is edifying to see how many still look twice at the beautiful marble stairs and perhaps wonder about its history.' Definitely worth a visit, a true link with the past.

Shortly before the official opening of the new Theatre Royal, managing director J. E. Pearce announced at a packed press conference in a city hotel: 'The policy of the management of the new Theatre Royal will be to present theatregoers with grand opera, musical comedy, drama and variety under conditions which have never before obtained in the theatrical history of the Irish Free State, and in fact are not excelled elsewhere.

'Every encouragement will be given to local artistes, and in addition, the finest talent it is possible to procure from all quarters of the globe, regardless of expense, will be engaged and presented to patrons under the most favourable circumstances and the most luxurious surroundings. Profiting by the past and present theatrical scientific research, the management will be in an advantageous position in offering theatrical productions which have never been surpassed, in lavishness, lighting or entertainment value.'

The resident manager of the new theatre would be Jack McGrath. Coming from a prominent Roscommon family, he had wide experience in the entertainment business, having been manager of the Savoy cinemas in Dublin and Cork. 'Our policy with regard to the new Theatre Royal will be to present at popular prices the cream of talent and the finest entertainment it is possible to secure,' he promised. 'The theatre is dedicated to the entertainment of the people of the Irish Free State and to visitors from all countries.'

The fourth and final Theatre Royal opened in Hawkins Street on 23 September 1935 in a blaze of publicity. A large, stylish art décor building, it was designed by the London-based architect Leslie Norton, in association with local architects Messers Scott and Good.

With a contrasting Middle Eastern/Moorish interior, it was built on the lines of the eleventh century palace and fortress complex known as the Alhambra in the Spanish city of Granada. However, some architectural commentators said that the atmospheric Moorish interior motifs jarred with the art décor exterior, although the critics were few. What mattered was that Dubliners had a brand new Theatre Royal.

With an audience capacity of 3,700 seated and 300 standing, and looking onto a 40-foot stage, the aim of the owners, the Dublin Theatre Company, was that the cine-variety venue would host the biggest acts in the English-speaking world – and it did. Built at a cost of £250,000 and scheduled to have a staff of 300 on an £800 weekly wage bill, the equivalent costs today would be €11 million with weekly salaries totalling €35,200.

By far the biggest theatre in Ireland and Britain, it was also claimed to be the largest in Europe, although several historians discovered that there was in fact a theatre in Germany with a capacity of 5,000. The large foyer, with its marble staircase, was supplemented by a lift on the left. It was agreed that Norton had done a magnificent job all round.

Referring to its capacity and the uncovered facts about the larger German theatre, a reader noted in the letters page of *The Irish Times*: 'Leave it to the Irish for somebody to spoil the party.' Still, Dubliners were content to say, even boast, that having the second biggest theatre in Europe on their very doorstep, swamping anything in London and Paris, was indeed an achievement any city would be proud of.

While it may have been dwarfed by the Radio City Musical Hall in New York, with its 6,015 capacity, which had opened two years previously, the building of the Royal to accommodate nearly 4,000 patrons was still a notable achievement for a small country like Ireland.

In comparison to today's theatres here, the Bord Gais Energy Theatre has a capacity of 2,111, while the Gaiety holds 2,000, the Olympia 1,240, the Cork Opera House 1,000 and the National Concert Hall 900. The London Palladium, the most famous variety theatre in the UK which has hosted the Royal Variety Performance more times than any other theatre up to the present day, even falls short of the Theatre Royal capacity, with seating for 2,286.

Prices at the Royal were set at five pence to 15 pence and, oddly enough, cheaper on Sundays. Shows were twice nightly, at 6.30 and 8.50 with one performance at 8.30 on Sunday night. Sunday seats could be booked in advance, with many having 'permanent' seats which could be booked by going along to the theatre, showing the previous ticket or tickets at the box office and booking the same seat or seats for the following Sunday.

However, this eventually led to a black market, with touts going to long cinema queues in town, particularly on Saturdays, and offering Royal tickets at much higher prices than printed on the tickets. The touts' line would be that the theatre was sold out, but they had some available, 'for the right price' of course.

The new Theatre Royal was formally declared open by the future Taoiseach, Dubliner Sean Lemass, at the time Minister for Industry and Commerce. As it happened, Lemass was a keen theatregoer who with Jimmy O'Dea had formed an amateur group called the Kilronan Players nearly 20 years earlier. He seemed the most appropriate person to open the Hawkins Street showplace.

Lemass said the opening of a new theatre, particularly one as large as the Royal, was of considerable interest to all citizens. 'The serious business of the state was done in factories, workshops and offices but all workers needed occasional recreation,' he said. 'The business of providing entertainment and the employment it gave constituted an industry of the first importance.

'If the magnificence of this new theatre was any indication of the entertainment it was going to provide, and I think it was, then it would prove a theatre of which they could all be justifiably proud.'

Accompanying the minister on stage was Dublin's Lord Mayor, the legendary Alfie Byrne and the most famous person to ever hold that office. The son of a docker and a one-time theatre programme seller, the silvery-haired Alfie with the big smile was known to ordinary Dubliners for his warm greeting by shaking everybody's hand. An immensely popular figure, he would hold office for an unprecedented nine years, from 1930 until the outbreak of World War II in September 1939.

Byrne told the audience that he was sure they would agree with him that 'they were assembled in the finest theatre in Europe.' On receiving a cheque for charity of £200 from manager Jack McGrath on behalf of the company, Alfie said: 'It was a happy and generous thought to remember on such an occasion those less fortunate citizens who were not in a position to number themselves among the patrons of the theatre. I will do my best to distribute the money in a way that would give most satisfaction to the audience.'

The night turned out to be very successful. In keeping with tradition, the show was a blend of music and comedy, song and dance and a speciality act. Six trumpeters from the No. 1 Army Band, wearing their new full-dress uniforms, sounded a fanfare as the curtain went up for the first time.

Francis Mangan, an American of Irish extraction, presented the show. A well-known producer of shows in Britain and Continental Europe including France, Spain and Switzerland, he had a flair about him and used his imagination to the full. Mangan brought his own troupe of 24 dancers from London, and these were augmented by local dancers including the St Helier Sisters. Danny Malone, a well-known Irish singer, sang some popular airs while Alphonse Berg and company performed a speciality act centering on fashion styles.

Tommy Dando, Royal organist in the 1950s, always invited audiences to 'Keep Your Sunny Side Up'

Joe Jackson, an eccentric clown with his knockabout antics, got the laughs as did an American comedian billed as Senator Murphy, who specialised in satirising the speeches of US politicians. Grace and movement was provided by the Corps de Ballet.

On the Compton organ, said to be the best of its kind in the world and combining the musical sounds of a full symphony orchestra and dance band, was Alban Chambers, the first of several to fill that role, the most popular being Tommy Dando, with his signature tune, 'Sunny Side Up.' Chambers had a distinguished career, and was official organist at Leeds Cathedral from his early teens. He played in several major theatres before coming to the Royal from the Astoria Theatre in London.

The 25-piece orchestra was conducted by a musician who was to become another big Royal favourite, Jimmy Campbell. An Englishman who considered Ireland his adopted country, Campbell was born in South Shields, County Durham and was taught music by his father. He began his musical career at the age of 18 at the local Scala Theatre and later broadcast from the BBC in Newcastle for three years as a solo violinist before moving to Preston.

By this time Campbell had formed his own orchestra and had developed a talent for orchestration and original musical arrangements which would bring him to London and the Prince's Theatre, Shaftsbury Avenue.

Campbell's ability in selecting musicians who would work well in an orchestra ensemble made him an obvious choice to form an orchestra at the Regal Rooms restaurant before moving to the Theatre Royal as musical director.

He was in that capacity for most of the fourth Royal's history except for a period between 1946 and 1951 when he left following a disagreement with the management. During those five years he worked as musical director at the Prince of Wales Theatre in London as well as in Blackpool, and did some broadcasting for the BBC.

Philip Ryan, the historian, said: 'Jimmy became a well-known and much-loved character in Dublin. His love and loyalty to the Royal was legendary and he was genuinely missed during a five-year exile, though being replaced by fine orchestra leaders like George Rothwell, Alan Beale and Roy Fox.'

Sadly, Campbell did not survive the demolition of his favourite theatre for very long. Less than 18 months after the wrecking crew moved in during early July, 1962, he suffered a heart attack on 1 November 1963 and died in the Adelaide Hospital, Dublin aged 58.

This writer has fond memories of seeing him in the Royal foyer greeting patrons with a warm handshake. With his neatly-trimmed pencil-slim moustache and dark hair parted in the centre and slicked down with Brylcream, he always looked dapper in his cream suit, shoes to match and a red carnation in his lapel. The Dublin comedian Cecil Sheridan, a Royal regular, is on record as saying: 'Jimmy Campbell *was* the Royal. He epitomised class and, of course, he was a superb musician.'

Special guest of honour on opening night was the tenor Count John McCormack, a popular Royal performer. Appropriately enough, he sang 'Bless this House', a well-known song written in 1927. He would later become the first artiste to record it, followed in subsequent years by the likes of Beniamino Gigli, Father Sydney McEwan, Josef Locke, Vera Lynn, Doris Day, Perry Como and others. The audience hung on to McCormack's every word.

Count John McCormack was at home with ballads as he was with Mozart and Handel

There were conflicting reports that McCormack had earlier visited the as yet uncompleted site some time before opening night and was prevailed upon to try out the acoustics. Much to the delight of the workmen, according to the story, he sang, unaccompanied, 'Believe Me If All Those Endearing Young Charms', written by the Dublin poet and songwriter Thomas Moore.

Another source, and supported by the comedian Tony Kenny, not to be confused with the younger singer of the same name, claimed that McCormack did actually appear on the unfinished site. When prevailed upon to sing, however, he is alleged to have said: 'Gentlemen, with all due respect, scales you can have for nothing, but as for songs, then you have to pay for them.' McCormack himself always denied he ever visited the unfinished site at any time but the conflicting rumours would linger on for many years.

The opening night was well received by the national press. Said the *Irish Independent*: 'The management had promised the public that they would show what could be done on their stage in their opening performance and they kept their promise nobly last night. It is doubtful if Dublin has ever seen a show more sumptuously dressed, or one containing a greater galaxy of stars than we saw in the New Royal Revue.

'The programme presented is quite equal to the best that can be shown on the stage of any of the most famous European or American theatres. To present such a performance in a small city like Dublin was proof of great courage and enterprise. It was rewarded by immense success and the audience left the theatre convinced that if the new Theatre Royal can continue to give such presentations at such prices, "house full" will be the usual sign, even in this vast theatre with a seating capacity of almost four thousand.'

The Irish Times reported: 'Those fortunate people who were able to gain admittance to the new Theatre Royal on its opening night had every reason to be pleased with the entertainment which was provided. To say that it was lavish is to express the fact mildly. It surpassed the expectations of everyone, and indeed there were not a few who were awed by the splendour of the night.

'From the moment the curtain went up until the end of the performance, the applause was almost continuous, every single artiste receiving his or her share of approval. It can safely be said that the theatre will provide something new, something more entertaining than has been Dublin's lot for a considerable time.'

In keeping with the promised policy of providing only the best entertainment, McCormack was back at the Royal the following month in the first of a series billed as International Celebrity Season Subscription Concerts on selected Saturday afternoons, with prices pitched from 75p to £3.

The tenor thanked his audience on stage for the big welcome, and did not disappoint with a selection of his favourites, including 'It's a Long Way to Tipperary', 'Macushla', 'The Rose of Tralee', 'When You and I Were Young', 'Kathleen Mavourneen', 'When Irish Eyes Are Smiling' and 'The Wearin' of the Green'.

McCormack was followed on 2 November by the tenor Richard Tauber for a short season. Tauber, who was not a German despite popular belief, but an Austrian from Linz, had a lyrical, flexible voice and fine breath control, singing with a warm, elegant legato. He was elegant in appearance too, although he had a slight squint in his right eye. This he disguised by wearing a monocle and which, when accompanied by a top hat, added to the elegant effect. For many people Tauber was the epitome of Viennese charm.

Tauber won over his audience from the start, and there was warm applause for his renditions of 'My Heart and I,' 'Love's Old Sweet Song,' 'Girls Were Made to Love And Kiss,' 'You Are My Heart's Delight,' 'One Day When We Were Young' and a selection of operatic arias. There were glowing reviews in the press.

In the third celebrity concert, the Austrian violinist Friedrich 'Fritz' Kreisler took to the stage and received warm receptions after every performance. Regarded as one of the greatest violinists of all time, he was known for his sweet tone and expressive phrasing. Like many great violinists of his generation, he produced a characteristic sound which was immediately recognisable as his own.

Although he moved in many respects away from the Franco-Belgian school, Kreisler's style was nonetheless reminiscent of the *gemutlich,* or cozy, lifestyle of pre-war Vienna. Of Jewish origin like Tauber, he foresaw the dangers in the rise of Nazism and the persecution of his race and left for the United States shortly after the outbreak of the war. He settled in New York, from where he continued his successful career.

Royal audiences were now being spoiled for choice. Following Kreisler for a short season came the celebrated American bass singer/actor Paul Robeson on 1 February. Robeson would always be associated with his superb rendition of 'Ol' Man River' from the Broadway production *Show Boat* first performed in 1927, and no Robeson show would be quite complete without it, in Dublin or anywhere else.

He sang many of his other popular songs such as 'Just Awearyin' for You,' 'Nobody Knows the Trouble I've Seen,' 'Mighty Like a Rose' and 'Swing Low, Sweet Chariot' but the audience was waiting for 'Ol' Man River' and there were repeated calls for the song. He admitted later that there was never any doubt that he would fit it in, and he duly obliged towards the end of his show.

With music by Jerome Kern and lyrics by Oscar Hammerstein II, two iconic figures of American theatre, 'Ol' Man River' contrasted the struggles and hardships of America's black people with the endless, uncaring flow of the Mississippi River. Robeson sung it from the point-of-view of a black dock worker on a riverboat and captured all the emotion of the occasion.

Happily, *Show Boat* is still as popular today with production companies as it was in the 1930s and the songs have lost nothing in the passing of the years. A version of 'Ol' Man River' sung by Robeson, with music by one of the doyens of big band music, Paul Whiteman, was inducted in the Grammy Hall of Fame in Los Angeles in 2006. 'Ol' Man River' has been recorded by many artistes including Frank Sinatra, Judy Garland and Bing Crosby.

There was a treat for classical music fans when the English conductor and impresario Sir Thomas Beecham was booked for the final concerts in the series starting on 15 February. From the early twentieth century until his death in March 1961, Beecham was a major influence on the musical life of Britain and for that matter Ireland.

Founder of the London Philharmonic with his younger colleague Malcolm Sargent and the Royal Philharmonic orchestra, as well as being closely associated with the Liverpool Philharmonic and Halle orchestras, he was just the man to help wash away the winter blues.

The audience and the critics praised Beecham's repertoire, one newspaper describing it as being 'eclectic.' His programme included some works from lesser-known composers over famous ones, though he did not neglect those whose music he was frequently associated with, such as Haydn, Schubert, Sibelius and the one he revered above all others, Mozart.

After the concerts for followers of serious music, the theatre management returned to a series of regular weekly variety shows, starting off with an American production called *Radio New York*, clearly a nod to New York's Radio City Music Hall. It was presented by Will

Will Mahoney, highest paid vaudevillian

Mahoney, a stage and film comedian who claimed Irish ancestry on his mother's side.

Mahoney was described as the highest paid variety star on the American vaudeville stage, allegedly earning $5,500 per week. As the top of the bill, he was single-minded and something of a perfectionist. He brought on stage a 17-foot-long xylophone platform on which he danced with small mallets attached to his shoes, the tunes matching his rapid patter and slapstick comedy. His acrobatics demanded concentration and skill, and attracted rounds of applause.

Several London productions followed, including a revue, *Stop Press*, a short season by the Carl Rosa Opera Company with a repertoire of six works, as well as a big C. B. Cochran revue *Streamline* followed by another London show, the old reliable *Peter Pan*. Before the end of 1935, there was a change of policy by popular demand when cine-variety was introduced, following the trend set by the Radio City Music Hall.

The first movie was *The Man with Two Faces*, which had just been released in the US and starred Edward G. Robinson, Mary Astor and Ricardo Cortez. It was a fanciful but entertaining yarn about a famous actor who tries to protect his actress sister from her sinister husband. A popular innovation, movies would continue to be shown alongside the stage shows until the theatre closed in 1962.

8

The Gorgeous Gael Comes to Town

The press labelled Jack Doyle the Gorgeous Gael and Jack the Playboy Puncher, but they could well have called him the Great Lover or the Great Charmer. The big handsome Corkman was of course more famous as a heavyweight boxer in the 1930s and 1940s with a hefty wallop in his right hand, but he was also a very good singer, with his fine voice somewhere between baritone and tenor. Doyle's fame was such that he needed bodyguards to protect him from admiring females and jealous males.

Though Doyle spent most of his life in Britain and America, he liked playing the Theatre Royal, and on his first visit in 1933 he packed the theatre for four weeks, with standing room only each night, such was his considerable appeal.

One veteran Irish newspaperman told the author that whenever Doyle appeared at the Royal, one particular English Sunday paper would send over both a male and a female reporter to cover the show. The male would review the show itself and the female would pick up the gossipy bits.

It must be remembered that there was no shortage of gossip with Doyle. What today's glossy magazines and newspapers hell bent on getting all the juicy bits and blowing them out of all proportion would have done with Jack can only be imagined.

Doyle's initial visit to Hawkins Street in 1933 came shortly after he lost on a disqualification in the second round for alleged low punching against the Welsh heavyweight Jack Petersen at the White City Stadium in London. He was considered a hero by Irish fans who maintained that he should never have been ruled out. 'He was robbed!' was the general cry in Ireland.

In his private life Jack certainly was a ladies man. With his innate charm, impressive physique and striking good looks, the 6 foot 5 inch Doyle 'could charm the birds off the trees with those looks and that voice,' as one contemporary critic put it. Certainly it was never too difficult to realise why people liked Doyle, especially the ladies. Besides his good looks, he was the ultimate flatterer. He was friendly, chatty and outgoing, and simply very good company, as I discovered in several interviews with him in Dublin and London.

To refer to Doyle's private life is a complete misnomer because he simply had no private life. Everything Jack did was out in the open, or at least was forced out in the open because there always seemed to be a reporter or two hanging around, whether he was relaxing in a hotel or performing in a theatre.

Doyle first fancied himself as a singer while warbling in the bathroom. As a kid, he used to play the harmonica. After all, he could always perhaps turn to show business when his boxing days were over, realising that a boxer's days are often limited. Jack had already dabbled with a career on stage when his manager, Dan Sullivan, a Cockney who claimed Irish blood arranged for him to make an appearance at the London Palladium to get him some publicity.

Sullivan, a true schemer, admitted in an interview with *The People* newspaper in 1954 that he invented a story that Doyle had signed up for a month of singing engagements around Britain at a staggering £750 a week. He claimed he produced a fake contract in order to 'validate' his claim and boasted that the newspapers fell for it.

Sullivan's next step was to call around and see the Palladium impresario George Black, a friend of some years' standing, and arranged for Doyle to get a 'secret' guest spot on the highly-popular Crazy Gang show that was destined to become something of a show business legend. Each morning for a week Jack sang and rehearsed a routine with the Crazy Gang comics Bud Flanagan and Teddy Knox. By the time the big day arrived, his performing technique was polished and professional.

On opening night Flanagan 'conveniently' spotted him in the audience and called him up from his seat in the stalls: 'Give us a song or two, Jack.' Sullivan had secured £50 worth of tickets for positioning people in the audience, stooges, and they applauded as encouragement for Doyle to get up on stage.

Jack's performance was the predictable knockout. His rendition of 'Mother Machree' brought such sustained applause – seemingly spontaneous but well rehearsed – that there were calls to do an encore. He then sang a duet and exchanged gags with Bud Flanagan. The audience loved it and so did Jack. Afterwards he was besieged by theatrical agents and recording bosses, and offered enough work to keep him on stage full-time for the foreseeable future.

Doyle accepted an offer from the Decca label and went into their London studios. The first record, in June 1933, was his show-stopper 'Mother Machree' on the A side and 'My Irish Song of Songs,' another Irish ballad rich in sentiment, on the flipside. This was followed a month later with two more Irish favourites, 'Little Town in the Old County Down' with 'Where the River Shannon Flows' on other side.

The publicity from his Palladium appearance and his recording debut gave his boxing career a tremendous boost, and a crowd of over 60,000 packed the White City Stadium for the Petersen fight. After his disqualification, his popularity did not diminish. There was considerable public sympathy for him, especially when he was suspended from boxing for a month and his £3,000 purse withheld pending an investigation.

In the meantime, Doyle decided to accept offers for theatrical engagements and opted for a British and Irish tour later in 1933, with the main dates pencilled in for the Theatre Royal and the Cork Opera House. Demand was so heavy for the Dublin date, which would open the tour, that the Royal management extended it to four weeks.

Jack appointed an Irish comedian of his acquaintance to act as his theatrical manager. Fred Curran, whose real name was Conway, was a stand-up comic in the mould of Tommy Trinder, one of the top English comedians of the day. Curran had been born in Galway but brought up in Manchester, where his parents had settled when he was a child.

Doyle loved Curran's droll, almost impish humour and greatly respected his knowledge of show business. Fred may never have succeeded in hitting the big time but after appearances in theatres all over Britain and Ireland, he knew everything there was to know about the entertainment industry and what made it tick. It was to him that Doyle entrusted his immediate future outside of boxing, which was stalling for him anyhow.

Curran, outwardly a mild, almost timid figure, nevertheless proved himself a shrewd entrepreneurial operator, quickly realising that the best way to project Jack on stage was to accentuate the duality of his talents as a singer and a boxer.

This he did by devising a programme in which Doyle would first sing a selection of his favourite songs before disappearing into the wings and re-emerging for a series of exercises and shadow boxing routines to musical accompaniment in a ring hastily erected on stage. In this way, he considered that Jack would be identifying with his by then oft-stated public persona – that he could sing like John McCormack and fight like Jack Dempsey, the former heavyweight champion of the world and his ring idol.

Doyle's unlucky defeat in the Petersen fight only increased his popularity in Ireland. There was a wave of sympathy for him, and the general feeling was that he was hard done by in London and should never have been ruled out. Jack's biographer Michael Taub recalled: 'That Doyle was held in the same high esteem as any noble figure of Irish republicanism who had been martyred by the British was evident from the reception he received at the Theatre Royal.'

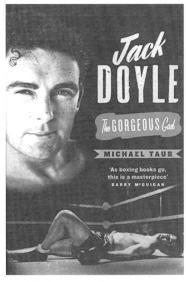

Michael Taub's biography of Jack Doyle

The demand for tickets for his twice-daily performances broke all existing box office records for the theatre. Crowds lined the streets around College Green and Hawkins Street awaiting Doyle's much-publicised arrival. When he arrived, he had trouble pushing his way through the crowds at the stage entrance around the corner in Poolbeg Street, finally making it on stage nearly 45 minutes later after shaking numerous outstretched hands and signing autographs.

Doyle was on a percentage of the takings, and his earnings averaged around £600 a week during the show's extended four-week run. Reviewers noted that his voice was a nice blend of Doyle soprano and McCormack tenor. 'Jack's material struck a perfect balance between pure schmaltz and acceptable sentimentality, and his delivery, as in the boxing ring, was executed with a perfect sense of the dramatic,' said one critic.

Jack set the scene perfectly with perennial favourites like 'The Hills of Donegal' and 'The Rose of Tralee' before a rousing version of 'Mother Machree.' Then it was exit for Jack the singer to the wings, a quick change from white tie and tails to ring gear for Jack the boxer as he pushed his massive frame through a series of callisthenics and shadow boxing routines. There were many 'Ooohs' and 'Aaahs' from the ladies in the audience.

When he finished his show on the final night and prepared for the trip to the Cork Opera House, where he would get another tumultuous reception, he promised the Royal management that he would be back. He kept his promise, returning in 1936 with his first wife Judith Allen, a visit that proved highly controversial to say the least, and later with his second wife, the fiery actress Movita in 1944.

After Cork, Doyle planned to go to America where he hoped to resurrect his boxing career, continue with his singing engagements and perhaps make it to Hollywood and a movie career. First, however, was the little matter of celebrating his 21st birthday in his native Cork, an event he promised would be the party to end all parties in the city's plush Imperial Hotel. It was. Jack never did anything by half.

Legend has it that the party lasted for several days. It was hailed at the time as the greatest social gathering the city on the Lee had ever known. Certainly it exceeded even his own expectations as it seemed the whole city converged on the hotel in an attempt to catch sight of him and to witness the comings and goings of the glittering event.

Doyle looked resplendent on full evening dress as he stood arm-in-arm with his mother Anastasia, or Stacia as she was known, at the top of the red-carpeted staircase while his guests trooped by one by one to shake his hand. Waiters scurried round with anxious looks but the dinner could wait for this was the food of life for Jack. Besides, he had to sing several songs for his wide circle of hometown friends.

With that little matter out of the way, Doyle set sail for America on the *S. S. Washington* with the aim of conquering the boxing world over there. It did not quite work out like that. While waiting around for fights, his singing kept him in demand in concert halls, theatres and on radio. Not too surprisingly, he even found love. It was in the shapely form of Judith Allen, a Hollywood movie starlet and a divorcee. Indeed, Judith would go through her life with no less than seven divorces.

They married, somewhat in haste, in a registry office in Ague, Mexico in April 1935. At the time she was the regular girl friend of the reigning world heavyweight boxing champion Max Baer, an insanely jealous man, but Doyle seemed to ignore such trivialities.

The quickie wedding was a romantic occasion but sure enough the judge who performed the ceremony obviously did not think so.

Omitting the normal routine of asking the groom and bride to kiss each other, instead he handed Jack and Judith a couple of business cards on which was printed the name of a lawyer, with the words Legal Mexican Divorces Secured. Quite clearly the judge was looking ahead.

Jack and Judith returned to California and took a house in fashionable Beverly Hills, complete with servants. A luxury limousine transported her to and from the nearby Paramount studios where she received $200 a week whether she worked or not. Doyle had nothing to do but sit around the house, read the newspapers, practice his singing in the bathroom and console himself by counting his and Judith's money.

Boredom, however, quickly set it. Nightclubs and parties beckoned. There were stories of his hard drinking and philandering and, inevitably, these reached Judith's ears. Rows and discord followed. The relationship became strained.

Both agreed to get out of Los Angeles for a while to save their marriage and make a New Year resolution in December 1935 to start afresh. They would put together a singing act and tour Ireland and Britain, and Judith could meet Jack's family in Cork. In the run-up to their departure across the Atlantic, Doyle was still seeing other women but Judith seemingly turned a blind eye to it all for the sake of trying to keep their decidedly shaky marriage together.

Starting with a very successful British tour in March 1936, they were booked to appear in Irish halls, the highlights again being the Theatre Royal and the Cork Opera House. The opening show in Ireland was scheduled for the Royal, where two years earlier Jack had been cheered to the echo. However, things were different now, as Doyle had feared.

He had suspected that public opinion in Catholic Ireland might be strongly opposed to his union with a divorced woman, but had underestimated the degree of hostility that would be directed at them. Jack's fears were heightened when he was told at the Gresham, then the premier hotel in the city, that 'their presence at the hotel would not be welcomed and that they should try elsewhere.' They eventually booked in at the Shelbourne, the No. 2 hotel.

The Corkman was emotionally hurt and humiliated but he soon realised the country would be against him. Church feelings were all powerful. The cheek of him! The great Jack Doyle, brought up a good Catholic boy in a sound Catholic home, taking a divorcee for a wife and expecting to be welcomed with open arms. The feeling was that he was setting the worst kind of example and one that undermined the very solid structure of the church and its teachings.

Red-faced bishops and priests bellowed fire and brimstone from the pulpits, like dragons on the loose, that here were two people 'living in sin' and should not be tolerated in a Catholic country. Feelings were running so high that Doyle became an outcast in his own native land, ostracised and disgraced. The press took up the chant. He was simply not wanted at any cost, neither Doyle nor his wife. Not at the Royal. Not even in the country. The message was clear: they should get out – and fast.

'Doyle should forget about appearing at the Theatre Royal or any Irish theatre,' wrote one correspondent to the *Irish Press*. 'Let him take his wife back to England or America or anywhere else for that matter,' said another. The signs were looking anything but good.

The evening before they were due to appear, an announcement was made from the stage that the opening performance on the following night was 'regrettably cancelled because Miss Allen is feeling unwell.' Nobody believed it. All ticket holders would be reimbursed. From the audience there were hisses, catcalls and shouts of, 'We don't want them here anyhow,' 'Yes, keep these two sinners away' and 'Go back to Pagan England, Doyle.'

One angry woman stood up in the stalls and shouted: 'Doyle was sent by the devil, and he should stay out of Ireland. He's not welcome. Nor is his wife.' So violent was the outburst from all parts of the theatre, and so long did it continue, that the announcer was not only embarrassed but scared, and could hardly make himself heard above the din.

A large notice was placed outside the theatre the next day announcing the cancellation as Catholic organisations carrying placards marched up and down Hawkins Street denouncing the 'sinful couple.'

Doyle was angry at being rejected in his native land. He maintained that his private life should have nothing to do with it. Judith was no less hurt. She had been longing for the day she could set foot in Ireland after hearing Jack's many wonderful stories about the land of his birth and the legendary friendliness of the people.

With the rest of his planned Irish tour cancelled, the couple continued playing British halls with no opposition before heading back to California. It would be another eight years before Doyle would return to perform at the Royal, this time under totally different circumstances.

Meanwhile, Doyle's name was linked with several Hollywood stars and socialites including the actress Carole Lombard as well as businesswoman Libby Holman who, apart from being a successful singer, was heiress to a major tobacco company. Michael Taub, Doyle's biographer, remembered: 'Jack was a giant in stature and with a giant appetite for life. A lady killer. He lived his life like a hell-raiser, and by the time he was 30, he had earned and squandered a £¾ million fortune.'

As well as being the toast of Dublin, London and New York, he conquered the social scene in Hollywood and he was as much at home in the movie colony as he was in the company of royalty. In the film capital, he soon became friendly with the likes of Errol Flynn, James Cagney, Bing Crosby, Pat O'Brien, Frederic March, Robert Taylor, Barbara Stanwyck and Johnny Weissmuller, the former Olympic swimming champion who became famous as Tarzan.

On the domestic front, however, things were no better between Jack and Judith, going from bad to worse. Doyle's dangerous liaisons with the opposite sex were obviously getting in the way of a lasting happy marriage. He was also going through money as though he had a printing machine at home and could turn out cash whenever he needed it. Jack's problem was that he could never hold on to it. He preferred the bright lights too much.

They had many rows in public and private, between his philandering and his heavy drinking, before Judith told him she was filing for divorce. She told her lawyer that Jack blackened her eye, consorted with other women, ignored her, embarrassed her publicly and threatened her with a pistol. 'Life with Jack is one long series of battles in and out of the ring,' she maintained. 'To be honest, I've just had enough.'

When Doyle was informed of these allegations, he was aghast, and insisted that life with Judith constituted the happiest days of his life. 'Judith and I are very happy together, and if I ever raised my hand to her it must have been in a dream,' he maintained. 'I can't believe all this. I would never strike a woman. One day she says I threatened her with a revolver but we didn't even quarrel so how could I have threatened her? We spent the evening together and sang to each other. I love Judith and I will always love her.'

She later changed her mind about seeking a divorce, delaying matters in the hope that Doyle would change his ways but the last straw came when Jack became involved very publicly with the rich Dodge family who ran the motor car empire. His marriage to Judith Allen was over, having lasted less than two years.

Doyle, in the meantime, had struck up a friendship with Horace Dodge Junior, son of the company's founder. Before long he had not only captured the affections of Horace's sister Delphine but also their 66-year-old mother Anna and even Horace's wife Mickey. There was nothing the bold Jack would not do for love or money, and it came as no surprise when Doyle was handed a cheque by Horace, said to be in the region of $10,000, with the stark warning never to contact Mickey or any of the family again.

Doyle's boxing career gradually wound down with the passing years and he concentrated on his singing. By now Jack had acquired a new wife, a fiery Mexican actress named Movita he had married in a registry office in California in January 1939, renewing their vows in Dublin in 1943. But their marriage was a tempestuous one, with constant reports of Doyle having affairs with a succession of women.

He was also drinking and gambling heavily, and more often than not sported a black eye in public. Their constant rows involved crockery thrown on many occasions. Certainly there was more fighting in the bedroom than love-making.

The press called Movita, whose real name was Maria-Louisa Castaneda, an archetypal Mexican firebrand, but she insisted such a tag was totally fictitious. 'We were both a bit hot-headed so let's leave it at that', she said. But it was not all battling. They had good times on holidays together.

On one vacation in Berlin just before the outbreak of World War II they met Hitler. Eugene Barrymore, a member of the famous American theatrical family, was a witness. 'They were at this beautiful hotel when in walked Hitler accompanied by his uniformed lieutenants, all of them bronzed and blond,' said Barrymore. 'Everyone stood except Jack and Movita. 'I'm Irish, I don't have to stand,' he told her. Now Hitler had an electrifying presence. He looked daggers at them so they shot up.

'When Jack had extended himself to his full height, Hitler was immediately taken by this beautiful hunk of manhood. He was shocked at Doyle's size, as Hitler was only five feet himself. When Hitler found out Jack was Irish, he got one of his associates to act as interpreter. Apparently, Doyle made quite an impression.'

Back in California, however, there were more rows and more recriminations. In a bid to save the bond, he and Movita decided to get married officially in a Catholic ceremony in Dublin in February 1943. They arrived in the capital complete with over 50 pieces of luggage containing wardrobes of fabulous dresses, hand-made shoes and dozens of Jack's suits, sports jackets and expensive monogrammed silk shirts and ties.

Jack Doyle and his second wife Movita relax at the Gresham Hotel before their Royal show in 1944

The couple wed at St Andrews Church in Westland Row, the street where Oscar Wilde was born, and the ceremony brought traffic to a standstill, with extra gardaí having to be rushed to the scene at short notice to control the great crowds. The reception in the plush Royal Hibernian Hotel in Dawson Street went on all day and night with gallons of champagne said to be consumed.

Ulick O'Connor, the Dublin author and broadcaster, recalled Doyle and Movita walking down Grafton Street, with Jack looking like a figure out of a Greek myth, in 1945. 'Down the street strode Jack Doyle, film star, lover, boxer and singer, 6 feet 5 inches and astonishing good looks,' said O'Connor. 'As he strode down the most fashionable street of the city with his Irish wolfhound and his film star wife, he seemed to epitomize something of the spirit of those Dublin years.'

The wedding was a prelude to an Irish tour in 1944 which would include playing the Theatre Royal, where seven years earlier the show with his then wife Judith Allen, a divorcee, had been suddenly cancelled over that public outcry led by the Catholic Church. Doyle had hoped that incident had been forgotten. True enough this time the headlines were different, and more favourable. The 'real' Jack Doyle was back.

Billed as the *Punch and Beauty Show*, it packed the Royal every night. Their duets turned out to be real showstoppers, especially 'South of the Border', co-written by an Irishman, Jimmy Kennedy, a former member of the Royal Ulster Constabulary from Omagh.

'The show was a spectacular success,' Movita remembered later. 'Jack had a boxing ring rigged up on stage, with girls in little dresses doing dance routines and acting as trainers while he shadowboxed and performed exercises. It was all done in the dark, with lovely fluorescent lights illuminating the stage. I thought it was a nice production number, very cute, very clever. We did two shows a night, plus matinees on Mondays and Saturdays. It went on for weeks and weeks.

'Crowds were forming as early as ten in the morning and the same people came back day after day, or so it seemed to me. It was truly amazing. We were on a percentage of the gate, and the theatre, which I believed was bigger than any other in Ireland or Britain, was packed for every performance. We were earning a fortune.

'We later took the show around the country with most of the acts from the Theatre Royal show and called it the Hit Parade. Again crowds flocked to see us, with full houses every night. You would not believe the receptions we got. The roads were choc-a-bloc wherever we appeared. The people were beautiful, and Jack was okay really. He wasn't bad at all because he didn't get drunk too much.'

Elderly residents in Longford Town recalled seeing Doyle and Movita on stage at the Odeon Cinema. John Hastings, now living in Middlesex, recalled: 'The show opened with 12 glamorous chorus girls showing their legs to the gents of the town in the front seats. The gents would normally sit in the two-shillings seats at the back during a picture show but they made sure they were not going to miss this treat. After all, it was not too often they would get to see a show like this.

'Jack announced the girls as the Doylettes as distinct from the Royalettes who were resident at the Theatre Royal in Dublin. As I recall, the show lasted a full week with packed houses every night. As you know, Jack was a bit of a lad, and not only with the ladies of the chorus.

'He was a loveable rogue and very tight with his money in bars. We heard later that he tried to leave town without paying the girls but one of them threatened to call the gardaí and, all apologies and kisses all round, he coughed up the money there and then. Yes, that was Jack Doyle all right.'

The show continued on an English tour, with more packed houses.

The English shows often featured the much-loved entertainer 'Two Ton' Tessie O'Shea, who later would be extremely popular at the Olympia. 'In my opinion Jack had the greatest personality, both on and off the stage, of anyone I knew,' recalled Tessie in later years.

'He was definitely a real lady-killer. We were all crazy about him. I suspect that apart from his handsome looks and his fine physique, it was his Irish blarney that really got through. I wish there were more Jack Doyles in the world. In my remembrance of him, he was a big leprechaun, and a charmer.'

The touring continued in Britain, and while everything looked happy on the outside, such was not the case in reality. Trouble was looming. Surprise, surprise, Doyle was up to his old ways again, with rows either over his womanising or his drinking, sometimes both, until Movita finally told him one winter's day in 1946 that she wanted a divorce. He replied it was not possible as they had married in a Catholic church. More rows followed until Movita suddenly walked out.

Jack heard no more from her until one day in 1960 he read in a newspaper that she had married the movie star Marlon Brando, a marriage that would also end in divorce eight years later. Once asked about her marriages, she was quoted as saying: 'The only true love of my life was Jack Doyle but we just couldn't live together. That was the sad part of it all.'

This writer was fortunate to have had an opportunity of interviewing Doyle several times for my newspaper, the *Evening Herald*, in the 1960s and 1970s. The last interview was in a Dublin hotel in Westland Row close to the birthplace of Oscar Wilde and long since pulled down.

Jack, living in London at the time with a new woman in his life, Nancy Keogh, who had Irish connections, was in town for a singing tour of Ireland. By an odd coincidence, our meeting place was across

Jack Doyle chats to the author in later years

the road from St Andrews Church where he had married Movita some 30 years earlier, a ceremony that brought traffic to a standstill.

Still handsome and heading for his sixties, with strands of grey running through his dark hair, Doyle remembered among other things the Theatre Royal with affection. He recalled with sadness how he heard of the Royal's demise:

'I read about it in an Irish newspaper in London,' he lamented. 'They should never have pulled it down. Some business people or the government should have stepped in and saved it. It was a magnificent theatre, certainly the best in Ireland or Britain. It had a massive stage which many visiting artistes commented on. I always loved appearing there.'

On a less serious note, he smiled: 'Maybe we could turn back the clock to those wonderful times, those big shows in Hawkins Street. I always felt I gave the audience what they wanted, good clean entertainment. That's what show business is all about, really.'

When I picked up the *Irish Independent* one morning just before the Christmas of 1978 and read sadly that Doyle had died of cirrhosis of the liver at St Mary's Hospital in Paddington, London at the age of 65, I remembered his comments from that final interview we had in Dublin.

'Have I any regrets, that I supposedly wasted my life on wine, women and song, and that I went through £250,000, an astronomical amount of money in those days, with little to show for it? None whatsoever,' he had said. 'I'll tell you now, Thomas. I saw a bit of the world.

'Yes, I was a playboy, and enjoyed the company of beautiful women, lived the high life, and mingled with the top movie stars and all that. Okay, probably I should have taken myself more seriously but so what. I had a good time, a wonderful time. I played the Royal, the biggest of the biggest, too. No, I've no regrets. What more can anyone say?'

9

The Russians Are Coming

By 1936 the Theatre Royal was losing money and some radical thinking had to be done – and done fast. It was one thing providing Dubliners with top shows and classy productions headed by visiting artistes but they were costing dearly. For a start, the fees had to be looked at. Fortunately, the famous theatre was saved from financial ruin by a Russian immigrant family.

Maurice Elliman and his wife Ettie arrived in Dublin in 1900, having fled Tzarist persecution in Latvia with precious little money and having to borrow the fare. They would have three sons, Louis, Abe and Maxie. Maurice started life as a grocer and became involved in the cinema trade initially by establishing a cinema seating business on Camden Street, opening his own cinema, the Theatre De Luxe on the same street, in December 1912. The original building still stands and is now the De Luxe Hotel and nightclub, looking almost the same today as it did before it finally closed as a cinema in June 1974.

Louis, who would become the best known sibling, graduated from the National University of Ireland and was subsequently apprenticed by his father to a chemist in South Richmond Street. After eight years he left that position, partly out of boredom but mainly because of little money, and headed for London. 'I was lucky in London as I became the Irish agent for First National Pictures, and I suppose my career, my true career, took off from there,' he would recall in later years.

'First National Pictures had been formed in California in 1917 by a group of exhibitors led by the businessman and film enthusiast Thomas L. Tally. Infuriated by the block-booking practices of Famous Players-Lasky, later becoming Paramount, and rather than be forced to buy a package of routine films in order to get a big name star such as Mary Pickford, the new company decided to make their own pictures and set out to lure top stars.'

Soon, First National Pictures, or First National Exhibitors Circuit as they were formally known, with over 5,500 members across the US, were in a position to sign up stars of the magnitude of Charlie Chaplin and Mary Pickford and became a key figure in the industry, especially as they had their own studio in Burbank, California. When First National was absorbed by Warner Brothers in 1926, Louis moved back to Dublin with ambitious plans, along with his father, to move into the Irish theatrical business, later encompassing cinemas all over Ireland.

Louis persuaded his father in the autumn of 1936 to buy the Gaiety Theatre, whose company now owned the Theatre Royal, and they soon acquired cinemas. The Royal, however, was the jewel in their crown. Nevertheless, earlier that year it looked as though the Royal might go out of business due to the high financial demands of the visiting artistes and the 'generosity' of the manager Hugh Margey, who insisted on paying them what they wanted rather than negotiating a particular fee.

When one entertainer in particular, the English singer and movie star Gracie Fields, was booked to top the bill at the Royal in July 1936, she negotiated a fee that left little room for profit. As if that was not enough, the Lassie from Lancashire, as she was known through one of her most famous songs, insisted that a film she had backed financially, John Millington Synge's *Riders to the Sea*, made in 1935 and set in the Aran Islands, should be shown during the week she was making her stage appearance. 'Gracie got her wish but she was one tough lady,' Louis recalled.

Louis Elliman would become the man who saved the Royal and the Gaiety during the days of World War II, whimsically known as the Emergency down here, when visiting stars could not travel. Affectionately known as 'Mr Louis' to his staff, he was effectively 'Mr Show Business,' running both theatres with a tight fist. Besides booking local acts for the Royal, he put on regular shows at the Gaiety including pantos, plays, variety shows and seasons by the Rathmines and Rathgar Musical Society and the Dublin Grand Opera Society, both still going strong today.

When the Dublin Grand Opera Society was formed in May 1941, the president, Professor John F. Larchet, paid tribute to Elliman. When they were unable to secure a suitable rehearsal room in preparation for their first production at the Gaiety, Louis came to the rescue by putting the rehearsal room in the Royal at their disposal. Louis is also on record as treating them generously from a financial point of view.

One Royal veteran recalled that there were other instances when Louis showed his hard business side. Some years later, when Radio Éireann approached Norman Metcalfe to broadcast a series of programmes on the Royal's Compton organ, Louis insisted on charging a fee for use of the organ. With the balance from the total budget so small, Metcalfe had no choice but to decline the offer. He never really forgave Louis.

Elliman was a very private person who rarely gave long interviews and was seldom photographed. Philip B. Ryan, the historian, described him as 'a slightly mysterious man, and the more one knew about him, the deeper the mystery became.'

On his death in 1965, three years after the Royal closed, there were many tributes from theatre folk. The actor Micheál MacLiammóir said: 'Louis Elliman was very good to us all, to be remembered in terms of brotherhood. He had the theatre in his blood and he was a friend to us all.' MacLiammóir's partner Hilton Edwards said: 'I have known Louis Elliman for 25 years and this city will be the poorer without him.'

Certainly, Elliman enticed all the big stars to the Royal. In 1936 he brought in Ramon Novarro, a romantic idol of silent pictures in the 1920s and known as the Latin Lover. Novarro, who was accompanied by his sister Carmen, was still a Hollywood idol in the 1930s and one night as he was leaving the Royal, six women tried to kidnap him and bundle him into a taxi. Luckily for Novarro, several members of the theatre staff were quickly on the scene and came to his rescue.

'This often happens back in America,' he said with a smile. 'Fortunately, I'm still around.' However, it was later claimed that it was all a publicity stunt devised by the Royal publicist Jack Lyons, although Lyons himself strongly denied he had anything to do with it.

Novarro was followed by one of the most popular American song and dance acts to play the Hawkins Street theatre, Ben Lyon and his actress wife Bebe Daniels. On the way to London for shows at the Palladium, they stopped off in Dublin for a week's engagement at the Royal, a practice followed by many other American artistes. This was the Lyons' first theatrical engagement and the historian Philip B. Ryan recalled that both of them were always very grateful for the management giving them an opportunity to perform their stage act in the capital. 'Ben and Bebe could not thank the management enough for their patience, help and above all their invaluable advice,' he said. They remained in Britain during the war and hosted very popular BBC radio shows such as *Life with the Lyons* and *Hi Gang*.

The Lyons were followed by the saucy, wide-faced English comedian Max Miller. With his wicked charm and fast patter, he was probably the greatest stand-up comedian of his generation. He wore flamboyant suits too big for him and ties to match, with a white trilby perched on his head. Miller's act would be punctuated by songs, some sentimental and other comic, some of which he wrote himself. Sometimes he would accompany himself on guitar or entertain with a soft shoe shuffle.

Although Max's material was risqué, he never swore on stage and disapproved of those who did. He used double entendre and when telling a joke would leave out the last word or words to let the audience fill them in. He would take from his pocket two books, one white and the other blue, explaining to the audience that these are joke books and asking them which they would like. They almost always chose the blue book which contained the naughty ones.

Miller's visit in the spring of 1936 was not his first time here. He had done an Irish tour in 1921. 'We played in Limerick during the Catholic retreat when no good Catholic must go to any sort of amusement,' he related. 'A priest stood at the door of the hall, taking down the names of any of his parishioners who dared to enter so we ended up with just a handful of people. We had to dress in a room beneath the stage, and had to go down some rickety stairs to get to it, and two steps were missing. This left a big gap and if you fell through it you landed in the cellar.

'I complained to a sort of dogsbody, who called himself the manager, that the girls didn't want to dress with the boys in the same room. He seemed perplexed. "Why? Have you had a row?" In the end we rigged up a curtain to cut the room in half. It meant the boys had to go through the girls' part to get to the stage. With the sights they saw and the conversations they heard, they were real men by the end of the week.

'In another town in Ireland, Cavan if I remember, six of us stayed in one house, paying ten shillings each. The landlady was determined to teach me an Irish jig. In the end I got board and lodging, dancing lessons and a spot of company for half a quid – not a bad bargain, eh? The hall was lit by candles. When the dance routines got under way, the movement made by the artistes blew out the candles and the stage manager had to keep a box of matches handy. The audience seemed to take it all for granted.'

Miller was twice banned by the BBC, first in the 1930s and then in the 1950s. But these incidents only helped his reputation as daring and naughty and would lead to increased box office sales. The Royal management tipped him off about his material, and he promised to keep it clean. He kept to his word, leaving out his famous, or infamous if you prefer, ditties and risqué jokes.

How he managed to keep it all clean and cut out the blue stuff could not have been easy as his regular material was his stock in trade but he did it. As the Royal manager, Hugh Margey, soon to be replaced, remarked later: 'Miller was a real pro, no doubt about that. Only a fellow like Max could pull it off.'

Jimmy Durante played the Royal for a week in the spring of 1936. The New York-born entertainer was on is way to make a movie in Britain with Richard Tauber called *Land Without Music* when his agent received a call to visit Dublin. Durante's distinctive, clipped gravelly speech, comic language butchery, jazz-influenced songs, and large nose helped make him one of America's most familiar and popular personalities of the 1920s through the 1970s. His jokes about his nose included referring to it as 'the schnozzle' and the word became his nickname.

As he strutted across the big stage Durante's act included his by now familiar material such as 'The Lost Chord,'

Jimmy 'Schnozzle' Durante with his wife, former showgirl Marjorie Little

'Umbriago' and 'Ink-A-Dink-A-Doo', the latter becoming his theme song, with words by songwriter Ben Ryan to music that Durante himself composed. At the end of his act, he threw his hat at the orchestra, and in response they flung dozens of hats at him, much to the amusement of the audience.

Interestingly, shortly before his Royal appearances Durante starred on Broadway in the musical *Billy Rose's Jumbo*, in which a police officer stops him in the street while leading a live elephant and asks him, 'What are you doing with that elephant?' Durante's reply, 'What elephant?' was a regular show-stopper. This comedy bit, also reprised in his role in the 1962 movie *Billy Rose's Jumbo*, based on the 1935 musical, is said to have contributed to the popularity of the idiom, 'the elephant in the room'.

By late autumn, the Theatre Royal was back in profit under the Ellimans. Visiting artistes were paid what the new owners felt were 'more realistic fees', but all existing contracts were fully honoured. If an artiste drew particularly good attendances, there would be a bonus for them at the end of the week. Manager Hugh Margey was offered, and accepted, a similar post as manager of the Savoy Cinema restaurant in O'Connell Street.

The English comedy act, billed as Old Mother Reilly and Her Daughter Kitty, were also on the Royal in 1936. In real life they were the husband and wife team of Arthur Lucan and Kitty McShane. Devised by Lucan himself, Old Mother Reilly was an Irish washerwoman and the double act was hugely successful on stage and in 15 movies.

They first met in the panto *Little Jack Horner* at the Queen's Theatre in Dublin in 1916 and performed several times there in individual acts. Later, in their famous double act, they were back in Dublin at the Tivoli Theatre on Burgh Quay, subsequently the *Irish Press* offices. By the time they played the Royal, they were very well

Arthur Lucan and his wife Kitty McShane, billed as
Old Mother Reilly and her daughter Kitty

established here, and their act went down very well. Typical of their sketches was:

Kitty: 'Hello,' and turning to the audience, 'Hello boys!'

Riley: 'Hello boys!' How dare you be so familiar.

Kitty: That's not being familiar. I'm saying 'Hello' to the boys.

Riley: I think it's familiar. You don't know them, do you?

Kitty: No, but I will before the night is out.

The big stars continued to grace the Royal stage, such as the American tap-dancing duo the Nicholas Brothers, who would later appear in popular Hollywood musicals in the 1940s such as *Down Argentine Way*, the movie that boosted Betty Grable to stardom, and *The Pirate*, in which they danced with Gene Kelly. This was shortly before Kelly, whose paternal grandfather came from Derry, made his most famous film, *Singin' in the Rain*, with Debbie Reynolds and Donald O'Connor.

Another family group, the Mills Brothers, was also a popular American act. Sons of a barber from Ohio, they concentrated on popular close harmonies of the day. Their programme for the Royal included 'Lazy River', 'Nevertheless', 'Someday You'll Want Me to Want

You, 'I've Got My Love to Keep Me Warm', 'Opus Number One', 'The Glow Worm' and what would be two of their biggest successes from the 1940s onwards, 'You'll Always Hurt the One You Love' and 'Paper Doll', their first major hit which would sell over six million copies in 1943. The management wanted them back but commitments in the US, including movies, club dates and recording sessions, prevented them coming. More's the pity.

Donald Peers, son of a Welsh miner who never heard his son sing because he vehemently disapproved of the variety stage, had yet to achieve his enormous success when he played the Royal in the late autumn of 1935 but the audience gave him a warm reception. The crooner obliged by singing the song that became his most requested number, 'In a Shady Nook by a Babbling Brook'. This writer has fond memories of his mother sitting down by the big Phillips radio in our Dublin Corporation flat and listening to Peers' BBC radio programme in the late 1940s. One of the early pop idols, at the peak of his career he used to get up to 3,000 fan letters a week.

Tommy Trinder, the popular English comic and son of a London tram driver, was at the Royal at the end of 1936. Trinder started his stage career at the age of 12 and would star in quite a number of successful comedy movies throughout his career. However, his fast-talking and quick-witted style was more suited to stand up comedy in front of a live audience.

Trinder found that in Hawkins Street. With his trademark trilby hat, the leering smile and the wagging finger, he won over his audience early on, especially with his catch phrases, 'You lucky people!' and, 'If it's laughter you're after, Trinder's the name'. Above all, too, he was clean, unlike some other visiting English comedians.

Dance bands proved to be hugely popular when they visited the Royal in the late 1930s, particularly in 1937 and 1938. Big name bands led by the likes of Nat Gonella, Billy Cotton, Ray Noble, Henry Hall and the man known as the Aristocrat of Big Band Music, Bert

Ambrose, graced the famous stage. Interestingly, Ambrose's singer in Dublin at the time was a little-known Londoner named Vera Lynn.

Vera would go on to international fame as a solo artiste and became the Forces Sweetheart during the war years with hits such as 'We'll Meet Again,' 'The White Cliffs of Dover,' 'Yours' and later 'Auf Wiederseh'n Sweetheart,' the first record by a UK artiste to top the US charts. 'I indeed recall singing at the Theatre Royal with Ambrose,' she remembered. 'A lovely theatre and warm audiences. It was particularly pleasing because I had always wanted to be the best singer with the best band, and Bert Ambrose had the best band.'

George Formby, the Lancashire entertainer with his saucy songs while strumming bouncy rhythms on his ukulele which gave him an instant rapport with audiences, drew packed houses at the Royal in 1937. He would return to Hawkins Street several times in the 1950s, and for a few years lived in Foxrock, County Dublin. One of Britain's biggest celebrities, Formby was earning more than £100,000 a year at a time when professional men such as doctors were on salaries of little more than £1,000.

Adored by millions of fans. including the British royal family, George was not a man blessed with outstanding musical or thespian talent, and it was said he could not read music. His appeal lay in the warmth of the cheeky yet endearing character he exuded on stage and in movies.

The Royal audience called out for his famous songs. George duly obliged with ditties which were the big hits of the day, and without which no Formby show would be complete,

George Formby with his wife and business manager Beryl

143

such as 'When I'm Cleaning Windows,' 'Leaning on a Lamp Post,' 'With My Little Ukulele in My Hand,' 'Mr Wu Is a Window Cleaner Now,' 'Count Your Blessings and Smile,' 'Bless 'Em All' and 'Chinese Laundry Blues.'

Formby's week was arranged in conjunction with the Irish premiere at the Regal Rooms Cinema next door of his latest movie *Keep Fit*. George played his by now familiar role of the working class underdog – the gormless, gullible, indefatigable and triumphant hero.

Formby's character is a weakling who overcomes obstacles to beat a corrupt rival in the boxing ring. *Keep Fit* also starred Kay Walsh and Guy Middleton, and was filmed at the Ealing Studios in West London, to this day the oldest continuously working studio facility for film production in the world, having started in 1902.

George's wife Beryl, a former clog dancer, was his full-time manager/agent, with fees starting at £35,000 per performance. As it happened, she continually hogged the limelight, always making sure to walk on stage at the end of her husband's performance to share the acclaim.

As George was receiving his applause on the Royal stage, Beryl walked out, and a surprised Jimmy Campbell, the orchestra leader, handed her a bunch of flowers intended for the next female performer. With a mock smile, Beryl said: 'For me? Thank you.' She was hurrying to George's dressing room with the flowers when a stage hand stopped her and said: 'Sorry madam, you can't keep those flowers. They are for a girl singer on next.' With a distinctly sour face, she reluctantly handed them back and stormed off.

While Beryl's business skill and tough character made Formby the UK's highest paid entertainer, both in movies and on stage, she was a domineering and tyrannical woman who effectively took over his life. Beryl was the boss. She even refused to let him drink on his own in a pub or go out with male friends for dinner in case he met some other woman.

At theatres, including the Royal, she stood in the wings with a clipboard and a stopwatch, monitoring every detail of George's performance and ensuring he did not get too close to any of the chorus girls. People in the entertainment business knew of her domineering attitude but apparently this trait was never made public until years later.

Nevertheless, it was no secret that their marriage was anything but a happy one. Many put it down to Formby's alleged affairs but this was never the case. He was a faithful husband, and there is no record of any unfaithfulness. The cracks in the marriage were caused by Beryl's iron fist. With her it was business, business, business, and money, money, money. She negotiated his contracts down to every minute detail, and allowed George just five shillings a day pocket money.

Utterly ruthless in contract negotiations, she thought nothing of harassing theatre managers or BBC executives. While there is no evidence or record of any hard bargaining for George's week in Hawkins Street, or his fee for that matter, both Beryl and the Ellimans were apparently happy with everything. This came as a pleasant surprise to Josef Locke, the Derry tenor and Theatre Royal favourite who would sell his seafront house near Blackpool to the Formbys in 1953.

'I never heard of any disagreement over George's fee but I can assure you that Beryl was a formidable woman, a tough lady indeed,' Locke recalled. 'She did all the business, going through contracts meticulously and checking the finer details. All the houses George and Beryl lived in, including the one I sold them, had to be called Beryldene, and their yachts were named Lady Beryl.'

Betty Driver, the actress who later played Betty Williams in *Coronation Street*, found that her own entire contribution to a particular movie with George was taken out on Beryl's orders. 'She was a monstrous woman, though very clever,' Driver remembered.

On one occasion Beryl flew into a rage when she learned that George had been to the studio canteen for a cup of tea with his co-star Irene Handl. 'She was such a nasty, spiteful piece of work to just about everyone, including George,' said Handl in later years. 'She was so twisted and conniving that it was impossible to work out what was going on inside that head of hers.'

An experienced if limited actress, Beryl often demanded the role of leading lady for herself so as that her husband would not have the opportunity to be intimate or too familiar with any female co-star. The director Monty Banks was so infuriated with her that he once said: 'The only time you will get me directing anything where that bloody Formby woman is concerned will be when she is playing the murder victim and the scene is for real.'

Yet Beryl was not without her passionate side. Her striking looks meant she had a coterie of male admirers, and according to Formby's diligent biographer David Bret, she had affairs with at least two actors in the 1930s. George, being a devout Catholic, refused to divorce her.

In later years she developed cancer, and within two months of her dying in 1960, George announced his engagement to schoolteacher Pat Howson, 20 years his junior. He confided to close friends that with his new fiancee he had achieved a happiness that he had never experienced with Beryl. 'My life with Beryl was hell,' he publicly confessed in an interview following her death. Sadly, just two days before the wedding set for 6 March 1961, Formby died of heart failure. He was only 56.

The cowboy star Tom Mix came to the Royal early in 1939. A former Texas Ranger and rodeo champion, Mix became one of Hollywood's best-known western heroes in silent pictures and early talkies. Between 1909 and 1935 he appeared in 291 movies, all but nine of which were silent pictures and was Hollywood's first western megastar.

Mix provided exciting escapist entertainment for cinemagoers, in marked contrast to the slow if authentic style established by William S. Hart and copied by other western stars of the period. Mix had much to do with establishing the successful formula that set the pattern for all western films to follow as well as helping to define the genre for all cowboy actors who came later, notably John Wayne and Clint Eastwood.

Cowboy star Tom Mix and Tony, billed as his Wonder Horse

Mix had retired from movies in 1934 and concentrated on world tours with Tony, billed as his Wonder Horse. Coming to Dublin as part of a European tour, he delighted Royal patrons with some sharp shooting and reminisced about his life on screen and the people he met along the way. On his return to the US where he continued a radio show which would run until 1950, he never failed to tell friends about the 'wonderful reception I had in Dublin' and recommended them to visit 'the old country.'

Another major cowboy star, Gene Autry, came to the Royal during Horse Show Week in August. Billed as the Singing Cowboy, Autry was a genuine cowboy, born on a ranch in Texas. 'I was working as a railroad telegrapher at a junction in Oklahoma when Will Rogers, the actor, heard me sing and urged me to go into show business,' he told a newspaper reporter in Dublin, where he had come on the first leg of a month-long European tour.

'I started singing on a local radio station, got my own radio show and made my first recordings. That led to a break into movies in 1934 and a 13-chapter serial called *Phantom Empire*, plus my first starring role in *Tumblin' Tumbleweeds* in 1935 and happily here I am.'

Arriving at the North Wall on Saturday, 5 August, Autry made his live radio debut on European radio with a 30-minute show on what was then Radio Éireann. Then at noon on the following Monday there was a welcoming parade down O'Connell Street which drew tens of thousands anxious to get their first glance at the cowboy hero. In the afternoon he opened a week-long engagement at the Royal. Autry was booked for three shows a day, with performances at 3.40, 6.00 and 8.40.

The show opened with Jimmy Campbell starting up the orchestra, and a film came on screen supposedly depicting Autry leaving his ranch by stagecoach for his Irish trip, and when the audience noticed that the coach was driven by his movie sidekick Smiley Burnette there were loud cheers. Autry rode onto the big stage on his famous horse Champion who swished his beautiful long tail and stood on its hind legs. Gene sang a number of popular songs from his movies and at the finish thanked his audience for 'the wonderful reception.'

It is worth noting that Autry was a hugely successful business-man, and his many interests over the years included his own film production company, a radio and TV chain, ranches, oil wells, a fly-ing school, a music publishing company and the Californian Angels baseball team. He was making movies up to 1953 and did his final one on a comeback in 1976.

Demand was such that a matinee was added on the Saturday, start-ing at 1.00. As if that was not enough, two extra Saturday performances were tagged on to the end of the schedule. This meant that he gave a total of 21 shows, with an estimated audience of 80,000, an unheard of figure not only then but right through the theatre's long history.

The Royal management were planning as a companion movie that week an Autry picture. When this was not possible, *Man of Con-quest* was shown, starring Richard Dix and Gail Patrick. It told the story of Sam Houston, the nineteenth century American statesman and soldier of Irish extraction and best known for his leading role in bringing Texas into the United States. However, next door at the Regal Rooms, Autry fans could catch Gene in *Mexicali Rose*, about a singing cowboy who fights corrupt oil men selling worthless stock from a non-existent well located on land belonging to a poor Mexican orphanage. It co-starred the regular Smiley Burnette.

In the Royal audience on the first night were two songwriters, Jimmy Kennedy from Tyrone and Michael Carr, a Dubliner. After the show, they visited Autry's dressing room and showed him a rough copy of a new song they had just written. Autry liked the look of it and, taking it back to America, it not only became one of his biggest hits internationally but was the title of his next movie rushed into cinemas in time for the Christmas market.

The song, 'South of the Border,' has since been recorded by many artistes including Frank Sinatra, Patsy Cline and Cliff Richards' former backing group, the Shadows. Jack Doyle also recorded it with his wife Movita. It is still popular today, 75 years on, with the Cork tenor Finbar Wright including it on a CD.

Louis Elliman reverted to three musical comedies by English companies in 1939. First was *The Desert Song*. A Sigmund Romberg operetta first performed on Broadway in 1926, it could probably be considered today as a combination of Zorro and Superman where a hero adopts a mild-mannered disguise to keep his true identity a secret from a beautiful and spirited girl. The best known songs, 'One Alone' and the title number, went over well with the audience. It was filmed three times.

The Desert Song was followed by *Balalaika* which also became a movie, in 1939. Set in Russia, it is centered around a captain of the Czar's Cossack Guards and a cabaret-cum-opera singer and secret revolutionary who fall in love on the eve of World War I, are separated by war and ideology and meet again in 1920s Paris. The title song, 'At the Balalaika,' was the show's most popular number, judging by audience reaction.

The third was *The White Horse Inn*, another winner with Royalgoers. An operetta set in Austria which had enjoyed huge success on Broadway and London, it was about the head waiter of an inn who is desperately in love with the owner, a resolute young woman who only has eyes for one of her regular guests. Filmed five times, all in Germany or Austria, *The White Horse Inn* is probably best remembered here for its hit song 'Goodbye', which will always be associated with the Derry tenor Josef Locke.

The English comedian Max Wall followed, and introduced Royal fans to Professor Wallofaski, a ludicrously attired and hilariously strutting character with his tragic clown's face and distinctive sadness in his voice. John Cleese has acknowledged Wall's influence on his own 'Ministry of Funny Walks' in the comedy series *Fawlty*

The Three Stooges, the madcap trio of Moe, Curly and Larry

Towers. Louis Elliman would recall in later years that Wall was one of the funniest comics to ever appear at the Royal.

Keeping up the comedy trend at the Royal in 1939, Elliman brought in the hilarious American comedy act, the Three Stooges, familiar to moviegoers in two-reel comedy shorts produced by Columbia Pictures in Hollywood. Consisting of Larry Fine and the two Howard brothers, Jerome, known as Curly, and Moe, they were touring Britain at the time and took the opportunity of visiting Dublin.

Audiences were delighted with the comic action, as they bopped each other on the head with mallets, tweaked each other's noses, gouged their eyes and kicked shins. Reviews were excellent, with the trio being described as 'simply hilarious' and 'just plain madcap fun all the way, just like in their films.'

Away from the public they were quite serious and lived quiet lives. They stayed on in Dublin for a few days after their Royal week and enjoyed the opera from box seats at the Ellimans' other theatre, the Gaiety. The Three Stooges and opera? Who would have believed it! As they were leaving the theatre, they signed autographs for delighted fans.

10

World at War and the Birth of Home Talent

By the beginning of 1940, the world was truly at war. The previous September, Hitler's forces attacked the Polish border, prompting Britain to officially declare war on Nazi Germany three days later. By New Year's Day, hostilities had escalated.

This resulted in stringent travel restrictions and meant that cross-channel acts, let alone American artistes, could not risk visiting Ireland. For the first few months, the war was largely confined to the sea and propaganda, and called 'the phony war' or the 'Bore war', a pun on the Boer War of 1899-1902. This allowed Germany to secretly prepare for the *blitzkrieg*, a land and air attack.

Travel by sea was considered dangerous. Throughout September and October over 20 British ships had been sunk by the menacing U-boats and mines, including the liner *Athenia*, with the loss of 112 passengers and crew, and the battleship *Royal Oak*, with 800 men lost. Nevertheless, two months into the war Elliman managed to put on a professional boxing tournament at the Royal featuring several British boxers on a cold, foggy night in November 1939.

Always a popular crowd-puller in Hawkins Street, this time the main attraction was between Tommy Farr, the Welsh heavyweight who had gone the full 15 rounds with the great Joe Louis for the world title in 1937, and Manuel Abrew, a Scot of African heritage.

'I was met at Dublin Airport by the Hibernian pipe band and played all the way into the city,' Farr remembered in later years. 'On arrival at my hotel, either the Gresham or the Shelbourne, I'm not sure which, to my dismay I was handed a letter marked 'From IRA headquarters.' On opening it, I read: 'If it's good Irish money you're after, you will be a dead man.' When I got to my room I was informed by the porter that two young ladies were waiting for me in the lounge.

'They told me that unless I handed over £100 to the Party Fund, there would be trouble. I laughed out loud and told them in no uncertain terms to get out of there. Secretly, though, I was scared. I went back to my room and immediately informed the gardaí. I also contacted the promoter, a Corkman named Gerald Egan. The outcome was that I was put under the protection of two burly detectives, who stayed outside my room all night.

'On fight night they smuggled me out the back door of the hotel, straight into a car and slipped into the theatre by a side door. I can tell you I was never so nervous in my life. My fears were lifted somewhat when I climbed into the ring. The theatre was packed and my manager told me all tickets had been sold out five days earlier.

'I knocked out Abrew in the third round but I didn't wait for the official verdict. I made my way to the dressing room on the double and was back in my hotel long before the theatre had emptied, with the two detectives at my elbow. As I made for my room, a messenger handed me a note which read: "Leave the £100 at the desk for collection if you want to get out of Dublin alive."

'My detective friends assured me that there would be nothing to worry about and they stayed outside my door. At daybreak, they drove me straight to the airport after arranging a flight to Liverpool an hour before my scheduled departure. I heard no more about the IRA threat but I can tell you I was never more happy to get out of Dublin and into Merseyside. Later on, whenever I heard or read any mention of the Theatre Royal in Dublin, my mind would always go back to that occasion.'

The British actor Robert Donat risked his life on a tramp steamer to make it to Dublin in April 1941 for a matinee at the Royal in aid of the Newspapers Press Fund. Donat, who overcame a bad stutter to develop a fine resonant voice, read extracts from James Hilton's novel *Goodbye Mr Chips*, for which he had won an Academy Award as Best Actor two years earlier in Los Angeles.

The supporting bill on the show, which drew a full house, included players from the Abbey Theatre, including F. J. McCormick and his wife Eileen Crowe in a one-act play *Never the Time or the Place* by Lennox Robinson. The show was compered by Lord Longford, the Irish peer and company director at the Gate Theatre.

Louis Elliman was now faced with a major decision – either close the Royal and the Gaiety, or develop local talent. 'The problem with the home talent is that many of them were inexperienced, essentially amateurs,' he recalled in a newspaper interview in later years. 'Certainly they had tremendous potential but they needed a bit of experience and that only comes from practice, practice, practice. Up to then, they had been mainly supporting acts, and many were in their late teens, or just turning into their twenties.

'If we were going to keep the theatres open, and that was the wish of us all, we would have to put them out there, and have them learn their craft as they went along. But we persevered. They were real troupers, all of them, and I could never give them enough credit. Thankfully we got through the war years, although it wasn't always easy, as you can well imagine.'

It was during this period that the Theatre Royal earned the great affection of Dublin audiences by helping to dispel the threat and gloom of the Emergency with pantos, sketches and humorous reviews.

One of the most successful of the home artistes during those dark days of the war years was the Dublin comedian Cecil Sheridan, who had made his initial debut at the Royal in 1937. The son of an upholsterer also named Cecil, and his wife, Catherine, his mother died of tuberculosis when he was six and he and his siblings were raised by his father.

Educated at Synge Street CBS, near the birthplace of the playwright, novelist, social reformer and Nobel Prize winner George Bernard Shaw, Cecil grew up with a bad stammer and in a bid to cure it he sought opportunities to perform in public.

Sheridan, a teetotaller all his life who disliked other people drinking in his company, made his stage debut at the age of 20 when he won £100 in a talent contest at Whitehall Carnival on the outskirts of the city. However, he continued to work in his father's upholsterer

Cecil Sheridan has his dancing shoes on for the Royalettes

business until 1937 when, after winning another talent contest, he decided to become a full-time stage performer.

Cecil always maintained it was the best decision he ever made. When he wrote to Louis Elliman and asked for an audition, he was accepted and so began a career lasting over 40 years.

Whenever he walked out onto the Royal stage dressed in a tatty old overcoat with his hands concealed up the sleeves and wearing a flat cap, the audience broke into spontaneous laughter. He simply looked funny. Then when he went into his monologue based on the henpecked husband, it brought the house down.

Cecil also worked at the Olympia and mainly at the Queen's, where in the early days he was a permanent in the resident company, but he always said the Royal was his favourite, often on stage with his diminutive sidekick Mickser Reid alongside him. 'The a-a-audiences were always very r-r-responsive,' he said in a newspaper interview in later years. 'They l-l-liked you and you l-l-liked them, and that was v-v-very important, all important.'

Cecil's stammer never interfered with his performances on stage, completely disappearing once he stepped in front of the footlights. But like many famous artistes in various branches of the entertainment industry, he was always nervous walking out on stage. 'Everyone experiences n-n-nerves going out on s-s-stage but mine wore hob-nailed boots,' he once admitted. 'But once you s-s-start, everything is f-f-fine. In any event, the s-s-show must go on.'

Cecil got on well with Louis Elliman, and there was one amusing incident when 'Mr Louis' was in the stalls one morning ready to take a rehearsal when he noticed no performers in sight. 'Where the hell is everybody?' he roared through a haze of cigar smoke. Cecil emerged from the wings and explained that there was a fellow from one of the newspapers taking photographs backstage. 'Photograph my backside!' bellowed Elliman. Said Cecil, retreating: 'Hold on a m-m-minute boss and I'll see if he has a p-p-plate left.'

Having fun with little Mickser Reid
are Cecil Sheridan, left, and Noel Purcell

On another occasion going into the theatre he happened to meet a newspaper seller who also had a stutter. 'H-h-how much do I owe you for the p-p-papers Billy,' Cecil enquired. 'I t-t-took the H-H-H-Herald every night and the M-M-Mail on Tuesday.' The frustrated vendor replied, after starting to count on his fingers: 'For C-C-Christ sake C-C-Cecil, you have me as b-b-bad as yourself n-n-now.'

Sheridan had a caustic wit in private life but former colleagues would remember him as a kind and caring man. He had a particular affection for his sidekick Mickser Reid and he ensured that Mickser worked as often as possible in his shows by writing special roles for him into his scripts.

Jimmy O'Dea, the resident comic at the Gaiety, was one of many who had a great respect for Cecil. O'Dea called him 'a true professional who knew the secret of projecting a comic persona and had an inbuilt sense of timing.' Cecil died in January 1980 and was fondly remembered at his funeral which drew a large crowd of mourners.

*   *   *

Early in 1940, the Dublin opera singer May Devitt shared top billing at the Royal with Richard Hayward, the Merseyside singer and actor who appeared in several movies in the 1930s. Reviews were good, particularly as far as the local girl was concerned.

'Davitt's voice is light, warm in tone and with a certain satisfying brilliance in its upper register,' enthused the *Irish Independent.* 'She blended well with Hayward from the start.' Hayward, who had a close affinity with Ireland and helped form the Belfast Repertory Theatre Company, said later: 'I enjoyed working with May. A lovely lady and fine artiste.'

Philip B. Ryan, the historian, said of her: 'May Devitt was not in the front rank of divas but she had great sex appeal and magnetism, two qualities that ensured a rapport with the audience in a theatre the size of the Royal.'

Southern Ireland may have kept out of the war but that did not stop the Ellimans from making a reference to our soldiers with a miniature tattoo in August called *The Roll of the Drum.* The colourful show, aimed mainly at encouraging men to join the army, and supported by the Irish government which saw it as a way to galvanise national solidarity, featured over 200 soldiers and the No. 1 Army Band conducted by Lt. Dermot O'Hara.

Together, along with the drums and pipes of the 2nd and 5th Infantry Battalions, they demonstrating arms drill and physical training. The show was produced by the army general staff and dedicated, as the programme indicated, to National Defence.

The production was one of the best presented at the Royal or any other Dublin theatre during the 1940s. Imaginatively staged by Charlie Wade, the theatre manager, it featured a blend of music and song aimed at pleasing all tastes. It ran for three weeks and broke all existing Dublin records for theatrical attendances, which was quite a feat considering the vast size of the Royal.

The singing was done by John Lynsky and Tom Peacock and the comedy was in the capable hands of Mike Nolan, Joe Duffy and Paddy Tyrell. The trio of funsters were effectively amateur entertainers and had learned their craft, like many others, at the Father Matthew Hall in Church Street on Dublin's north side. This venue was considered an ideal training ground for performers seriously interested in going into entertainment, whether in variety, operetta, drama, dancing, musical comedy or whatever.

Originally built in 1890 by the Capuchin friars as a temperance hall dedicated to the memory of the Tipperary-born teetotalist reformer Father Theobald Matthew, for many years it staged the annual Feis Ceoil, a cultural festival of music and dance. First organised in 1897 for the purpose of stimulating musical studies in Ireland and encouraging native performers and composers, prizes aggregating £800 were distributed among the successful competitors.

The Father Matthew Hall is now a three-story office block, but the Feis Ceoil is still going strong with more than 170 competitions nationwide. Many famous artistes have gone through the Feis including tenors John McCormack and the latter day Finbar Wright, broadcaster Sean Og O Ceallichain, author James Joyce in a brief singing career and Maureen O'Hara, who would go on to fame in Hollywood movies as the Queen of Technicolour. 'Winning the Feis Ceoil started it all,' remembered Maureen fondly.

Subsequently, Tyrell became a permanent member of the Happy Gang at the Queen's Theatre, a team of performers assembled and christened as such by another Dublin comedian Danny Cummins who got the idea from the more famous Crazy Gang on the London stage. Tyrell did sketches as well as developing a popular series called *Thanks for the Memory* in which he and Gloria Greene, a former usherette at the theatre, sang duets each week requested by the Queen's audience.

This writer had the pleasure of meeting Tyrell on several occasions in his retirement years at the Dublin fruit market where he had a stall and found him to be a good companion. Like most comedians, he was quite serious away from the footlights. Friends would say he rarely talked about his stage work but always said he enjoyed his years with the Happy Gang as well as his occasional appearances at the Royal.

Following the success of *The Roll of the Drum* in 1940, there were two further productions with an army flavour during the war years, *Tramp, Tramp, Tramp* and *Signal Fires*, with several of the same artistes as well as new faces making up the company. The pantomime in the 1941-'42 season was *Cinderella* and included Noel Purcell and Mike Nolan as the Ugly Sisters.

Purcell would be a Royal favourite right to the end when the theatre closed for the last time. A star on stage and in movies, Noel was the quintessential Dubliner who never lost his local accent. His fine recording of the 'Dublin Saunter', composed by Leo Maguire and about 'Dublin can be heaven with coffee at 11 and a stroll in Stephen's Green,' is still played on Irish radio programmes, and is as popular today as it was when he first recorded it in 1954.

Born in Lower Mercer Street, off which a new road was built in 1991 named Noel Purcell Walk, Purcell was a big Royal favourite in the 1940s and 1950s, particularly in the Nedser and Nuala sketches during the war years featuring Noel and another Dublin actor, Eddie Byrne.

Written by the Cork scriptwriter Dick Forbes, the routines had Purcell as the dame Nuala and Byrne as her scheming husband.

Pauline Forbes, another big Royal favourite, played their daughter Fionnula. In real life, Dick and Pauline were father and daughter. Their comedy act brightened many a life for harassed Dubliners experiencing the dark days of the war.

Purcell also had a very successful movie career and estimated he made close on 100 films in almost 40 years in front of the cameras as a fine character actor, nearly always with his long, white beard. 'Purcell's characters usually liked a tipple or two,' said the movie historian and author David Quinlan, 'but was nobody's fool even when intoxicated.'

Pauline Forbes, daughter of scriptwriter Dick and a performer in her own right

Among Noel's co-stars were the likes of icons such as James Cagney, Gregory Peck, Orson Welles, Brigitte Bardot, Jack Hawkins, Danny Kaye, William Holden, Peter Sellers, Sophia Loren, Marlon Brando, Laurence Harvey, Kirk Douglas, Peter O'Toole, James Mason, Paul Newman and many more.

Nevertheless, he always found time to fit in his Royal shows whenever shooting schedules permitted. It is to his eternal credit that he did the Royal pantos for most of the 1940s and 1950s. 'To me, the Theatre Royal was something special, very special,' he said in an interview. 'There was always a great camaraderie there, and I made many life-long friends at the Royal. I could talk about the theatre for hours.'

Noel's first job on leaving school at the Christian Brothers in Synge Street was as a carpenter. It was whilst making some scenery for a stage production that he became interested in acting, which

Peter O'Toole chatting with good pal Noel Purcell

would determine his life. His early years were mainly spent touring halls and theatres in Ireland and Britain before becoming a regular at the Olympia, and sometimes at the Queen's, and finally the Royal. But the Royal was his 'real home', as he so often said.

It was Eddie Byrne who introduced the popular 15-minute quiz show *Double or Nothing* in 1942. The dark-haired and good-looking Byrne had been brought into the Royal in 1940 on a trial basis as a newcomer but stayed on for five years before leaving for Britain and going into movies, where he had a successful career that lasted well into the 1970s. His daughter Catherine Byrne is a well-known actress and is best known nationwide for her TV role as Dr Judith Dillon in the RTÉ soap *Fair City*.

Double or Nothing was a big success on the Royal. The husky-voiced Dublin singer Peggy Dell saw an American one-reeler at the Queen's Theatre one night called *Take It or Leave It* and suggested to Louis Elliman that it might form the basis for a stage quiz on the Royal. 'I think it might be something that would suit Eddie Byrne down to the ground,' she said.

After 'Mr Louis' got hold of the film and watched it, he offered it to Byrne but he rejected it. 'I told him I was the wrong man for the job, that I was an actor and that he should look for somebody else,' Byrne recalled in later years, but Louis, being Louis, got his way and the quiz turned out to be an unqualified success.

'What happened was that members of the audience would be invited on stage to each answer four questions on the subject of their choice,' Eddie remembered. 'They would be asked: "Will you take the prize now and go away, or is it double or nothing?" The first correct answer earned two shillings and if they kept getting the answers right, it was doubled until it reached 15 shillings. If they failed to answer a question correctly, they got nothing.

'I must say it got off to a poor start because people at first were shy about coming up from the audience. But once they got used to the idea, they rather liked it. As the quiz got more popular, the prize money was increased. Sponsors were sought and they donated prizes, and eventually Louis and the management were offering a Friday night jackpot prize of a new Vauxhall car. That's how successful *Double or Nothing* was.'

The formula was that the orchestra would play the theme music and the combined Royalettes and Rockettes dance troupe did a routine as they sang the theme song:

> If it's Double or Nothing you've been waiting for
> Then here is Eddie, who's ready to give you some more
> If you can answer questions right, you know
> He will give you two four, eight, 16 or so.

'Those figures were used mainly to suit the rhythm of the song, as the actual cash prizes for four correct answers progressed from 2s 6p, roughly 12 1/2p today to £1, or €1,' said historian Philip B. Ryan, 'but the contestants could collect their winnings at any stage. If someone after three questions had won 10s, or 50p today, it was theirs for the taking.

'There were four contestants, usually the first four in a mad rush to the short row of steps to the stage as £1 was a lot of money is those days. On stage they would be seated in front of the quizmaster who was himself standing at a podium with a cup-like attachment at the side and into which he dropped the money nosily as it was won. On Friday nights the big prize was the new car.

'Eddie Byrne was always impeccable in evening dress and the epitome of the perfect compere. Although Eddie could give the impression of being somewhat aloof or tetchy, he was never condescending, although he once got very cross with a contestant who tried to send him up. In Dublin, however, rumour spreads on its own lubricant of malice, and is usually started by someone who is jealous of or dislikes the victim.'

Ryan remembered that on one occasion, a young lady said in reply to Byrne's usual question that she was a parlour maid. 'You mean you are a skivvy!' he was alleged to have said. A remark like this would certainly not go down well, and many people felt that it was typical of Byrne to say such a thing.

While he was a very capable performer, Byrne was not always popular with everybody because of his sometimes smart remarks. He was often the butt of a joke by a contestant, although his successor Eamonn Andrews, another Dubliner, said: 'Eddie was personable, fast-talking and confident. He was made for the show.'

One evening in the bar, two old ladies were seated near Eddie, who was on his own. One of them approached the compere with her hand outstretched. 'Mr Byrne, this lady here is my good friend Alice, and we want to shake your hand. We are thrilled to meet you,' she gushed. 'You know, we come here every week to see you in *Double or Nothing* and we wouldn't miss it for the world.'

'That's very nice of you,' said Eddie. 'I hope you enjoy the show.'

'Oh, yes. We're along every week. Isn't that right Alice? We never miss even one week.'

'That's really nice to hear,' said the compere, who was beginning to get a bit bored at this stage. 'But tell me, why do you come absolutely every week? Not even missing one week.'

'Well,' said the old lady confidentially, 'we know that one of these nights somebody is going to beat you up and we want to be here to see it!' Ouch!

Eddie Byrne, left, and Noel Purcell take a break on the roof of the Royal

When Byrne left to pursue what turned out to be a very successful movie career in 1945, playing alongside Noel Purcell in several films, the quiz was taken over by Eamonn Andrews. Byrne, like Noel Purcell, was very busy before the cameras and is mentioned in David Quinlan's book *The Illustrated Directory of Film Character Actors* as 'an actor who seemed to be turning up in every third film during the 1950s.'

During 1954-1959, he had parts in no less than 29 films, more than four a year, and as it happened, many shown in his old 'home,' the Royal. Byrne had his first role as a seaman in the early 1940s, a strange premonition considering his role in 1977 as the naval officer General Vanden Willard in *Star Wars Episode IV: A New Hope*.

Several years before he died of a stroke in August 1981, he said in a newspaper interview that while he made a very good living in films, he enjoyed his years at the Royal, 'working with so many wonderful performers.'

Sean Mooney, a popular baritone during and after the war years

Another Irish star to emerge at the Royal in 1942 was the local young baritone Sean Mooney. He was a competitor in the weekly Radio Éireann competition *Newcomers' Hour* and later sang with the church choir at the Star of the Sea Church in Sandymount on the Dublin coastline. When Louis Elliman was looking around for a singer for his show *Round and About*, he asked several members of the Royal company if they knew of anybody suitable.

Noel Purcell remembered Sean singing in the church choir and recommended him. Mooney went for an audition on the Tuesday afternoon and by Sunday afternoon he was on the Royal stage as a professional. His strong voice delighted audiences both at the Royal and the Capitol later as well as appearing in the Dublin Grand Opera Society productions at the Gaiety, including *The Bohemian Girl* and *Faust*.

In 1950 Sean recorded his most famous song 'If We Only Had Old Ireland Over Here,' later put on record by Josef Locke, Connie Foley, Foster and Allen and the American country singer Hank Locklin. Nor did he confine his singing to the variety stage. In later years, he did cabaret spots around Dublin and the writer well remembers him doing a week's engagement at the Braemor Rooms in Churchtown, still in fine voice and where his popular rendition of 'If We Only Had Old Ireland Over Here' brought the house down.

Elliman was introducing new acts into his shows and they soon learned the traditions and practices of theatre life, such as never whistling in the dressing room, never actually mentioning *Macbeth*, just the Scottish play, never wearing a watch on stage, and always walking around the entire stage before the curtain went up so that you 'own the stage' even if there were are other artistes with you. The new acts included the comedian Jack Cruise and crooner Frankie Blowers.

Cruise, a Dubliner and first cousin of the portrait painter Leo Whelan, left secondary school at St Vincent's CBS in Glasnevin at 18 and started his working life as a trainee ledger clerk in Kennedy's bakers, a well-known bread company in the city. In his spare time, and always being interested in acting and drama, he joined an amateur theatrical group.

In 1936, at the age of 21, while performing in the panto *Jack and the Beanstalk* at the Father Matthew Hall he created what was to become one of his favourite characters, John Joe Mahockey from Ballyslapdashamuckery.

John Joe was an astute countryman, or culchie to use the Dublin expression, who wore a flat cap with an enormous peak, navy blue suit, white shirt, red tie and a large pair of brown hobnailed boots. When Cruise left Kennedy's bakery in 1945 to work full time as a professional, he joined the Royal company and was appointed house manager and press officer. He also appeared regularly on the Hawkins Street stage as a comedian as well as scripting many shows, and was on stage for the Royal's final production in 1962.

Cruise was always guaranteed to get the laughs whenever he got into his John Joe Mahockey character, which was often. He introduced John Joe to holidaymakers at Butlin's Holiday Camp in County Meath in 1951 and over the next eight years produced and starred in 80 different shows at the camp.

Jack divided his time between the Royal and Mosney as well as the Olympia Theatre where he produced and starred in several very successful pantos including *Aladdin and the Wonderful Lamp, Cinderella, Jack in the Box* and *Ring Out the Bells* up to the early 1970s. He died in May 1979, aged 63.

Blowers, a devotee of Bing Crosby, was probably the most relaxed singer to ever play on any Dublin stage, let alone the Royal where he was a regular performer. Audiences had little trouble making comparisons between Blowers and Crosby. Indeed, he was known as Ireland's answer to the iconic American entertainer, with his easy flow and smooth style, especially in songs like 'Buddy Can You Spare a Dime', which was Blowers' own favourite, 'My Blue Heaven', 'The Folks Who Live on the Hill', 'Sweet Sue' and 'Where the Blue of the Night Meets the Dawn of the Day', Crosby's signature tune.

Former colleagues would remember Blowers arriving at the stage door in Poolbeg Street on his old English BSA bicycle, manufactured by the Birmingham Small Arms company and known in Dublin as 'upstairs models', wheeling it inside, taking the trouser clips from his ankles and going into his dressing room to get ready for the show. 'Frankie was always early, in all weathers', recalled one veteran stage hand. 'He was a real pro, no doubt about that, and that's the very reason he was so good at his job. The audiences loved him, and he loved them.'

Crooner Frankie Blowers and the Royalettes

When time permitted, Blowers also was the vocalist with Joe Coughlan's band at the Ballerina Ballroom in Parnell Square, where many a romance blossomed in the intimate surroundings. The Ballerina was this writer's favourite among all the city's dance halls in the 1950s, and there were many to choose from.

When the Royal closed in 1962, Blowers moved to the Gaiety Theatre and also did guest spots in *The Good Old Days* at the Eblana in the basement of Busaras, Dublin's central bus station. He also had a residency at the Green Isle Hotel on the Naas Road where he was entertainments manager. 'But the Theatre Royal was his real home and he was always happiest there,' remembered his daughter Lynda Doherty. 'He was devastated when it was pulled down, as was everybody else.'

Meanwhile, Blowers also resumed his ballroom engagements at the Ballerina as well as doing stints with Phil Murtagh at the Metropole in O'Connell Street, Jimmy Greer at the National in Parnell Square and the Crystal in South Anne Street where the lights shone on a revolving crystal ball, sprinkling coloured lights on the dancers. Ah! What memories.

Johnny Butler, the bandleader whose name will be fondly remembered by dancers who quickstepped, slow waltzed and foxtrotted to his music at the Ballerina, the Olympic, the Bar-B and other ballrooms, claimed he discovered Blowers at a club in Dun Laoghaire.

'It was at the Workman's Club where I used to play,' he recalled. 'Those were the days when there were no microphones and you sang through a megaphone. There was this young man sitting on the bandstand in front of me and imitating playing a trumpet. I asked him if he could sing and when he said he could, I got him up on the stage and he sounded just like Bing Crosby.

'He told me his name and that he was 17 so later I brought him into the city and he started singing with my band or the Vincent Phibbs band which I directed. Later on he would sing with other bands and of course at the Theatre Royal where he was a great favourite.

'One night after singing at the club in Dun Laoghaire he missed the last tram so he slept in an armchair at my home until the following morning. He just loved to sing. He was a wonderful guy, no doubt about that.'

There was also a dark side to Blowers. The general public was completely unaware of this aspect of his life and who only saw the tall, dark and handsome singer up there on stage. He had developed a serious drink problem, a fact acknowledged by his daughter Lynda. Before going out on stage at the Royal, there were many occasions when members of the cast would have to try to sober him up. Often he would be so drunk that another resident singer, Sean Mooney, would have to deputise for him.

Blowers died in October 1973 of a heart attack following a stroke. He was 54. At the time his diary showed many upcoming dates for concerts around Dublin. Johnny Butler was among a large gathering of mourners from many walks of life and not only show business at Mount Jerome Cemetery in Harold's Cross.

'Frankie Blowers was one of the true gentlemen in a very tough and competitive business,' said the bandleader, having flown in from the US for his first visit to Dublin in 16 years. 'He was one of the nice guys. But you know, I think too that in some ways he was too timid for the music business. I often thought he should have been in something else, like a salesman. But he remained the perfect gentleman and a fine singer. I've no hesitation too in saying that the Theatre Royal was his favourite stage, his real home in a way. He would often refer to the Royal in conversation.

'Frankie was a very private man and disliked the razzmatazz that's associated with show business. I don't think many people knew either about his lifelong hobby of making model trains and planes. I know personally that he made a clockwork train for his daughter that took a year to assemble and couldn't have been bought from him for pure gold. He would tell you the trains and the planes were all for Lynda's sake but you know, don't let that kid you. Frankie was the one who loved the results of his craftsmanship.'

* * *

In the 1942-'43 season, the Royal was continuing to show a profit, thanks to Louis Elliman's shrewd control and the policy of including new movies in the programme. It would not be quite true, as has been suggested, that only second-rate movies were shown at the Royal.

It should be remembered that Elliman was a very influential person in the Irish entertainment field and always made sure the Royal got first-run films, and good ones too. What he did not have was the luxury of the international stage stars as he had before the war but made the best of it by putting on top variety shows with all local artistes.

Another innovation by Louis was the establishment of an art department in the old premises of the *Freeman's Journal* around the corner in Townsend Street. This building itself was full of history as the *Freeman's Journal* was the oldest nationalist newspaper in Ireland, first published in 1763 and merging with the *Irish Independent* in 1924. It was immortalised in James Joyce's *Ulysses* as the place of employment of Leopold Bloom who sold advertising for the paper.

Now it was creating a piece of theatrical history. Under the direction of Fergus O'Ryan, assisted by James Mahon and overseen by Elliman, although Louis never interfered with their work, they designed posters, programmes, hand-prepared glass projection slides and anything related to Royal artwork.

An apprentice in the department was Mahon's 14-year-old brother Thomas, who was assigned the tricky task of touching up film posters featuring international female stars. This work involved deftly raising necklines and lowering hemlines with a bottle of printer's ink and a brush to meet with the strict censorship in vogue at the time. When one particular Hollywood star of the 1950s saw her 'doctored' picture in the foyer of the theatre, she exclaimed to the manager Phil Donohue: 'Is that really me?'

Interestingly, after the Royal's closure, the talented Mahon brothers went on to have successful careers as designers elsewhere – Thomas designing the Apple Records label for the Beatles and James in the ESB. However, they never forgot how the Theatre Royal gave him their first start in life with their chosen careers, and often recalled to families and friends about many of the famous stars they met. 'What memories,' James was once quoted as saying.

The Royal panto of the 1942-'43 season was *Red Riding Hood*, a show which provided Eddie Byrne with one of his best stage roles as the wolf, described by the *Irish Independent* as 'a truly terrifying creature and a part which truly stretched his capabilities as an actor.' The cast of over 100 in a show that each member blended so well included Jimmy O'Dea's future wife Ursula Doyle as Robin Hood, Olive Briggs as Maid Marion, Renee Flynn as the Fairy Queen and Johnny Caross as Felix the Cat.

The film accompanying the panto was *About Face*, a comedy concerning two army sergeants, one dumb-tough and one mild-mannered, who get into a saloon brawl, crash a high-society party, and end up in a car wreck. The cast included William Tracy, Joe Sawyer, Jean Parker and the always dependable Margaret Dumont, best remembered as the stately, statuesque lady who triggered many laughs as the perfect foil for Groucho's antics in seven Marx Brothers movies.

Elliman was now supervising the production of the shows under the pseudonym of T. R. Royle. This presented no real problem for members of the company and staff as they knew only too well who it was but they still called him 'Mr. Louis' as before.

Following *Puss in Boots*, the first series of shows under the billing 'T.R. Royle presents' was called *Royal Flush* and these featured Noel Purcell and Peggy Dell, with occasional spots filled by Harry Bailey, Cecil Sheridan and Sean Mooney. Eddie Byrne, following a break, was also back by popular demand with his quiz show *Double or Nothing.*

Since the start of the war, the Royal shows had also featured an occasional high-kicking chorus line, the first being an English troupe of girls called the Violettes. They were led by Alice Delgarno, a Scottish choreographer and dancer, and Babs de Monte, a Londoner who designed the costumes.

The Violettes mainly consisted of former Tiller Girls, the first all-girl, high-kicking dancing line-up across channel and founded in 1890 by John Tiller, a theatre director from Lancashire and credited with being the originator of precision dancing.

In the 1920s and 1930s, at the height of their fame, there were eight troupes of Tiller Girls performing across the world including the Folies Bergere in Paris, the London Palladium

Comedian and sometime fiddle player Harry Bailey with his wife

and on Broadway. They played the Royal shortly before the outbreak of the war in 1939. Within each troupe the girls were matched very precisely by height and weight. Tiller had noticed in other groups that the overall effect of a chorus line of dancers was often spoiled by lack of discipline. He found that by linking arms, the girls could dance as one.

But Tiller was a hard taskmaster. In training and rehearsals, he was relentless with the girls, repeating every movement time and time again until they were perfect. Tiller worked them so hard that at times they were so exhausted they had to be carried home by their parents – their feet too blistered to walk.

The American equivalent of the Tiller Girls was the Rockettes, then and now the resident troupe at Radio City Music Hall in Manhattan and who, for their Christmas production alone, do five shows a day, seven days a week. Troupes of Tiller Girls are also around today, with the company run worldwide by the founder's grandson Bernard Tiller.

The Violettes were booked by Louis Elliman to play the Royal for one week in the autumn of 1939. Most of them were former Tiller Girls and were highly trained and thoroughly professional. They blended in well with the show and Elliman was so impressed he asked them to stay on for another week.

'I had been looking around for a good line up of dancers for some time with no success as we couldn't book cross-channel acts because of the war but the Violettes seemed to be the answer,' he told a newspaper reporter in later years. 'We booked them for a third week and then a fourth but by then some of them pulled out as they had commitments in London and regrettably could not stay on in Dublin.'

Dalgarno and de Monte stayed on with the remaining ones, and Elliman started recruiting Irish girls to join what he hoped would become a permanent Royal line-up, Soon 'Mr Louis' had what he wanted – a dancing troupe.

Over the next few months, the last few English girls left for the London stage. Dalgarno and de Monte liked Dublin and remained, encouraging Elliman to recruit Irish girls. Soon it was an all-local ensemble. There were always about 18 on hand with 12 on stage, the remainder to be called in for holiday periods, weeks off, sickness or whatever.

By 1943 Elliman had named them the Royalettes, and with occasional changes of personnel, remained very much part of the Royal scenario up to the night the theatre closed for the last time 19 years later. The average age of the girls was 19.

A third party, Christine Kealy, was in charge of make-up, using glycerine and red ochre during and immediately after the war because of shortages. Christine also looked after the girls' hair-dos as well as being the wardrobe mistress, a difficult enough job considering the great many changes they had to make.

Most of the girls auditioned came from dancing schools with a good sense of rhythm or were natural dancers who just needed a little polishing. But few had any training in ballet. The wide routines required classical dancing and some acrobatics, so Dalgarno and de Monte had to decide how loose-limbed a girl was and how high she could kick.

The Royalettes soon built up a reputation for precision, innovation and glamour, and there is little doubt that they contributed greatly to the box-office takings. The girls received regular standing

The Royalettes relaxing in their dressing room after a Christmas show

ovations. Although ultra demure by today's standards, the Royalettes had a pleasantly sensual cachet in a 1940s-1950s society where public sexuality was severely frowned on. Part of their mystique was their good looks and unattainability.

Louis Elliman took every opportunity to make it clear to everyone that 'we have in the Royal a troupe of dancers on a par with anything in London, Paris, New York or anywhere else. There is no doubt about that.'

But the work was hard for the pay, which was £21 5s a week, and the girls, wearing slacks and turbans, were in the theatre at 10.00 every morning for rehearsals. They worked until 12.00 on the empty stage to the sound of a piano, often played by Gordon Spicer, who was on the Compton organ for the shows. As well as finalising routines for the two shows, one in the afternoon and the other at night, they were also working on the following week's shows.

'Yes, we were a family, if you like, but the point was that the work was really tough, even terrible,' de Monte would recall. 'We were thinking up new routines the whole time so as to present something new and fresh each week. It was really amazing what we did, to be honest. I remember once the wardrobe mistress Christine Kealy having to make 55 costumes in five days, can you believe it?

'We rehearsed every single day, seven days a week, from 10.00 to 12.00 noon, then there was a break for lunch before going out on stage for the first show. After that, there was a rehearsal for the evening show starting at 8.00. You must remember we were an ensemble and we had to attain precision and perfection. It was like you were in the army.

'Now to get two people together to do exactly the same thing is difficult enough but you can only imagine having 12 girls doing it. Let me say though that the girls never complained, at least not to me or Alice. Nor do I ever remember them making any complaints about money. They were dancers and their life was the theatre.'

Grace Bourke went straight from school to become a Royalette at 16. Described by Babs de Monte as 'a lovely little girl and a very live spark on the stage', Grace would later marry Eamonn Andrews when she retired from the dance troupe and would be known as Grainne. She came from a theatrical background as her father was the impresario Lorcan Bourke who produced plays at the Olympia Theatre in Dame Street and her mother Kathleen was stage manager. The family had a theatrical costumers business close to the Olympia.

In an interview in later years, Grainne described life as a Royalette as particularly gruelling. 'We would rehearse with the other dancers from 10.00 in the morning to midday before breaking for lunch and return to the theatre for the first of the twice-daily shows,' she said. 'The stage show had usually three big dance routines and a number of backings, such as the chorus back-up for the *Double or Nothing* compere.

'Every Sunday afternoon a new show opened and the same evening Alice and Babs would begin planning the following week's routines. Unison, Babs believed, was what appealed to audiences. She used to say that we used to stop the show with one of our routines. However, it's fair to say that we lived a somewhat nomadic existence and with the two shows and the rehearsals, we wouldn't get home until midnight.

'When we broke for meals, we were not allowed to bring in fish and chips. Romance was certainly out for the girls. If any happened to have steady boyfriends, the lads were told to go. It was as simple as that. When I left the Royalettes to work in the family's theatrical business in Dame Street, the contrast of doing something more relaxing and less stressful was incredible.'

Frankie Blowers' daughter Lynda Doherty recalled: 'My mom was Georgina Tinkler, one of the Royalettes, and I've happy memories of those times. Mom and dad would have me in the dressing room and I would meet the girls and many of the stars and we'd have tea. Dad

Crooner Frankie Blowers and Georgina Tinkler, a former Royalette, on their wedding day

had the No. 1 dressing more often than not.

'There were four dressing rooms to accommodate the Royalettes. The stage was massive. It went back and back, with an enormous amount of scenery. My mother did tell me the work was very hard, with two shows seven days a week as well as rehearsing for the following week's show. Remember too, Thomas, they were not paid very well either. I suppose they just loved what they did. When my mother married dad in 1948 she had to leave the Royalettes as married women were not expected to work in those days so she became a housewife.

'Interestingly I saw great movies at the Royal too and I think I must have seen *The Magnificent Seven*, that marvelous western with Yul Brynner and that great cast, about 125 times. I knew it off by heart, all the action and all the dialogue.'

Another former Royalette who did not wish to be named remembered: 'Yes, it was really hard work, but we got through it. You could call it back-breaking work if you like and it was. I remember Alice Dalgarno as a very, very tough taskmaster, like a drill sergeant, and getting us to do it again and again and again until we got it right, at least they way she wanted it.

'I would go home at night with blisters on my feet and they just ached. But there you are. That's show business. This was what you wanted and it was a question of take it or leave it. It was that simple. Some of the girls left and were replaced right away by the substitutes Mr Louis had in the wings, so to speak, but the majority stayed. I must say though that I enjoyed my time as a Royalette, despite the hard work. Jobs were not too plentiful in the 1940s either. But you know what they say, the show must go on.'

It was Father Cormac O'Daly, chaplain to the Catholic Stage Guild, who encouraged the girls to recite the Rosary in their dressing rooms between shows. Besides reminding them to keep the faith, the prayers were also to ensure that they did not have 'bad thoughts' when they went out on stage while performing their

Georgina Tinkler in relaxed mood

high-kicking routines. It must be remembered that several of the 'dirty raincoat' brigade were often in the front row seats gawking up at the girls so maybe some of those should have said the Rosary too.

Rose Brennan, the Dublin singer who made her debut on the Royal stage at 16 and would later find fame in Britain as resident vocalist with the Joe Loss Orchestra, said: 'The Royalettes dressing room was like a convent. The girls had holy pictures on the walls and recited the Rosary. It was another world. Visiting musicians, whose advances were always rejected by the girls, dubbed the Royal the Virgin Island.'

It is not clear if all the girls, particularly the Irish ones, participated in the Catholic ritual of the Rosary, and while Father O'Daly always encouraged everybody to do so, it was reported that one or two of the older ones donned plastic raincoats, known as mackintoshes, and slipped out quietly.

They made their way across Poolbeg Street, into Corn Exchange Street and into the upstairs lounge of the White Horse Inn bar on the corner of Burgh Quay, a pub frequented by many *Irish Press* staff, and where they exchanged 'juicy bits of gossip' as one put it. The girls would down a few glasses of 'liquid refreshment' before making their way back to the theatre without anybody, least of all Father O'Daly, who was coming to the end of the prayers, noticing their absence.

There was another bar opposite the stage door in Poolbeg Street, Mulligans, still in the same spot since 1872, but the White Horse Inn, later known as the Dark Horse Inn, was apparently the most popular. Nevertheless, if some of the male artistes wanted a little bit of privacy in knocking back a pint, they would make their way into Mulligans.

If they were anyway late, the stage doorman always knew where to find them. It should be noted that there were always a number of bars in the theatre but somehow 'getting out of the building' for a little bit of privacy somehow seemed a more comfortable and enjoyable option.

11

Scriptwriter with the Right Note

The Theatre Royal during the 1940s owed much of its success to the scriptwriter Dick Forbes. A proud Corkman from Prince's Street, with its tight community spirit, Forbes in his lifetime was a drama coach, drummer, tap-dancer and playwright, with a keen interest in railways and shipping. He was also 'a voracious reader' in his own words.

With his fertile imagination, however, Forbes' scriptwriting was his real forte and he could turn seemingly ordinary situations into hilarious moments and develop them, something that Louis Elliman recognised early on. Dick had hit upon a winning formula and his revues went down exceptionally well with audiences depending on local talent for their entertainment.

As well as writing the Royal scripts, Forbes collaborated with Harry O'Donovan on Jimmy O'Dea's BBC radio series *Irish Half Hour* which was very popular on both sides of the Irish Sea. In the series, Forbes also performed an old music hall song called 'Killaloe', about a teacher of French who comes to a little village in the West of Ireland.

One of three sons of a master tailor, he was small of stature but big on ideas. A Shakespearean actor early in his career, Forbes had a keen interest in all of the Bard's plays and would be willing to take on a role at short notice with little rehearsals. 'I knew most of the dialogue anyhow, and I would just have to brush up on it before going on stage, he said.

When Dick was a young man, his father took him to South Africa where the senior Forbes started a clothing business in Cape Town. Dick became homesick, however, and was sent home to study law with the idea of making it his career. But he soon felt he was not really cut out to be a lawyer and in 1920 joined the IRA when he was despatched to the organisation's Flying Columns.

These were groups who ambushed the British forces and the Royal Ulster Constabulary whenever they ventured out from their barracks. On one of these dangerous missions, Forbes was captured and sent to England where he spent 18 months in Shrewsbury Jail.

On his release, he decided to pursue the considerably less dangerous career as an actor/entertainer and toured Ireland in fit-up companies, once forming an act with the twinkle-toed song and dance man Jimmy Harvey, who later became a member of the celebrated Happy Gang at the Queen's Theatre.

Forbes was also an underrated drummer, and while hitting the skins with a band in Waterford, he met a Yorkshire woman who ran a dance academy in the town. It was love at first sight for Dick and Muriel, and their marriage produced two daughters – Pauline, who would subsequently become a regular Royal performer, and Twinkle.

In his spare time Dick also did a lot of writing, including the penning of revue scripts for the Olympia Theatre and the Cork Opera House. An indication of his talents was that in 1936 his play *Silver Jubilee* was produced at the Abbey Theatre following a nationwide competition for new playwrights. The play came first from an entry of 117.

Forbes was introduced to Louis Elliman by Noel Purcell and it was a match made in heaven. Dick contributed to some of the early shows, although his first attempt, *Thro' Erin's Isle*, did not cause much comment. It was the series that followed called *Something in the Air*

Noel Purcell, left, with English actress Peggy Mount and Eddie Byrne

that really clicked for him. A spectacular production with elaborate costumes and more importantly a strong cast, the Dublin theatre critics gave it excellent reviews. Philip B. Ryan, the theatrical historian, recalled that 'nothing like it had ever been seen in Dublin.'

Eddie Byrne sung the introductory song while Noel Purcell performed a weekly spot called Schoolboy Howler. There was also a comedy act featuring Byrne and Purcell, sometimes joined by Forbes himself as well as another great Royal favourite over the years, Albert Sharpe.

Sadly, Irish theatregoers did not see enough of this talented Belfast actor and former member of the Abbey Players as he subsequently went to Hollywood where he established himself as a fine character actor. He is fondly remembered by moviegoers for his seminal role in the whimsical 1959 movie *Darby O'Gill and the Little People* in which he played the caretaker who claims to have befriended the King of the Leprechauns, portrayed by Jimmy O'Dea.

The movie may have its critics who claim it is 'utterly stage Irish' but it was a big hit worldwide and is currently on DVD. Leonard Maltin, the esteemed movie historian and reviewer, described it as 'a delight and a movie with dazzling special effects'.

Albert had a busy career in Hollywood and besides playing alongside Sean Connery in the *Darby O'Gill* picture, he worked with the likes of Fred Astaire, Gene Kelly, Joseph Cotten, Jennifer Jones, Peter O'Toole, Vincent Price, Trevor Howard, Deborah Kerr, Jane Powell and Cyd Charisse. He also starred in the Broadway musical *Finian's Rainbow* at the 46th Street Theatre, which ran for two years and later became a movie featuring Fred Astaire.

Sharpe got his first taste of the entertainment business when, during holidays from St. Mary's Christian Brothers Grammar School, he sold programmes at the Empire Theatre in Belfast. When he left school, he became an assistant to magicians and later joined a Shakespearean company and toured Ireland and England. It was not until Sharpe joined the Abbey Players in the early 1940s, however, that his career took off.

'From my work in the Abbey, I made my first movie, *I See a Dark Stranger*, in 1946 and when the Broadway producers were looking around without much success for somebody for *Finian's Rainbow* a year later, the Abbey producer Ria Mooney recommended me and I got the role of Finian,' he said in an interview in 1965. 'I was 62 at the time and the New York papers were calling me 'an overnight star on the Great White Way'. It ran for two years so between the stage and movies I was kept busy.

'When Disney selected me for the *Darby O'Gill* picture. I was in semi-retirement at the time. Off all the work I did, I guess everybody remembers me for *Darby O'Gill*. I've no complaints with that, not at all,' he added with a chuckle.

Sharpe lived in quiet retirement in Belfast in the mid-1960s and said that while he enjoyed his movie career which covered 14 years, his happiest days were on the stage. 'The Abbey and the Royal and those wonderful theatres in Belfast were just magic,' he recalled. He died in his native city in February 1970 at the age of 84.

In the Royal show *Something in the Air*, Elliman introduced a second group of dancers in addition to the Royalettes. They were the Rockettes, an obvious nod to New York's Radio City Music Hall. They were all around 16 or 17 years of age. As soon as the Rockettes became proficient Louis transferred them to the Royalettes troupe. Eventually the remaining Rockettes moved over to the Queen's Theatre where they had a successful run.

Passing Parade of 1943 was billed as 'an extravaganza,' with a large cast that included Jack Cruise, Albert Sharpe, Sean Mooney and Phil Donohue, who would later become manager of the Royal. The crowds came along and the show got good reviews. The panto that year, and the first of what was to be many written by Dick Forbes, was *Puss in Boots*. Playing Puss was Rita Conroy who, like Cruise and so many others, learned her craft at the Father Matthew Hall. Noel Purcell played the dame and the cast also included Eddie Byrne.

Byrne was back with his popular *Double or Nothing* quiz in the first show of the new year, *Royal Salute to 1944* which featured several speciality acts including the Cook Brothers who had an entertaining cowboy routine. The most important guests on that show, in February 1944, however, were boxer Jack Doyle and his wife Movita.

Remembering the furore over what had happened with Doyle when he arrived here with the divorcee Judith Allen in 1936 which caused the nearest thing to a revolution, the bold Jack was taking no chances this time. He was now a married man, having wed the fiery Mexican actress 12 months earlier in a lavish ceremony in Dublin.

The Doyle-Movita show was billed as *Home from Hollywood* and they started by touring the country, with the Royal the last stop. When his agent told Jack that one engagement was in Ballyjamesduff, a former market town in Cavan with a population of around

1,000 residents, he shouted down the phone: 'Where?' After being assured it was a nice pleasant town and the fans would turn out in big numbers, he was still apprehensive. 'Ballywhere?' he exclaimed. 'Where the hell did you dig that up from? Have they electricity there, or gas lamps?' Nevertheless, the show went well and the Doyles were pleased.

Now here he was finally at the Royal for a week in a big show. Both sang several songs, including the expected 'Mother Machree', and got a warm reception. 'Really, Mr Myler, it was great to play the Royal after the disappointment in 1936', he explained to this writer in later years.

'I had no doubt that the audiences would be very responsive on my second visit and they were. Movita too was over the moon with excitement, and the moment we came off stage she gave me a great big hug and said, "I love you, honey". All told, a very happy period in my life.'

Jimmy O'Dea, a Gaiety regular, was back at the Royal in April with a brand new show called *Variety Fair*, written in collaboration with his regular scriptwriter at the Gaiety, Harry O'Donovan, with a big input from Dick Forbes, who penned the Royal sketches.

Noel Purcell was in the production too, in sequences called the *Golden Budda* in addition to his regular solo spot plus the introduction of comedy sketches entitled Nedser and Nuala, played by Eddie Byrne and Purcell. Byrne was also continuing with his popular *Double or Nothing* spot so it can be ascertained therefore that artistes had to work hard in the absence of foreign stars.

Nedser and Nuala were supposedly a working-class Dublin couple, with Byrne as Nedser and Purcell as his wife Nuala, who was constantly at war with her deceitful and distinctly work-shy other half. Their daughter was played by Pauline Forbes, another Royal regular and, as mentioned earlier, Dick's daughter in real life. Louis Elliman felt that all three worked so well together and his intention was to keep the act going on and on. More importantly, audiences loved them.

The summer series of shows was called *Royal Bouquet*, which *Evening Herald* theatre critic John Finegan described as 'brilliant in its colour, movement and variety, and on a par with any of the shows presented in the Hawkins Street theatre. The Royal does not need foreign artistes when we here in Ireland have so many talented performers available.' Not surprisingly, Nedser and Nuala were back with more fun and frolics.

The *Royal Bouquet* show also featured spots for Jimmy O'Dea, May Devitt, Ginnette Wadell, Michael Ripper and the ever-popular Royalettes, along with the Rockettes adding touches of glamour to the production.

The final show of the year before the panto opened was *Royal Parade* which had a stirring opening ensemble with the girls dressed in military-style uniforms and emerging from each side of the audi-torium. Regular patrons never thought they would get so close to the girls, a dream come true for the lads.

The panto, which had its gala open-ing night on 17 December, was *Mother Goose* which John Finegan described as 'beyond all doubt and argument the greatest and most spectacular panto Dublin has ever seen and which will hardly be seen again in anybody's life-time.'

Finegan and this writer worked side by side on the *Herald's* editorial desk in the 1970s and he often mentioned the panto in conversation. 'It indeed was a superb show, brilliantly staged with lots

Programme for the 1944 panto
Mother Goose

of singing, dancing and most important for the young folk, lots of comedy', he once said during a chat about theatres, and in particular, that 1944-1945 Royal panto. 'There was no shortage of "Look behind you" lines too.'

The panto was so elaborate with no detail overlooked that part of the back wall behind the stage had to be knocked down and an extension built to accommodate the scenery. It featured Noel Purcell as Mother Goose and Eddie Byrne as her husband Nedser Gander. The seemingly rubber-boned Johnny Caross, a one-time boxer and carnival speciality act, was Jemina the Goose.

Others in the strong cast included Iris Lawler as principal boy and who had come from the Gate Theatre. Jimmy Campbell had left the Royal company and returned to England. His place was taken by George Rothwell, who had previously been on the Compton organ.

Pyke's Theatre Pye
(By kind permission of Evening Herald)

Caricatures by Evening Herald artist Bob Pyke of Royal performers in the 1944 panto Mother Goose

Purcell agreed with John Finegan's lavish praise of the show. Before opening night Purcell commented to a newspaper reporter: 'I think this is the best panto that Dick Forbes has ever scripted, so now it's up to all the performers, from the top of the cast to the bottom, to give it their best shot.'

History has proven that everybody worked their hardest to make it work – and they succeeded admirably. At the end of the six-week run it was estimated that some 258,000 people, roughly a third of the population of the city at the time, had seen the panto, with many no doubt seeing it more than once. Many people came from the provinces too, especially when word got around that it was a show not to be missed.

In the summer of 1945, Max Elliman, a brother of Louis, died after a brief illness. Max had been house manager of the Royal and he was one of the most popular figures in the Dublin theatre world. He got on well with the performers and was forever courteous. Always interested in show business, not surprising since he came from a theatrical family, he vowed when he was

George Rothwell, Royal bandleader and organist during the mid-1940s

around 14 that he would do what he could to promote entertainment. It was the only job he ever wanted.

Max was manager of the Corinthian Cinema on Eden Quay, which in the 1920s had shown some of the finest films of the silent era including *The Birth of a Nation* and *Metropolis*. He also managed the Queen's Theatre on Pearse Street before moving to the Royal.

'Maxie was especially liked by pressmen,' wrote Liam McGabhan in the *Irish Press*. 'He had a casual off-hand manner that hid a rare generosity, and a reporter was always welcome in any of the theatres or cinemas he managed. Whenever he was pressed for a story of the theatre world, he gave the details quite frankly with nothing "off the record". Maxie trusted his man implicitly as to how a story should be treated. He took criticisms of the films and shows with fine good humour. Maxie had a fine sense of appreciation and never kept a pressman waiting. We shall miss him.'

Elliman's replacement was Jack McGrath, who had previously worked as manager and who, interestingly, later attained the rank of colonel in the British Army in World War II before being invalided out following a spell as a prisoner of war. His assistant was another of the Elliman brothers, Jack, who had the position as publicity director as well as deputy manager. The two Jacks worked well together, sharing ideas and suggestions and bringing them before 'Mr Louis.'

In late July, Louis Elliman approved a new series of revues called *Royal Brocade*, a colourful production with a different show each week. The shows had the regular company plus two newcomers to the cast, Maurice Keary, a tenor who had starred in the Gaiety's lavish production of *Show Boat*, and Norman Barrs, an actor from the Gate. Dick Forbes continued to write lively and witty scripts up to his death in August 1949 and the overall result drew full houses.

'Everyone in the company had three shows to deal with at the same time,' said the historian Philip B. Ryan. 'First they had to know and perform the current show, which was not to be confused with the previous week's show, and then every Sunday afternoon Dickie Forbes distributed the scripts which had to be committed to memory for the following week's show. What must be remembered is that the Royal was a very special place that needed expert management and stage skills. It contained everything that a theatre needed. It was a self-contained world with its own special community of workers of every description who lived, ate and slept the Royal.'

Sean Mooney, the baritone and a regular Royal performer, recalled: 'We were all one big happy family – from the front of house staff, ushers and usherettes, the orchestra, the backstage staff of scene shifters, electricians, carpenters, scene painters to the performers. Everybody was friendly. There was no animosity, no rows. Most were known by their Christian names but respect was given where it was due.'

*   *   *

Despite his considerable success on radio and television across the Irish Sea, particularly with *This Is Your Life*, Eamonn Andrews always attributed the Theatre Royal for providing him his big break with the popular quiz show *Double or Nothing* in the 1940s. The format would later be copied by Radio Luxembourg and led to British TV quizzes such as *Double Your Money, Take Your Pick* and more recently *Who Wants to Be a Millionaire.*

'Of all the theatres in Dublin in the 1940s, the mammoth Theatre Royal topped the lot,' Andrews would recall in his autobiography. 'First-class productions, plus the inclusion of an item which took Dublin by storm, *Double or Nothing*. It also catapulted into the limelight a personable, fast-talking young Dublin actor named Eddie Byrne. Not a little of the quiz's success was due to Byrne's handling of it.'

Andrews had always yearned to be a writer or a poet. The son of a Dublin carpenter, he became an amateur boxer with St Andrews BC in York Street close to St Stephen's Green after a boxer friend gave him a hiding. A scholarship won under the severe and rigid Christian Brothers School in Synge Street helped to get him a job in an insurance office before becoming a freelance broadcaster with Radio Éireann and radio critic with the *Irish Independent.*

It was Louis Elliman who offered Eamonn his big opportunity. The owner of the Royal was so impressed with the success of *Double or Nothing* compered by Eddie Byrne that he decided to put a similar one on in the Savoy Cinema in Limerick which he also owned. When Andrews' name was suggested, Elliman immediately agreed to give it a try. At this time Eamonn was driving an old Morris car that could just about make the road journey to Limerick and back, over 100 miles each way.

The prospect of the quiz intrigued him. He had seen Byrne doing the show, mostly at weekends and agreed that it was Eddie who made it such a success, although he was once amused when the compere got very cross with a contestant who tried to send him up. But Eamonn felt he would love to give it a go in Limerick. It would involve two shows a day for seven days a week, at £30 a week.

His only problem was making the long journey back in time for his work on Radio Éireann which consisted of introducing records. It was a hectic schedule, and though he enjoyed himself on stage, he was sometimes fortunate to make the Savoy in time for the show. Once he was so breathless that he could scarcely ask the questions.

Andrews often got a close friend, Dermot Cafferty, who in later years would become his partner in a business empire which included the Gaiety Theatre, to act as chauffeur so as to keep to his schedules. Other times a member of the Savoy Cinema agreed to drive him back to Dublin.

Once, on the way back to Limerick with another friend, the old jalopy careered off a wet road and hit the side wall of a garda station, knocking off a drainpipe before skidding to a halt. Eamonn alighted, apologised for the damage and paid the station sergeant 30 shillings. With so little time to change, the audience were quite surprised when their compere walked out on stage with mud on his trousers and shoes.

The Limerick gig lasted several months. When Byrne left to pursue a movie career in Britain, he recommended to Louis Elliman that Andrews would be the ideal compere to replace him on the Royal for *Double or Nothing*. 'Although Eamonn wasn't a creature of the theatre, rather a radio man, he was young, ambitious and personable,' recalled Byrne.

'I felt he had the charisma to carry the quiz. Indeed, I knew that he was described as a nicer person than me. I had to make the quiz controversial and that seemed to be my attraction, and people disliked me for that. I felt that Eamonn would always put them at ease, which he did.'

'The publicity that surrounded my takeover made my debut a huge ordeal,' Andrews remembered in later years. 'While the Savoy had been small and intimate and cosy, the Theatre Royal was one of the largest cine-variety theatres in Europe. I was gripped by excitement and a tingling fear in the moments before I went on. The fear was tingling inside me as I introduced the first contestant and I was far more nervous than he was.

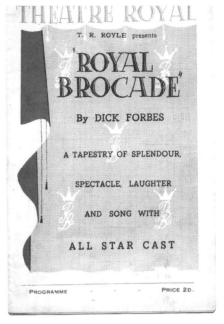

Programme cover for
September 1945

'In my nervousness I made a tentative wisecrack. From the darkness beyond the footlights a fantastic sound rolled down to me – the sound of an audience laughing. Suddenly my tenseness eased and my fears vanished. I knew then that it was going to be all right.

'Whenever I stopped to think of my shyness I was astonished at what I was doing for a living. I still did radio work but usually there was just an inanimate microphone and me, perfect for someone so withdrawn. Yet here I was, running onto a huge stage, painfully aware of all my deficiencies and performing before huge audiences.

'The Royal show made me more well-known in Dublin and people would come up to me in the street as though they knew me. I found it very exciting and flattering, and the more people I met, the more the main burden of shyness wore off. At parties, though, I was still painfully shy.

'People never seemed to understand the huge difference between talking to up to 4,000 unknown, and unseen, people from a stage and standing up in a living room under close scrutiny from perhaps a small gathering of friends whom you can see very well.'

Besides the star prize of the car at the weekend, the nightly prizes were modest. They would last until the weekend to increase audiences' interest but there was always a reserve question to stump the audience and drag out the quiz. One of those questions was: 'How many sixpences piled on top of each other would it take to reach the top of Nelson's Pillar?' It did not matter what the contestant replied. It was always the wrong answer.

Gus Smith, Andrews' biographer, recalled Jimmy Sheil, who was the Theatre Royal manager at one time, saying that Byrne was more meticulous than Eamonn. 'Eddie worried too much about the quiz, whereas Eamonn was more casual,' Sheil recalled. 'Eamonn didn't mind making a mistake or the audience having a laugh at his expense. He often walked on stage wearing white socks with black shoes and dinner suit.

'One night I found him waiting in the wings wearing his so-called matching gear. "For the love of God, Eamonn," I begged him. "Go to your dressing room and change those awful socks." In fairness, he rushed off and changed. Another thing was that I used to warn Eamonn never to go on stage without make-up, and while he never did, he hated anything on his face. He used to say it was effeminate. He was always a man's man.'

The Dublin singer and Royal performer Rose Brennan recalled: 'I always thought that in handling *Double or Nothing* on the Royal, and I'm sure in Limerick too, the quiz relied more on Eamonn's personality than it did with Eddie Byrne.

'In a way I suppose Eamonn was a contradiction,' said Rose. 'He could be shy yet he had tremendous ambition. Compared to the pros at the Theatre Royal, he was totally untheatrical. He was still an insurance man. Although he may not have been completely at ease on stage he was always very popular because he was a nice man. I think he disguised the fact that he was very intelligent and very clever.'

Andrews always spoke very fondly of his days at the Theatre Royal. '*Double or Nothing* was good fun,' he remembered. 'As the weeks and months went by, it continued to be in great demand and the management had hefty commissionaires standing by to stop would-be contestants battling each other to get on stage. It came on during the second half of the stage show.

'The show was a great target for university students short of ready cash and I often suspected we were supporting

Programme for February 1946

half the higher education facilities of the city. One student I learned later was the actor Peter O'Toole, and it wasn't hard to imagine him producing that altar boy look to win the audience's sympathy and prompt me to give him a few clues so that he could pick up the prize money. O'Toole did become something of an eccentric.

'But then, in the late 1940s, the Theatre Royal had a handful of characters who, at times, would have made Peter, at his most predictable, seem like an usher at a funeral. The theatre was like a miniature, self-contained town, a secret garish society visited sometimes by the outside world.

'Even the resident organist Gordon Spicer was someone who never ceased to amaze me. A dour Yorkshireman who had studied music at Oxford University, he was a musician of infinite delicacy but drunk most of the time. His face was almost permanently bruised and seldom without sticking plaster on a cut, caused by falling on the stone steps leading to the flat where he lived with a dog, Danny, and his housekeeper Dottie.

'The offer as quizmaster of *Double or Nothing* in the Royal came out of the blue, although it shouldn't have been a surprise because I had been doing it in Limerick. Based in Dublin would mean no more travelling forwards and backwards down the country. I really enjoyed the quiz and I got on very well with the contestants. You can't beat the Dubs, the real Dubs.

'It was through the Royal that I got my big break into Britain. In 1949 Joe Loss and his orchestra played the Royal and Joe's manager Leslie McDonnell asked me would I be interested in touring with the band and compering the same kind of quiz.

'I would be paid £40 a week, good money then. At first I was reluctant but held out for £50. Joe and Leslie agreed and I got the boat over to England a few weeks later, opening at the Finsbury Park Empire in London. Luckily, it all started from there and you know the rest.'

Quiz master Eamonn Andrews weds Grainne Bourke, a former Royalette

As it happened, Andrews had a further happy link with the Royal in November 1951 when he married Grace Bourke, a former Royalette, at the Corpus Christie Church in Dublin. Grace, who preferred the Gaelic equivalent Grainne by which she would always be known, had long since left the troupe to dance solo in shows presented by her father Lorcan and stage managed by her mother Kathleen at the Royal and other theatres.

Subsequently she moved into the family's theatrical costumers business in Dame Street beside the Olympia Theatre, as recounted in Chapter 10. The happy couple, who lived in Portmarnock, a seaside district on Dublin's north side, regularly visited the Royal and often said they always enjoyed the shows there.

When Andrews left the Royal to work in Britain, his place was taken by Roy Croft, the concert compere and a member of the travelling theatres, 'the fit-ups'. Born Harry Roycroft, he got his stage name by dividing his surname in two. He had been resident presenter at the Capital Theatre for four years when Louis offered him the opportunity of moving to the Royal.

'Roy had an ebullient charm and an engaging personality that enabled him to make friends easily,' remembered RTÉ broadcaster Brendan Balfe. 'He soon discovered that his chosen career path as a trainee solicitor was not exactly a barrel of laughs so he decided that show business was for him.

'After a productive career in broadcasting, he became entertainments officer for Guinness Brewery, which he described as "going around Ireland drinking the black stuff." As a raconteur, he was unequalled. He died in Dublin in September 2013 at the age of 91.'

Andrews passed away suddenly in November 1978, and Grainne died in April 1989 after a short illness. There is a 7 foot 10 inch bronze statue of Eamonn in the foyer of the RTÉ studios in Donnybrook. He was a former chairman of the independent RTÉ Authority which launched Irish TV on a snowy New Year's Eve in 1961.

12

Rock 'n' Roll Years

The 1950s were unquestionably the Theatre Royal's best years. Virtually every international star who played the London Palladium included the Hawkins Street venue in their itinerary. The Roaring Twenties was the jazz age, and the Turbulent Thirties a decade of hope. The Fabulous Forties saw Hollywood at its scintillating best despite the war years, but the Fifties were something special, certainly as far as the entertainment industry was concerned. New stars, new singers, new bands came on the scene, the music world spearheaded by the sensational breakthrough of rock 'n 'roll – and the Royal was ready for it.

It was a decade when Ireland was prepared for an escape to the world of gloss and glamour, and where better than to head for Hawkins Street for a stage show lasting for over two hours and followed by one of the latest movies. Yes, a great form of escapism for those who stayed in Ireland.

In the 1950s some 363,000 people received passports, travel permits or identity cards to enable them to leave the country. Emigration hit this writer's family when our parents had to say a sorrowful goodbye to their two boys, my brother Pat and I, as we walked up the gangplank carrying our bags and on to the mailboat at Dun Laoghaire bound for Holyhead, where we would catch the train for the long, tiresome journey to London, then known as the Big Smoke.

Those were the days long before the internet, mobile phones and the social network. Indeed, there were relatively few telephones, with only just 43,000 lines for the entire country, with even only the luckiest of homes having one. Getting a phone could take months as most lines were allocated for business. It is hard to imagine how people communicated at all in the 1950s. But communicate they did.

There were changes too in the entertainment business. With the bleak years of World War II almost a distant memory, new stars and singers began to emerge. These would include the likes of Frankie Laine, Johnnie Ray, Kay Starr and Tony Bennett. Slow in the initial stages, the trend reflected the growing influence of American black music known as rhythm and blues, or r&b, which, in a more sanitised form, would become established as the decade wore on as rockabilly and rock 'n' roll.

Louis Elliman was aware of new faces gradually emerging on the entertainment scene mainly in the US and let it be known that the Royal would welcome them and meet any changes full on. 'It's our job at the Theatre Royal to provide the very best of entertainment for our patrons,' he told a board meeting in January, 1950 during the circus season which finished at the end of the month.

It was back to the full company in February with the regular home performers before the popular Welsh singer Dorothy Squires did a week at Easter. Familiar to Irish listeners on the popular BBC radio show *Variety Bandbox* where she was resident vocalist, she had a fine crystal clear voice.

From the outset she won over the audiences with renditions of 'A Lovely Way to Spend an Evening,' 'I'm in the Mood for Love,' 'A Tree in the Meadow,' 'The Gypsy,' 'It's a Pity to Say Goodbye' and 'Anytime,' a big hit for the American singer Eddie Fisher.

The 100-strong American Air Force band took to the stage in May and revived memories of the Glenn Miller swing era of the 1940s with their fine renditions of Miller's hits. These included 'American Patrol,'

'Pennsylvania 6500', 'Tuxedo Junction', 'String of Pearls', 'Chattanooga Choo Choo', 'At Last', 'Little Brown Jug' and the haunting Miller signature tune 'Moonlight Serenade', which they kept until last.

'Big band music was still tremendously popular, and we tried to get the Air Force band back for a second visit but they had commitments in Britain and the US', recalled Elliman. 'We did very good business with them and they went down very well with our audiences. It proved to us that there was a very big public for people who enjoyed the music of the 1940s, and the 1930s for that matter.'

One morning in May, 1950, Elliman got a phone call from Frank Sinatra's European representative Lew Grade who ran a very successful agency in London. Grade said the singer, who was touring Britain at the time, had a few spare dates and was anxious to appear at the Royal, which he had heard a lot about.

Sinatra had yet to achieve the mega-stardom he would reach in a few short years and in many ways he was struggling with his career. This was three years before he made a spectacular comeback with an Oscar-winning performance in the movie *From Here to Eternity*, to be followed by his subsequent worldwide success as a recording artiste. In short, he was struggling.

Additionally, Sinatra had walked out on his wife Nancy, his childhood sweetheart, after 11 years. He would be accompanied on tour by his lover at the time, the tempestuous Hollywood screen goddess Ava Gardner, whom he had been transporting around Europe. Nancy said at the time: 'My life with Frank has become most unhappy and almost unbearable although I do not contemplate divorce proceedings in the foreseeable future.'

Elliman said he could book Sinatra for a week but only on the condition that Gardner would not accompany him. In those pre-permissive days, and remembering the furore over the Jack Doyle-Judith Allen controversy, Louis knew only too well that because of the notoriety attached to the couple, and fearing a backlash from the church and other religious groups, it seemed too much of a risk for Catholic Ireland. Grade insisted that it was Sinatra and Gardner or nobody so the deal was off the table.

In any event, a week of Sinatra concerts could well have lost money. Frank's singing career had hit a slump since the bobbysoxers' years of the 1940s when he could do no wrong. Now, his record sales were going poorly and his bad relationship with the press did not help. On the British tour he had done badly in places like the Finsbury Park Empire in London with many empty seats while the Bristol Hippodrome lost £8,000 on

Frank Sinatra and Ava Gardner were not welcome at the Royal

the Sinatra week, which followed a series of concerts at the theatre featuring Billy Cotton and his band which drew full houses.

Gardner, who would subsequently marry and divorce Sinatra, remembered in later years when she lived in London: 'I had been looking forward to going to Dublin and so had Frank. My two good friends in the movie business, John Ford and John Huston, the directors, had told me a lot about Ireland and they had connections there. It was a pity the concerts were cancelled. Still, there you go. That's show business.'

Sinatra eventually made it to Dublin – nearly 40 years later. In May 1989 he played the old Lansdowne Road rugby ground, now the Aviva, for two nights with Liza Minelli and Sammy Davis Junior, substituting for Dean Martin who was ill. He was back in October 1991, this time for three nights at the Point, on Dublin's docklands, and now the 3 Arena, when he was accompanied by Steve Lawrence and Eydie Gorme. Even though Ol' Blue Eyes' memory was beginning to fade by then, it is quite possible that his mind could well have drifted back to the Dublin of 1950 and the Royal shows that never were.

Elliman quickly put Sinatra out of his mind and concentrated on the theatre's remaining schedule for the year. In November the English theatrical impresario Emile Littler brought over the stage production of the Broadway musical *Annie Get Your Gun* which packed out the Royal for its 11-night run. It was a big success and got enthusiastic reviews. 'A terrific production with lovely melodies', said the *Irish Press.*

In early December, the veteran Canadian movie star Beatrice Lillie did a week at the Royal which went down very well. When informed that the proceeds of the concerts would go to the St Vincent de Paul charity in aid of the Sunshine Fund which happily still provides summer holidays for children living in disadvantaged areas of Dublin, she expressed huge delight. 'I couldn't think of a more deserving cause', she told a press conference. 'And thank you for asking me to your lovely city.'

Called by one US newspaper in the 1930s as 'the funniest woman in the world', it took a while for her humour to register with Dublin audiences but once they got used to it, it was fine. She told funny stories and anecdotes about her friendships with the likes of Winston Churchill, Noel Coward, George Bernard Shaw, Charlie Chaplin and others. Movie fans would remember her with Julie Andrews and Mary Tyler Moore in the 1967 Oscar-winning musical *Thoroughly Modern Millie* in which she played the nasty hotel owner Mrs. Meers.

After the success of the local circus in the 1949-1950 Christmas season, the Royal management once again dispensed with the traditional panto and booked another circus. This time it was the famous English company Chipperfields with a history going back 300 years. The programme said 'Royal Bengal tigers, a herd of elephants, Percheron stallions and Royal Cream ponies as well as clowns from all over the world – France, New Zealand, Denmark, Sweden, Spain, Australia, China and India.'

Chinese and Indian acts often presented problems for the stage management. Where could they go to eat? Ostinellis Italian restaurant provided the solution. Situated beside the Royal and Regal cinema and opened in 1945, it was owned by the Rank Organisation and was the only ethnic restaurant in the city at the time.

'The strange aromas of curries and other exotic dishes frequently wafted from the dressing rooms and into the backstage corridors,' recalled the theatre historian Philip B. Ryan. 'One Oriental act with the circus prepared their meals on a fire lit on the concrete dressing room floor. Apart from any other consideration, this makeshift method was most unlikely to meet with the approval of the Dublin Corporation fire officer Austin McDonald.'

Following the circus, it was back to local revues in January 1951. Jack Cruise scripted and starred in *High Times* with the regular cast including the high-stepping Royalettes. Noel Purcell had shaved off his famous white beard to appear as Mrs. Mahockey, the mother of John Joe, played by Cruise. During the run, however, Purcell got an urgent telephone call from London to appear in the movie *Appointment with Fear*.

'Can you do it, Noel?' asked the producer Betty Box. 'The film has a good little story, about a pedigree cow named Venus which has to be rescued from one of the German-occupied Channel Islands. It's an adaptation of the novel of the same name by Jerrard Tickel, a Dubliner who spells his Christian name with a J. Anyhow, you'd like the story but I'd need to know now as production starts soon.'

'Could you postpone it, Betty?' pleaded Purcell. 'I don't have my beard just now and in any event, I'm contracted at the Royal for the week.'

'I'll give you a couple of weeks to grow it,' said the persistent Box, who rarely would make a movie unless her good luck omen, Noel

Purcell, was in it. 'As I say, the picture has a good cast and it's headed by David Niven and Glynis Johns. Kenneth More is in it too.'

When Purcell replaced the receiver after telling Box he would see what he could do, he decided to grow the beard again and make an attempt to conceal it with heavy greasepaint for his dame role on the Royal. But to no avail. The bristles started to come through, and midway through the week, Mrs Mahockey was quietly 'buried' and was replaced by her 'twin brother'. It could only happen in show business.

On the following Sunday, Purcell was on an early morning flight to London to continue his burgeoning movie career. 'Louis Elliman was always very accommodating regarding my film commitments and I was forever grateful to him,' Noel would recall.

Tommy Dando joined the Royal company from England in 1950 and proved to be immensely popular with his well-known tunes on the big Compton organ. It was said that he had the largest singalong audience in the world. Dando, who would remain at Hawkins Street until the end in 1962, was as well-known as any of the stage performers.

Perched on his little seat and dressed in his traditional white dinner jacket, he would rise from the pit to great applause into a 'rainbow of light', as the author Deirdre Purcell so aptly put it, a little ball hopping shakily from word to word on the screen. Dando's signature tune was 'Sunny Side Up', written originally for the 1929 movie of the same name. His singalong would last about 15 minutes before he and the organ sank slowly out of sight before the orchestra took his place.

Towards the end of January 1951, Eileen Joyce, the talented Australian concert pianist, played the Royal for a week. Eileen was compared in popular esteem to top artistes like Very Lynn, the Forces Sweetheart during the World War II years, and the evergreen Gracie Fields. Thanking audiences for 'a lovely Irish welcome,' her repertoire included beautiful interpretations of Chopin's 'Piano Concerto No 1,'

Rachmaninoff's 'Piano Concerto No 2', John Ireland's 'Concerto' and Beethoven's 'Emperor Concerto'.

The debonair Jimmy Campbell was back in Hawkins Street in April with his full orchestra after a five-year absence in England. It seemed that time had stood still for Campbell, who was dapper as ever.

'It's great to be back in my favourite place, the pit in the Royal,' he told members of the company. 'I've really missed you all and I can tell you I'm here to stay.' They gave him a round of applause.

Carmel Quinn, the Dublin singer, was another popular entertainer at the Royal around that time, she recalled in an interview with the author during a brief holiday in her hometown. With her scrapbook on the table in front of her, she said: 'My very first connection with this famous theatre, and my first break, was in 1951, if I remember correctly, when I heard that auditions were being held on the stage for a forthcoming show. I went there by myself, not for an audition but just to see how things work. I sat in the back so as not to be obtrusive and just watched what was going on.

Singer Carmel Quinn has fond memories of playing the Royal

'Jimmy Campbell was holding the auditions. He was a very talented orchestra leader and on this occasion he was looking for that one voice – that voice that upon hearing it would just make the listener and the audience as a whole take notice. I listened to the various hopefuls – all were sopranos. Each would begin to sing and Jimmy listened intently, and then would kindly say something to the effect of "Thank you. We will be in touch."

'When the final singer had auditioned, Jimmy turned to close the session and put away his music when he noticed me sitting up in the back seats. "Can I help you," he asked. "Have you come for an audition?" I said I had come to see what this was all about and maybe in the future I could try it out. "Do you sing?" he asked. I said I could, but I had planned it for another time. "Well, you're here now," he said, "so why don't you come up on the stage and sing for me."

'I told him I had no music with me but he said not to worry. "Do you know Brahm's Lullaby," he asked. I told him I did and then he told his pianist to accompany me. His pianist had been playing the entire time for all the sopranos so when he began to play in the same key, I started to sing an octave down.

'Jimmy Campbell listened as I sang the entire song. Upon my completion he asked me why I sang the song in an octave down. I said that Brahm's Lullaby is a lullaby and it's what you sing to try and put the baby to sleep with soothing tones. I said a higher register voice would only keep the baby awake. "Okay," he said finally. "You might just fit the bill." Next thing I knew was I got the job.

'The first night I choose a relatively new song, one that was not heard by many up to then. It was called "The Isle of Innisfree". It was composed by Dick Farrelly. He was a garda as well as a songwriter and he wrote the words and music while on a bus journey from Kells in County Meath to Dublin.

'"The Isle of Innisfree" later became a very famous song. It's a haunting melody with lyrics expressing the longing of an Irish immigrant for his native land. When the movie director John Ford, who had strong Galway connections, later heard the song, he loved it so much that he chose it as the principle theme for his film *The Quiet Man*, with John Wayne, Maureen O'Hara and a strong Irish cast. Maureen made a recording of the song but the words were her own composition.

'When I chose the song for the Theatre Royal, one of the band members Bobby Murphy said to me at rehearsals: "Oh Carmel, don't sing that song. Nobody knows it. Sing something else." I replied: "Bobby, how will anyone know the song if it is never sung. I think it has a lovely melody." I sang the song.

'The audience was quiet upon my finish and then, in a thunderous roar of applause and a standing ovation, they showed their approval. I knew I had chosen the song wisely. At the end of the show I had no other song to sing so I did a reprise. This went down very well again.

'Mine was a one-week engagement. I sang "The Isle of Innisfree" on both the afternoon and the evening shows. I still have that very first review of the show and the mention of myself. The reviewer said: "Carmel Quinn, the young Dublin girl with an unusual voice, was a big hit." That was nice.'

Carmel left Ireland for the US in 1954 and settled in Leonia, New Jersey and made her big breakthrough by coming first on the *Arthur Godfrey's Talent Scouts* radio programme. She went on to appear on the TV version of the show called *Arthur Godfrey and Friends* and had a very successful career both on television and in concerts.

Still hale and hearty at 91, Carmel fondly recalls the Theatre Royal. 'It was at the Royal where I got my first break and I will never forget that,' she said, closing her scrapbook. 'Like so many people I was very, very saddened to hear back in the 1960s that it was closing and was being pulled down to make way for an office block. Progress! Is that what they like to call it?'

The first major international star to play the Royal in the post-war years was Bob Hope. The British-born comedian, who moved to the US with his parents when he was four years of age and subsequently became an American citizen, was on the last leg of a UK tour and looked forward to his Irish trip in May 1951.

Hope's constant companion on tour was the blonde Hollywood actress Marilyn Maxwell. Their affair was an open secret in Hollywood and whenever he had been asked about it by the British press, seeing that he was already married, his regular answer would be: 'She's just a friend.' When Hope arrived in Dublin with Marilyn by his side, Irish reporters were too discreet to bring up the Maxwell issue and contented themselves with questions about his movies and concerts.

Jean Greenberg, who was Maxwell's personal secretary for 26 years, claimed that Hope asked Marilyn to marry him while they were in Dublin but she turned him down because she knew Dolores, his wife of nearly 20 years, would never give him a divorce, the two of them being Catholics.

Hope was supported on stage by his straight man, the English actor Jerry Desmond, and got full houses all the week. Swaggering onto the stage and his eyes scanning the vast theatre, he cracked: 'You know folks, this is some garage.' The audience responded with peals of laughter. At one point, he looked towards the wings momentarily and said: 'There's a guy standing on the side called Harry Bailey and he's writing down all my gags. It ain't fair.' More laughter, though it is doubtful if Bailey, one of Ireland's top comedians, was pleased.

Not everybody was enamoured by Hope's overall style, however. Eddie Byrne felt that while Bob was a master of the fast one-liners, he was often inclined to basically tell the same jokes over and over again in concerts. 'But there is no taking away from him that he was a real trouper.'

Philip B. Ryan, the historian, described Hope as 'a somewhat cold, glib performer off stage.' On the other hand, Marion Fossett, ringmaster of Fossetts Circus, thought the comedian was 'a real gentleman' when she met him in 1994. 'Bob was 91 at the time and he was in Galway for a golf tournament,' she recalled. 'While being driven to the golf club, he noticed our circus and told the driver he wanted to see the show.

*Circus ringmaster Marion Fossett gets a hug from
movie veteran and Royal performer Bob Hope*

'After the performance, we all met for drinks and I can tell you it
was a great honour for us as we were all huge Bob Hope fans. My dad,
now sadly passed away, was thrilled to bits to meet the great man and
had a lovely chat. On leaving, Bob gave me a great big hug and it's not
every Irish woman that can say they were kissed by Bob Hope. The
local Galway newspaper devoted a whole page to the visit and the
golf tournament. It was wonderful.'

Another Hollywood great Judy Garland came to the Royal in July.
The Barbra Streisand of her day, Garland may have been just 4 feet 11
inches in her stocking feet but she was a giant in the entertainment
business. Fred Astaire called her 'the greatest entertainer who ever
lived and was renowned for her unique voice with its tremendous
range.'

When she came to Dublin, Judy had starred in some of MGM's best
musicals including *Strike Up the Band, Little Nellie Kelly, Ziegfield Fol-
lies, Babes on Broadway, For Me and My Gal, Meet Me in St Louis, Till
the Clouds Roll By, In the Good Old Summer Time* and *Easter Parade.*

Ahead of a run at the London Palladium, she did two weeks at the
Royal, two shows a day. It looked a heavy schedule but Judy insisted

Judy Garland greets fans at her Dublin hotel

she was up for it. At a packed pre-show press conference at the Royal which went on for an unprecedented two hours, Garland said her maternal grandmother was an immigrant from Dublin named Mary Eva Fitzpatrick, a descendant of Patrick Fitzpatrick, who moved to America from County Meath in the 1770s.

Asked by a reporter to name her favourite movies, she replied: 'Well, my own favourites would of course be *The Wizard of Oz, For Me and My Gal, Meet Me in St Louis* and *Easter Parade.* My favourite co-stars? I suppose it would have to be Gene Kelly, who had Irish descendants as you probably know, and of course Mickey Rooney. I made a few pictures with them. Then there was the delightful Fred Astaire, who I co-starred with in *Easter Parade.* We all got on very well together, I'm delighted to say. Gene and Fred were complete perfectionists and you had to do your act, dancing or otherwise, over and over again until they were satisfied.'

Looking around and indicating the surroundings with her hands, she said: 'You know, I've heard a lot about this famous theatre from friends and associates in the business and I can't wait to step out on that famous stage, which I'm told, is very big. But after working for so many years on the massive sound stages at MGM, that shouldn't present too much of a problem for me, I would imagine.'

In reply to a question as to what songs she would sing, she said: 'I guess I'll try to fit in as many as I possibly can, and hopefully somebody's favourite will be included. Yes, I will certainly sing 'It's A Great Day for the Irish' which, as some of you may or may not know, was written especially for my 1940 movie *Little Nellie Kelly* by one of MGM's musical directors, a man named Roger Edens.'

When Garland noticed a group of girls across the room who turned out to be from the Metropole Restaurant in O'Connell Street with autograph books at the ready, she interrupted the press conference. Walking over to them, she signed their books and shook their hands. 'It's nice to meet you, girls,' she said. 'I'll arrange tickets for you at the box office if you let the manager know when you can come.' Back she went then to the waiting reporters to continue the press conference. 'What a star,' said one of the girls.

Not surprisingly, reviews were excellent, and good publicity for the English tour that was to follow. 'It was the audience, some 4,000, who actually chose Judy Garland's songs for her at the Theatre Royal last night,' said the *Irish Press*. 'Smartly dressed and taking part in good humoured repartee with the fans who had come to see her, Ms Garland quickly got down to business, flung off her shoes at the edge of the stage because she explained her feet were hurting her, after calls for requests from all over the theatre.

'The dynamic film star, accompanied by an excellent pianist named Buddy Pepper, obliged with favourites such as 'Little Nellie Kelly,' 'It's a Great Day for the Irish,' her perennial hit 'Somewhere Over the Rainbow' and a Gaelic version of 'Pretty Girl Milking Her Cow,' *'Cailin Deas Cruidte Na Mbo'.* Her stage presence is easy and friendly, and she had about a dozen encores. At her press conference earlier, she was very friendly and courteous and never failed to answer a question. A real, genuine star in every sense.'

By the end of her final night she had performed to over 50,000 people, an unprecedented figure for an entertainer in Ireland. During her two-week stay, she always made a point at some stage of opening her dressing room window high above Poolbeg Street and singing a few bars of a song, 'just for the folks who couldn't get tickets for the shows,' as she would explain later.

Pauline Forbes, a regular Royal performer, had a slightly different view of Judy's opening night, always taking into consideration that many artistes can be very critical of other performers, not excluding greats like Judy Garland. 'While it was a great show, I don't think it went down quite as she would have wanted it to,' recalled the daughter of scriptwriter Dick Forbes. 'Judy was having a bad time of it with her husband Sid Luft. When she kicked off her shoes and sat at the edge of the stage to sing 'Somewhere Over the Rainbow' under just one spotlight, I felt that vocally it was not so good but because she was who she was, it was very moving. Overall, though, she was a wonderful performer.

'In the wings, she had what we took to be a drink of water and one of her people kept daring me to drink some. "Go on, have a sip," he said. I thought it might be a drug or something but he kept insisting I try it and it turned out to be Scotch and ginger ale.'

One man who had no complaints with the Garland weeks was Louis Elliman. 'The afternoon shows were not packed, as I would have expected but there were full houses for the evening performances,' he said. 'Certainly Judy was a superb performer, a real pro, and we don't see her like too often, unfortunately.'

The supporting programme was led by Vic and Joe Crastoritan who combined a fast music-and-song variety act while the local artistes were comedian Harry Bailey and the Royalettes. Jimmy Camp-

Orchestra leader Jimmy Campbell meets some friends backstage

bell as usual conducted the orchestra. Garland had hoped to return to Dublin at some stage but commitments in the US kept her busy.

Elliman was delighted that Noel Purcell was in a position to fit in the Christmas panto starting in early December 1951. It was *Robinson Crusoe* in which Noel played Mrs Crusoe. It was his seventh consecutive Royal panto with the exception of 1946-1947 when he was away filming. Also available for the panto season in between movies was Eddie Byrne as a very nasty Captain Hook.

The cast included some members of the Happy Gang. They had been regular performers at the Queen's Theatre in Pearse Street before the Abbey Players moved in following a fire at their own theatre in Marlborough Street three months earlier. The Queen's effectively became the Abbey until July 1966 when the present Abbey on the same site was rebuilt. The Queen's was demolished three years later and is now an office block.

The minstrels were back at the Royal for the first show of 1952 following the panto season. They had been featured in a segment of a big Royal production in 1943 called *Something in the Air* but now had their own show entitled *The Royal Minstrels.* While artistes performing in black face with only the white around the eyes showing and wearing black wigs would certainly not be considered politically correct in today's climate, this form of entertainment was hugely popular back then.

The Royal Minstrels performed a variety of songs but mainly calypso spirituals from America's Deep South. Audiences loved them, judging by the rounds of applause they received. So did the critics. 'The Royal Minstrels show bears the stamp of lavish setting and extensive production,' said the *Irish Independent.* 'The show signalises the return to Dublin of that great comedian Albert Sharpe, who resumed a long standing partnership with Noel Purcell. Jimmy Campbell, complete with black face and white suit, and his black-faced band, kept the show moving at a fast pace.'

When Elliman visited Hollywood in 1950, mixing business with pleasure, he saw a show featuring Katherine Dunham and her Caribbean dancers. Backstage he chatted with Katherine and got a promise they would come to Dublin at the first opportunity.

Katherine kept her word and did a week's show at the Royal in May 1952. Not surprisingly there were full houses for the Chicago-born entertainer, once described by the *New York Times* as 'a major pioneer in black theatrical dance.' Wrote the *Irish Press*: 'Audiences last night were impressed by the intricate and colourful dance routines.'

Elliman also met Danny Kaye during his trip to Hollywood and asked the American star would he consider playing in Dublin. Kaye explained that he had movie and stage commitments but promised Louis: 'When I'm over your side of the world, I would be delighted to play there.'

As with Katherine Durham and others, Kaye fell under Elliman's persuasive chatter and kept his promise. In the early summer he cabled the Royal boss to say he was playing the London Palladium and would be happy to come to Dublin. Elliman knew that the rubber-faced New Yorker, with his idiosyncratic style of delivery and rapid-fire nonsense songs, would go down very well with audiences here, if his bravura performances on the cinema screen were any yardstick.

Danny Kaye, one of the most popular visiting artistes to play the Royal, arrives at Dublin Airport

Arrangements in the press that Kaye would play the Royal for one week with two shows daily resulted in the expected huge demand for tickets. There were long queues in Hawkins Street and around in Poolbeg Street, and postal bookings were so heavy that the management had to employ extra staff to cope with the demand. When Kaye stood on the stage during the morning rehearsals, he seemed genuinely nervous of its enormous size but Billy Kelly, the stage manager, assured him: 'You'll be fine, Danny. The audiences will love you.'

'Kaye was a most charismatic performer,' said historian Philip B. Ryan, 'and as is usual with such people of genius, his various films did him less than justice. This is the strongest, irrefutable argument in favour of live theatre – the bond and rapport between audience and performer.

'Danny did nothing spectacular. Indeed that was the charm of his act. Audiences were not invited to sit back and marvel at the talent of the famous movie star. He talked amusingly, and would suddenly sing "Ballin' the Jack", complimented by extraordinary graceful movements, giving the song a dignity that it never really possessed. A spotlight would focus on his hands held high above his head while he sang "The Ugly Duckling", and gradually, unbelievably, the weaving hands magically became the duckling. It was bewildering and enchanting.

'The audience encouraged Danny to give more and more, and on the first night show he sat on the edge of the stage and warned them: "You now, the last buses will be leaving shortly." This prompted a huge roar from the audience and there were shouts of "We don't care," "We're here for the night", and "Carry on, Danny". Finally he told the orchestra to go home and he would continue with the show with his pianist Sam Praeger until nearly midnight.'

Towards the end of the week, letters started to arrive in his dressing room from grateful taxi drivers. They explained that Kaye's shows resulted in the best week they had ever experienced, taking patrons to their homes, many great distances, after his final midnight curtain. 'A big, big thank you from the taxi drivers of Dublin, Mr Kaye,' said one letter writer, wistfully adding: 'When are you coming back?'

Billy Kelly, the stage manager, recalled: 'Kaye used to kid me about my weight and I said to him one day during a rehearsal: "Okay, Danny, let you and I do a little dance on stage now and I'll show you how fit I am." He agreed and I can tell you in the end that he was very impressed with my footwork. He never kidded me any more after that. He was a wonderful guy and a great talent.'

In early November it was time for a return to classical music with the arrival of Jussi Bjorling who was billed as 'The Swedish Caruso.' Bjorling, who would tragically die of heart failure eight years later at the age of 42, delighted his audiences with arias from popular operas including *Il Travatore*, *Rigoletto* and *Cavalleria Rusticana*.

If Bjorling appeared confident going out on stage, the Hollywood star Betty Hutton, who followed Bjorling a week later, was a bundle of nerves before her music struck up. It was no secret that she always suffered a severe bout of stage fright, despite her public persona as an exuberant performer with boundless energy. She was known as 'The Blonde Bombshell.'

Hutton had appeared in major Hollywood movies but the prospect of walking out on a stage, any stage but especially one as big as the Royal, terrified her, even though she had played on Broadway. However, once she got out there or in front of a movie camera, all her fears evaporated like petrol spilling on the ground.

Stage manager Billy Kelly remembered: 'I recall Betty on her first night. She was really a bundle of nerves in the wings but again, once her music came up and she went out, she was fine. She would come to me before each performance and ask: "How's the crowd, Billy? How will I do?" I would assure her that they were wonderful and they would love her. "Get out there and do your stuff, Betty. Give them all you've got." She did too. She lived in fear of making a bad impression. Sure enough, after each show, she'd rush to me in the wings, give me a big hug and say: "You're a darling, Billy, you really are." She really was a great lady and a real trouper. One of the best the Royal ever had.'

Hutton's programme included several songs popular at the time as well as some from her movie musicals. But the biggest cheers came when she sang a selection of Irving Berlin tunes from her biggest movie *Annie Get Your Gun*. This show had been presented at the Royal two years earlier by an English company but in Hutton's show, it was something else! Dressed up as a cowgirl and complete with gun, she belted out numbers like 'There's No Business Like Show Business,' 'You Can't Get a Man with a Gun,' Doin' What Comes Natur'lly, 'Anything You Can Do' and the soft, romantic ballad, 'They Say that Falling in Love Is Wonderful.'

Babes in the Wood was the panto for the 1952-1953 season, with Noel Purcell in top form as Dame Wimple of Waffle. 'This is the best show from Hawkins Street since the late Dick Forbes' *Mother Goose* in the 1945-1946 season,' said the *Sunday Press*. 'Additional dialogue by Tim O'Mahony, as it says in the programme. Take a bow, Mr O'Mahony. We hope to hear more of you. Noel Purcell as the nurse is back at the top of his form. He even does little fragments of dances which recall his riotous ballet Spring Song. In Eddie Byrne, Jack Cruise and Phil Donohoe he has a trio of double-eyed gold-plated villains to contend with.'

Purcell had particular reason to remember the show as one of the visiting acts was W. H. Wilkie's Chimpanzee Family, one of which gave Noel a bad bite during rehearsals. A quick visit to the doctor resolved the problem but from then on he kept a respectable distance from the chimps. 'You can never trust those perishing monkeys, can you?' he remarked to Cruise.

Noel also managed to fit in the first Royal show in January 1953 called *Royal Cavalcade* before being called away for *The Crimson Pirate*, an action movie in which the lead stars Burt Lancaster and Nick Cravat swashbuckled their way across the Mediterranean.

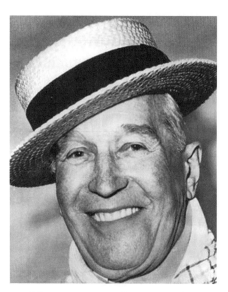

The suave French entertainer Maurice Chevalier

Elliman continued his policy of bringing big names to Dublin and announced that the French singer and actor Maurice Chevalier would give two performances at the Royal, each of 80 minutes duration, at the end of the month. Chevalier's large fee, believed to have been in the four-figure bracket, and his busy commitments elsewhere, prevented a longer stay but his shows attracted full houses. Dressed in his trademark boulevardier outfit of straw hat and bow tie, his swagger and twinkling, roguish blue eyes caught and captured the attention of the audiences.

Chevalier's selection of songs included 'Louise', 'You Brought a New Kind of Love to Me', 'Valentine', 'Ma Pomme' as well as several from the songbooks of Richard Rodgers and Lorenz Hart. 'The printed programme listed scores of Chevalier's songs but he would choose as the spirit moved him', remembered Royal manager Jimmy Sheil. 'I thought he was a very complex man, though, but probably the apparent complexity of the man might not be unconnected with the Parisian's presence on a cold, wet, overcast and generally depressing day in Dublin.

'I took him shopping for a white bainin-type jacket, after which we had lunch in the Gresham Hotel which was eaten in virtual silence. Afterwards I took him to see the trees along the Liffey and the public urinals, or *pissoires*, on Eden Quay and Burgh Quay in the hope that this would stir memories of Paris and the Seine but his reaction was remorse and unresponsive.

'In any event Chevalier stood in the wings that evening as his theme music "Louise," or as some call it "Every Little Breeze Seems to Whisper Louise," was played and what a transformation when he went out. Suddenly there was a wide, dazzling grin, his straw hat almost balanced on his nose and he stepped onto the stage, the epitome of the debonair song and dance man. He was charming and gallant to the ladies in the front rows and how he enjoyed singing. This was a happy man.'

After the show Chevalier thanked Jimmy Campbell 'for helping me along with some fine music' and signed autographs for members of the orchestra. 'I found him quite a pleasant fellow and wished him all the luck in his career, which was going pretty well at that stage,' recalled Campbell in later years. 'I did hear he collaborated with the Nazis during World War II but also that he was vindicated. Come what may, he was a superb entertainer.'

Despite the demise of many of the big bands in America, most of them survived in Britain. Three outfits, led by Joe Loss, Geraldo and

Harry Roy, all fit in dates at the Royal in July and August, 1953. Another welcome visitor that time was the jazz-influenced US bandleader Stan Kenton who brought his 39-piece orchestra here because they could not play in Britain.

There was an internal dispute at the time across the Irish Sea which began two years earlier in the Festival of Britain. It involved the British and American musicians' unions over issues concerning rates of pay, copyright and working conditions. However, in the words of one Irish reviewer: 'The core of the whole problem was that the unions simply could not come to terms with rock 'n' roll and other dance crazes.'

Bill Fuller, the Kerry-born impresario who had a string of ballrooms in Ireland, Britain and the US, took full advantage of this and in August he had Kenton play the Royal for one afternoon and then had them perform in the Bar-B ballroom in Woodbrook, near Bray, County Wicklow that evening.

'I put advertisements in the Irish and British newspapers and a boatload of fans arrived in their hundreds in Dun Laoghaire that morning,' recalled Fuller, whose wife was the Dublin singer Carmel Quinn. 'Kenton and the boys went down very well in both venues and played standard hits like 'Fascinating Rhythm', 'Body and Soul', 'Rhapsody in Blue', 'How Deep is the Ocean' and their best-known number, 'Peanut Vendor'.'

The name Francesco Paolo LoVecchio may not ring any bells in the public arena, but when this Chicago-born singer and songwriter changed his name in his twenties to Frankie Laine, he would in time become one of the most popular singers in the world. 'That's My Desire', which he recorded in 1946, remains a landmark event as it effectively marked the beginning of the end of the big band era and, to a large extent, the crooners, certainly across the Atlantic.

Laine was at the height of his success when he played the Royal in September 1953 for one week. Already well-known here as his records were regularly played on Radio Éireann's sponsored programmes and Hospitals' Requests, he was also in several movies.

Billed as 'Mr Rhythm', he was in full command of the stage as he belted out his big hits to an appreciative audience which included this writer. Songs such as 'Jezebel', 'Sugarbush', 'Way Down Yonder in New Orleans', 'Answer Me', 'Granada', 'Your Cheatin' Heart', 'I Believe', 'Mule Train' and 'That's My Desire' were enthusiastically received. At the finish, he thanked the audience for 'a lovely warm reception and one that I will always

Frankie Laine, who dominated the charts in the late 1940s and 1950s, meets his fans

treasure.' Before leaving for the Gresham Hotel, he sang a few bars of 'Jezebel' from his dressing room window and gave the eager fans down below a big wave.

Laine was still touring in the 1970s and did a cabaret spot at the old Drake Inn in the Dublin suburb of Finglas. When this writer visited his dressing room later and asked him if he remembered his week at the Royal in 1953, he said: 'Sure, as if it was only yesterday. The audiences gave me a wonderful reception and I had a ball. I'd heard about the Irish audiences back home and I finally experienced them. No, I didn't know the theatre was pulled down to make way for an office block. Very sad. They should always hold on to these old theatres like they do in London.'

Bob Hope was back at the Royal in late September for two nights. This time the comedian had a different girl with him, Gloria de Haven. A former band singer and star of several Hollywood musicals, she was typically cast as a vivacious, glamorous lead or second lead. Not surprisingly, she soon caught the attention of Hope, who always had an eye for the ladies and, predictably, she was soon on tour with him. As the local press had dealt with the issue concerning his previous lady companion, Marilyn Maxwell, they discreetly made no reference to Gloria in any of their reports. 'That's his own business,' said one scribe.

Hope joked with the reporters at his press conference: 'I played the Royal before, two years ago as you know, but I found it safe to come back. I reckon they've probably forgotten about me by now.' He had his regular straight man Jerry Desmond on stage and their cross-talk and general repartee kept the audience in good humour. 'A genuinely funny man,' said the *Irish Press*, 'and he is welcome to our shores anytime.'

There was no panto for the 1953-1954 season. Instead Elliman decided to put on a specially mounted show called *Trumpet Call* featuring the Royal company. It would be part of a national festival called An Tostal.

13

Celebration of All Things Irish

An Tostal, or the Pageant, was a festival inaugurated as a celebration of Irish life and culture, with the emphasis on drawing tourists into the country during the off-season at Easter. It was the brainchild of an executive at Pan American Airlines who pitched the idea to the Irish Tourist Board, then known as Bord Failte. He explained that his inspiration was the very successful Festival of Britain.

A forerunner of The Gathering in 2013, An Tostal was launched by the Taoiseach, Sean Lemass, on Easter Sunday, 5 April 1953, with a big parade through O'Connell Street in Dublin. There was also a series of regional parades as well as arts and sporting events, with fully licenced bars open until midnight.

Towns all over the country began a clean-up plan, thus starting the National Tidy Towns Awards still running today. An Tostal ran for three weeks annually until 1958 when it died out in most centres with the exception of Drumshambo in County Leitrim, where it continues to run every year.

Louis Elliman responded to An Tostal with a special three-week show at the Royal called *Trumpet Call* featuring officers, non-commissioned officers and members of the Defence Forces, as well as massed pipe and drum bands. It was a very colourful production with the civilian cast including Jack Cruise, Eddie Byrne, Bob Hennessy and Phil Donohoe, who would later become manager of the Royal.

Noel Purcell was there too, and performed a song he had recently recorded called 'The Man Me Mother Married,' plus the perennial favourite 'The Dublin Saunter,' or as many called it, 'Dublin on a Sunny Summer Morning.' Adding their usual glamour to the show were the Royalettes. 'With fond memories of wartime shows like *The Roll of the Drum, Signal Fires* and *Tramp, Tramp, Tramp*, it was almost like old times at the Royal,' remembered *Evening Herald* theatre critic John Finegan.

By Easter Sunday 1954, An Tostal had somehow lost much of its lustre, with a drop in the number of spring visitors from abroad. This also happened to be the Marian Year. Starting on 1 January, it would involve 12 months of commemorations dedicated to the Virgin Mary. It marked a mini-construction boom as the faithful erected shrines, statues and replicas of the Lourdes Grotto in parishes across the land.

The Ireland of 1954 as was a much different country than it is today. The reciting of the Rosary was carried out in most households, giving a boost by the onset of the Marian Year. If money was scarce and immigration still a drain, people managed to dig deep in the pockets or purses to support the work of Catholic missionaries abroad, with one report revealing that contributions to the Mission to Lepers for the previous year had hit an all-time high of £2,177.

Big movies of the year included *On the Waterfront, The Caine Mutiny, Seven Brides for Seven Brothers, The Barefoot Contessa, A Star is Born, Three Coins in the Fountain* and the Hitchcock thriller *Rear Window*. John Wayne headed the list of the top money-making stars followed by Martin and Lewis, Gary Cooper, Marilyn Monroe and James Stewart.

On the music scene Bill Haley and the Comets were shooting up the charts with their latest hit, 'Rock Around the Clock.' The exciting new sound with its driving rhythm-and-blues dance beat was revolutionising the popular music scene around the world including Ireland. It would be three years, however, before the band's busy American schedule would allow them to tour abroad. A line in Elliman's diary noted: 'Keep a watch on Haley.'

Meanwhile, the Royal shows continued to flourish. Borrowed from the Gaiety, Jimmy O'Dea was back in April in place of Noel Purcell who was away filming. O'Dea headed the cast of *Fun on Tostal*, which included the Queen's comedian Danny Cummins, straight man Vernon Hayden, comedienne Maureen Potter and the Royalettes.

A month earlier the Roy Rogers show was on stage. A former migratory fruit picker in California, Rogers had succeeded Gene Autry as 'King of the Cowboys' with a series of lively 'B' westerns, often with his sidekick George 'Gabby' Hayes. With the decline of the westerns, he moved his act to television and it was essentially this show he took to Dublin.

Rogers was accompanied by his wife Dale Evans, who co-starred with him in his movies, and his famous palomino Trigger, billed as 'the smartest horse in movies and TV.' Appearing in four shows, on the afternoon and evenings of 18 and 19 March, Roy and Dale sang several of their movie songs including 'South of the Border,' written by Jimmy Kennedy, the prolific songwriter from Omagh, 'On the Old Spanish Trail,' 'Tumbling Tumbleweeds,' 'Happy Trails' and 'Along the Navajo Trail.'

Time restraints did not allow them to spend much time here but they visited St Augustine's School, part of the St John of God Community Service for those with intellectual disability, in Blackrock, County Dublin, and spent a pleasant hour meeting the pupils and staff as well as signing autographs.

On the last week in April, Vivian Blaine did a week at the Royal. A former dance band singer and an established star of stage and screen, the cherry-blonde entertainer sang popular numbers from *Guys and Dolls* in which she starred on Broadway and in the movie.

They included 'Adelaide's Lament,' 'I've Never Been in Love Before' and 'I'll Know.' Both the *Irish Independent* and *Irish Press* likened her to the bubbly Betty Hutton who had played the Royal two years earlier. The only difference was that while Hutton had been as nervous as a kitten in the dressing room, Blaine could hardly wait to get out there. 'In the wings, she was like a racehorse waiting for the off,' remembered Billy Kelly, the stage manager.

Woody Herman was one of the most popular bandleaders of the period and often played swing that was experimental for its time. With the dispute involving visiting American musicians still going on in Britain, the enterprising promoter Bill Fuller booked Herman and the band, known in the 1950s as The Third Herd, for one Sunday afternoon performance at the Royal in May.

When the mailboat arrived in Dun Laoghaire it was packed with British fans anxious to hear the band. Not surprisingly, there were no spare tickets to be had. On stage they swung into their big hits including 'The Sheik of Araby,' 'Somebody Loves Me,' 'Laura,' 'Caldonia' and Herman's most famous and requested number, 'At the Woodchopper's Ball.' Several young people in the audience started jiving in the aisles but ushers quickly intervened and told them to get back in their seats 'unless you want to start a riot.'

On the Sunday evening Fuller had the band in the Bar-B ballroom in Bray, County Wicklow – and this time the fans let their hair down and jived to their heart's content. Strictly speaking, jiving was banned in practically all ballrooms but Fuller gave the all-clear to the Bar-B, especially as he owned the hall!

Lena Horne, the American singer and movie star who became a pin-up for black US soldiers during World War II, played the Royal for two nights in May to full houses. She gave fans some fine renditions of some of her hits including the song she will always be acquainted with, 'Stormy Weather.' Mary Kenny, the author and columnist, recalled that Horne, who died in June 2010, a week short of her 93rd birthday, 'was the epitome of glamour.'

By now, Hawkins Street was the place to see and hear the greats. Nat 'King' Cole, the Afro-American singer who specialised in the easy listening field, came in June and delighted fans of all ages with his soft, melodic baritone voice. Nat, who could well have been called the 'Sultan of Cool,' included all his major hits such as 'Sweet Lorraine,' 'It's Only a Paper Moon,' 'Get Your Kicks on Route 66,' 'Mona Lisa' and the ultra-smooth 'Unforgettable.' He was back in Dublin in 1960 to open a record store in nearby Tara Street and delighted the big crowd with 'Mona Lisa.' It was clear that Cole loved the Irish and they loved him.

Nat King Cole, fondly remembered for his smooth vocal delivery on a succession of hits

If Cole was the smoothie, Guy Mitchell was the direct opposite. With his energetic, happy-go-lucky style, the American typified 1950s pop music more than any other performer. Mitchell pulled in full houses for a week in September as he bounced into a medley of his big hits including 'She Wears Red Feathers,' 'Sparrow in the Treetop,' 'There's Always Room at Our House' and 'Christopher Columbus.' Nor did he omit his softer ballads such as 'My Heart Cries for You' and 'The Roving Kind,' as well as singing a few bars of a song from his dressing room window between shows.

Mitchell was still on the road in the 1980s and this writer had the pleasure of meeting him at the Braemor Rooms in Churchtown in suburban Dublin. 'When my Irish agent Willie Kane asked me to return to your lovely city, how could I refuse?' he said in the dressing

Guy Mitchell, a big hit at the Royal in the 1950s, was back in Dublin for cabaret shows in the 1980s and brought along his grandson

room. 'I well remember the Theatre Royal back then, a wonderful theatre. I'm darned if I can remember the local artistes though but I do remember these lovely girls, the Royalettes, isn't that what they were called? Ah, those were the days.'

Gracie Fields, the English entertainer who first appeared on the Royal stage at the age of 14 in 1912 and returned in 1936, was back again in October for one night and sang her big hits. It will be recalled that in 1936, the wily Lassie from Lancashire had (a) negotiated a fee with the Royal's general manager Hugh Margey that was so high it left a potentially small margin for the theatre and (b) insisted that a short film she had put money into, John Millington Synge's *Riders to the Sea,* was shown during her week.

Happily for the management this time, there were no such demands, probably as she was now 56 and was on what was billed as 'Gracie Fields Final Tour: Your Last Chance to See and Hear the Legend.' Pat Maxwell, the celebrity photographer, remembered Gracie being very nervous in the wings. 'In her nervousness she constantly twisted and loosened the scarf that she always held during her performances,' he remembered. 'Then, like many another star, she walked out and the confidence seemed to ooze from her as she sang "Sally, Sally, Pride of Our Alley."' At the end of her show, her fellow-Lancastrian George Formby walked out on stage and presented her with a large bouquet of flowers – and a kiss.

There was no panto at Christmas as Elliman wanted 'something different,' as he put it. Instead, he presented what John Finegan of the *Evening Herald* described as 'a bright and spectacular show for young and old.' Perhaps Elliman had a premonition when he called the show the *The Bells Are Ringing*, as a big production with the same title opened on Broadway in 1956, running for two years. In 1957 a London version was staged on the West End and was followed three years later by a Hollywood movie starring Judy Holliday and Dean Martin. As someone said: 'Should Elliman have had copyright on the title?'

The cast of the Royal show included comedians Harry Bailey and Hal Roach as well as Mick Eustace, who came over from the Queen's where he was a member of the Happy Gang. An accomplished pianist with a fine tenor voice, Eustace's most popular role was as Mickser, a clown-like figure whose trousers were too short, his black jacket too long and wearing his regular bowler which highlighted the chalk whiteness of his face.

Eustace was always complaining about the frequency and long rehearsals for shows, both at the Queen's and the Royal. It was no secret that he had a lucrative sideline in doing weddings. 'I probably made more money at weddings than I did on the stage,' he said in later years. 'Those bloody rehearsals were interfering with the nuptials and nobody cared a damn.'

On the Christmas show, too, was the popular close harmony group known as the Four Ramblers who had started their musical careers as singers on a 15-minute Radio Éireann programme sponsored by Donnelly's sausages. Val Doonican, the Waterford-born entertainer who would become one of the highest-paid stars on British television in later years, was a member of the group.

'The Theatre Royal is a far-off memory but it's very vivid in my mind,' Doonican recalled in an interview with this writer. 'I felt very privileged to have played there. It was a truly magnificent theatre, with its huge auditorium, lost of dressing room space and boasting a pit orchestra of up to 20 musicians that, by general standards, was quite unique. Jimmy Campbell was the orchestra leader and I had never worked with such a big orchestra.

'We played there many times but that Christmas show in the 1950s was the longest as it lasted several weeks. I remember it as being a very extravagant and spectacular production which starred local acts as well as imported ones.

'One of the entertainers on the show was a lady speciality act called Karinga who introduced two huge alligators from a box. But with a flick of her fingers, she was apparently able to hypnotise them. She also handled two big snakes as you and I would handle a garden hose.

'I was sitting in the dressing room with the Ramblers after one particular afternoon show when an announcement came over our speaker that all artistes come out on the stage immediately. The manager announced that one of Ms Karinga's snakes had gone missing and to be careful but the evening show would still go on.

'As you can imagine, there was panic. This creature could appear anytime, anyplace. Anyhow, we did our evening spot but before we finished, who pokes its head from the backcloth but our friend the snake, its head wandering searchingly a few feet from us.

'The audience thought this was great fun, and part of the act, but we were speechless. Suddenly, Karinga comes out from the wings, grabbed the big snake by the neck, gave a sharp pull, and its long body whiplashed through the air to the floor. She then picked it up, wrapped it around her neck and snapped: "Shame on you, scaring everybody like that." With one smack on the nose, she turned to us and said: "Sorry boys, do carry on." We did somehow, but we still weren't the better of our scary experience.'

Josef Locke, the Derry tenor with his substantial stage presence who had last appeared in Hawkins Street in 1944, returned to a tumultuous reception in March 1955. Locke, whose real name was Joseph McLaughlin, was now a major star in Britain and was

Val Doonican remembered the alligators and the snakes on stage

hugely popular particularly in Blackpool where he often did summer seasons.

At the Royal, Locke sang a mixture of popular Irish ballads such as 'I'll Take You Home Again Kathleen', 'Dear Old Donegal', 'Galway Bay' along with excerpts from operettas as well as the Richard Tauber favourite 'My Heart and I'. There were also familiar favourites with an Italian flavour like 'Come Back to Sorrento' and 'Cara Mia' but he could never leave without singing his big favourite 'Goodbye' from the show *The White Horse Inn*. It got rapturous applause.

The American singer Johnnie Ray arrived in April 1955 with much fanfare and was backed by the Vic Lewis band. At various times in his career Ray was known as the 'Prince of Wails', the 'Nabob of Sob' and 'Mr Emotion' because of his highly passionate style of singing and apparent ability to cry at will. Considered as having an important influence of popular music of the 1950s, Ray is regarded as a link between the young Frank Sinatra of the 1940s and the Beatles era of the 1960s, catching and holding the attention of the mainly young record-buying public to an enormous degree.

*Johnnie Ray, the 'Prince of Wails'
and the 'Nabob of Sob'*

Like a comet, Ray streaked to the top of the music charts in 1951 with his own composition, 'The Little White Cloud That Cried.' On the B side, as it happened, was 'Cry.' But when 'Cry' became an even more requested song, his record company quickly switched sides and 'Cry' became his identity song. It was a million-seller all over the world and stayed at No. 1 for a record 11 weeks.

Unlike singers such as Frank Sinatra, Perry Como and Dick Haymes, Ray was the first to take the microphone off the stand and roam, run and scream all over the stage, a common enough sight today. But back then, it was innovative. 'Ray had the Royal jumping,' said *The Irish Times* as the young fans yelled and screamed as he fell to the floor, puling at his hair, before getting to his feet and belting out hits including 'Please Mr Sun,' 'Walking My Baby Back Home,' 'Somebody Stole My Gal,' 'The Little White Cloud That Cried' and of course 'Cry.'

Mind you, Ray's performances, including his four shows at the Royal, with their overt sensuality and hysterical audience reaction, made him *persona non grata* to parents of young people worldwide, including this writer's. But he enjoyed quite phenomenal success with the young during the 1950s, revolutionising popular music and symbolising many of their frustrations and desires.

Interestingly, Ray also sang 'Such a Night,' which had been recorded by the Drifters. The song was banned by Radio Éireann and several US radio stations because of what they considered suggestive lyrics, about a long kiss in the moonlight. But there was no controversy with Ray performing it on the Royal, simply because the theatre management was unaware of the singer's actual programme.

In any event, Elliman would hardly have dropped the curtain on Ray considering his magnetic drawing power at the box office. Elvis Presley would record the song on a 1960s album without generating any fuss when moral attitudes were gradually changing. 'Never mind "Such a Night,"' said one excited fan leaving the Royal. 'Such a show.'

Before leaving for his hotel following the shows, Johnnie did what was expected of him. Opening the window of his dressing room, he gave his adoring fans down below a few bars of 'Cry' and 'Walking My Baby Back Home,' which were greeted with the predictable yells and screams.

Ray's show was followed by musicians of a more serious nature, maintaining Elliman's mantra that the Theatre Royal was for everyone. The celebrated Chilean pianist Claudio Arrau was on stage in May for one week. Regarded throughout the world as one of the supreme keyboard masters of all time and an intensely serious musician, he told newspapermen on his arrival in Dublin, expressing the words with his hands: 'An interpreter must give his blood to the work interpreted.'

Arrau did not disappoint, entertaining patrons with a selection from his wide repertoire from Baroque to Beethoven, Schubert, Chopin, Liszt and Brahms. After every performance, he would announce from the stage: 'I will always be grateful for the people of Dublin for the wonderful reception you have given me. Thank you all.'

The feast for lovers of classical music continued in June when the Spaniard Andres Segovia was in Hawkins Street. His programme included his own transcriptions of classical or Baroque works. 'Segovia impressed with his expressive performances – his wide palette of

*Heartthrob Dickie
Valentine, a big favourite*

tone and his distinctive musical personality, phrasing and style', noted *The Irish Times.*

Rawicz and Landauer were an immensely popular duo and played to full houses for a week in July. Having carved out a formidable reputation as a two-piano team and well known for their ensemble playing, they went down very well with fine arrangements including the waltz from Tchaikovsky's 'Eugene Onegin', Khachaturian's 'Sabre Dance', Debussy's 'Clair De Lune' as well as polkas and Strauss waltzes.

As a break from the serious side of things, Elliman brought over the British heartthrob Dickie Valentine for a week in August. Louis' business instincts knew that Valentine would be a great crowd-puller especially with the younger crowd, and he was proven right.

Voted Britain's No. 1 vocalist by the *New Musical Express* and subsequently named five times in all, the handsome Valentine, whose real name was Richard Maxwell, had a rich, melodic voice that had the teenagers screaming.

Having established himself as a singer with the Ted Heath Orchestra, Valentine had to have garda protection arriving and departing here, with fans blocking Hawkins Street and Poolbeg Street. On stage, he was magical as he sang his big hits including 'Mr Sandman', 'Finger of Suspicion', 'Broken Wings', 'A Blossom Fell' and 'All the Time and Everywhere'. December was still four months away but there were calls from the audience for one of his most popular numbers, 'The Christmas Alphabet'. Mr Valentine was only too happy to oblige.

The Regal cinema next door re-opened following renovations which had begun in May. First opened in 1938 with the screwball comedy *True Confession* with Carole Lombard and Fred McMurray, it had fallen into disrepair. Now, with seating capacity increased to 900 after the side balconies were removed, it was back in business under the Rank Organisation. The opening movie was the Walt Disney live-action adventure *20,000 Leagues Under the Sea* starring Kirk Douglas and James Mason. The Regal would be pulled down along with the Royal in seven years.

The Dublin close-harmony group the Harmonichords did a week at the Royal in November to very good business. Consisting of two brothers, Declan and Con Cluskey, as well as their friend John Stokes, they played harmonicas. When the Harmonichords later moved to England, they became the Bachelors.

'I have very happy memories of playing the Royal in the 1950s and 1960s,' recalled Declan in a recent interview with this writer. 'It was the Royal which started us off on our long careers and we were always very grateful for the break. We were effectively the first of the Irish boy bands to invade Britain.

'All the big international stars performed at the Royal and as we had an Equity card, we could get time off work, get into the theatre for free and watch the acts. The Royalettes brought a nice touch of glamour to the shows, too. There was a story going the rounds that I had a hot romance with one of them back then. I do recall we used to be in the back of a BMW but I won't go into that. Good Catholic boys and all that as we were in those days. There you go.'

Before Christmas, another new entertainer Joe Lynch made his debut in Hawkins Street. A Corkman who had made his name in Radio Éireann's first comedy series *Living with Lynch*, which went out on Sunday afternoons, the show later transferred to the Royal and was called *Laughing with Lynch*. It had the same cast and was highly praised by the critics. Lynch went on to TV later and starred in programmes like *Coronation Street* and RTÉ's *Glenroe.*

Noel Purcell, now a fully-established character in movies, with quite a number of good roles, returned to the Royal panto for the first time since *Babes in the Wood* two years earlier. This time, and without his trademark beard, he topped the bill in *Mother Goose*, repeating a role he played at the Royal in 1944, the Gaiety in 1937 and the Olympia four years earlier.

With colourful scenery designed by the Dubliner Michael O'Herlihy, who would later go on to Hollywood and direct TV shows such as *Star Trek, Hawaii Five-O, The A-Team, Gunsmoke* and *M*A*S*H*, the production attracted full houses. May Devitt was principal boy, with an urchin-style hairdo, and the big cast included favourites such as Pauline Forbes, Jack Cruise, Frankie Howerd, Cecil Nash, Frankie Blowers, Sean Mooney and the Royalettes, with Renee Flynn leading the Royal Singers.

Also in the line-up was the Waterford-born comedian Hal Roach, who would subsequently become a major star on the cabaret scene, mainly in Jury's Hotel, Dublin. 'It was always a great joy to work in the Royal with all those fine artistes,' he recalled. 'There was a great camaraderie on and off the stage and we all seemed to get on so well together. Like us all, I was deeply saddened when the old theatre was pulled down to make way for that hideous office block. I still shudder when I think if it.'

The Irish Times gave the show a good review, concentrating on Purcell's lead role. 'Film, stage and radio success has not changed Noel from what he essentially is, the typical, warm, unaffected Dublin man in the street. One of the best of all Panto dames, his power over children is one which many parents will envy, particularly at Christmas. It is this last mentioned quality which makes the scene in which little volunteer 'jockeys' are called from the audience to race mechanical horses across the village green, one of the comedy highlights of the show.'

The *Evening Herald*, however, felt the fun-making was a trifle flat. John Finegan, one of the foremost critics of the day, said: 'A few of the sketches tend to be tedious. This is possibly due to the fact that the scripwriters felt they could leave more than a fair share of work to the principals, having regard to their names and standing. But the cast made the most of the material.'

With most of the international artistes booked up with London engagements, Elliman concentrated his plans for 1956 in the main on the regular company, often with guest stars from the Gaiety or the Queen's. There was also the question of finance. These past few years had taken a heavy toll on the Royal coffers, with expensive acts being brought in, even though the company was in the red.

In any event, 'Mr Louis' felt the public enjoyed good, strong local shows, promising to return to the international acts the following year, always depending on their availability. However, he did make one exception, the flamboyant American pianist and showman ex-traordinary Liberace, who was in the UK at the time. Arrangements were made for the entertainer to play the Royal for a week in November 1956.

Arriving in Dublin to be met by a barrage of reporters, and oozing charm and good manners, Liberace made no reference to a court case in London a few weeks earlier when he won a libel action for £8,000 and £27,000 in legal costs against the *Daily Mirror*. The case was a result of an article by their waspish Irish-born columnist Cassandra which was laced with sexual innuendo, a definite no-go area then.

Liberace said he hoped 'the customers would like my piano-playing and my mode of dress which comes from a lavish wardrobe that includes rhinestone, white mink, sequins and gold lamé.' It is said by music critics of the modern age that Liberace's attire and mode of presentation left its mark on the likes of Elton John and Queen.

Had he heard of the Theatre Royal? 'Who hasn't?' he replied in typical diplomatic fashion. Had he received any bad reviews? 'Yes,

The flamboyant Liberace in a reflective mood in the dressing room

one was so bad that I cried all the way to the bank.' In later years in America, he would say: 'You know that bank I once cried to? I bought it.'

Playing to full houses, and sitting comfortably at his candelabra-lit white cream piano, continually smiling ever so sweetly and sometimes singing in a light voice, he did a selection of Gershwin favourites, cocktail jazz, movie themes, boogie-woogie and a little Rachmaninov.

Phil Donohoe, who was co-manager of the Royal at the time, recalled: 'Liberace's press conference ahead of his opening show was the biggest ever held in Dublin. Hordes of English newsmen came over to have another look at this extraordinary fellow. Before going on stage we all wondered about him. Would the audience be hostile? How would they react to a man who sings to his mother?

'We needn't have worried. At the end of his first show he had them eating out of his hand. We just couldn't get him off the stage with the applause. Off stage he was the height of courtliness. A gentleman. Of course, the bigger the star, the nicer the person, I found.'

The Christmas panto for the 1956-1957 season was *Red Riding Hood*, last staged at the theatre in 1943. It starred Cecil Sheridan, taking over from Noel Purcell who was away filming. Sheridan, who also wrote the script, played Granny Grapefruit and the cast included Cecil Nash and his daughter Veronica, who was making her Royal debut, Mickser Reid, Billy Livingstone and Mick Eustace.

The Royalettes were on loan to the Gaiety and, in a switcharound, the Gaiety Girls were at the Royal.

Wilson, Keppel and Betty, a novelty act popular on British stages, came to the Royal in early February 1957 for a week. They did not play for laughs but radiated good humour, capitalising on the fashion for Ancient Egyptian imagery. Their 'sand dance', accompanied by ballet music, was a soft-shoe routine performed on a layer of sand to created a rhythmic scratching sound with their shuffling feet, while performing a parody of gestures from Egyptian tomb paintings, combined to references to Arabic costume.

As popular as acts like Wilson, Kepple and Betty were, however, big changes were gradually taking place in the entertainment business, particularly in popular music. The sensational new sounds of rock 'n' roll were taking over dramatically. So it was that Elliman, who kept abreast of all trends, booked the chart-toppers Bill Haley and his Comets for two nights in late February. It will be recalled that three years earlier Elliman had scribbled 'Bill Haley' in his diary for a future engagement, and now the American band was in London.

Haley's recording of 'Rock Around the Clock' was featured in the 1956 movie *The Blackboard Jungle* and the song soared into the top of the charts worldwide, becoming a veritable anthem and rallying cry with the rebellious younger generation. The movie was booked into the Carlton Cinema in O'Connell Street and youths ripped up the seats with flick knives, threw bottles and other missiles from the balcony and engaged in fist fights, often with chains. Gardaí, led by the fearless Jim 'Lugs' Branigan, had to be brought in for every performance to maintain law and order. 'I saw that bloody film so many times I was sick of it,' Branigan once told me. There were even calls in Dáil Éireann for the film to be banned.

Wasn't Cardinal Stritch, the Archbishop of Chicago, quoted in the *Irish Independent* as saying that rock 'n' roll had 'tribal rhythms and such a throwback to tribalism cannot be tolerated for Catholic youth?'

And didn't the Catholic hierarchy in Ireland say rock 'n' roll should be outlawed?

When Haley was booked for the Royal, there were fears that riots would break out among young fans but a large force of gardaí was on hand, both inside and outside the theatre. The shows were greeted with loud and prolonged applause as Haley and the Comets blasted out a selection of their hits, including 'Rock Around the Clock', 'See You Later Alligator' and 'Shake, Rattle and Roll'.

Bill Haley and the Comets who changed the face of popular music with the new sound of rock 'n' roll

Not all were enamoured by Haley, however. Declan Cluskey of the Harmonichords, who would soon become the Bachelors, felt that the show was ruined by the sound system. Probably looking at it from a musician's point of view, he said in an interview with this writer in 2014: 'We were in the audience and noticed the system was very basic, with two tannoy horns on each side of the stage. I can still see them, about 20 feet or so up. Remember, this was the famous Bill Haley and his Comets and they had this weak sound system, with nothing more than a 31 watts amplifier. To give you an example, we did a concert in Great Yarmouth recently and they had 47,000 watts.

'People told us that all they could hear was Haley's electric guitar. Nothing else. To us personally, they simply sounded like a very bad country band. Sadly, you couldn't hear the instruments that made rock 'n' roll.'

Nevertheless, all this was lost on the audience who cheered and clapped the band's every number. Bad sound or not, this was the great Bill Haley and his Comets you were talking about, and you daren't say anything derogatory about them.

When Haley appeared in his dressing room window, all he could see down below was a sea of cheering, singing, dancing fans having the time of their lives. It was later confirmed that the crowd numbered over 2,000. An *Irish Press* reporter noted that 'gardaí had formed a line and with batons drawn, moved through the crowd. Several bottles were thrown and the glass shattered on the ground but thankfully nobody was injured.'

It was the audience which came in for sharp comment in the *Evening Press* social diary the next day. Whatever about the show itself, Terry O'Sullivan, who took no prisoners in his writings, said: 'Some of the patrons were grotesque absurdities who would have been better off at home saying their prayers. Others had an occasional eruption of self control while for the many, the visit of Bill Haley acted like a bad medicine.'

After the madness of Haley and the Comets, who soon left for a British tour, it was back to the serious stuff. With the 1957 Dublin Theatre Festival scheduled for May, Elliman felt it might be a good idea to invite the Royal Ballet to Dublin for the occasion. They had just finished a full-length version of Tchaikovsky's *Swan Lake* with Margot Fonteyn in London and the reviews were very good. 'I felt the Royal Ballet would go down very well, particularly with Fonteyn appearing,' he said. Louis' instincts were proven right, with full houses for a week. Boxing fans were well catered for too, with films of big fights flown in from the US five or six days after they happened.

14

Hollywood in Hawkins Street

Hollywood proper came to town on the evening of Sunday, 9 November 1958, when the Royal staged a show billed as *Shake Hands with the Irish*. The title coincided with a movie being made at Ardmore Studios in Bray, County Wicklow called *Shake Hands with the Devil* with James Cagney in the lead role.

Louis Elliman had recently been elected chief barker of the Variety Club of Ireland and, when the first annual variety concert came around under his remit, what better way to mark it but with a show at the Royal – and to have Cagney, described by Orson Welles as 'maybe the greatest actor to ever appear in front of the camera,' as the main attraction.

The idea was that Cagney would perform his famous song and dance routine exactly as he had done it in his 1942 movie *Yankee Doodle Dandy* in which he played the famous theatrical impresario George M. Cohan. Playing completely against type, the role won Cagney the Best Actor Oscar. The film company said Cagney would be free from filming on Sundays and he himself would be delighted to do it.

'Cagney was one of the coolest performers of all,' recalled the celebrity photographer Pat Maxwell. 'I had been with him earlier in the day and had driven him from Wicklow, where he did a bit of sightseeing, to his hotel in Dublin. As he prepared to go on stage to face an

Hollywood great James Cagney in good company with the Royalettes backstage

audience of nearly 4,000, he chatted nonchalantly to me without a care in the world. When the orchestra struck up, he danced in a soft shoe shuffle towards the microphone and went into his big number, 'Yankee Doodle Dandy.'

'This was followed by a neat piece of footwork before he moved over to the pillar on the right side of the stage and proceeded to dance his way up until gravity prevented him from reaching the top. Then he fell back and, like a cat, landed on his dancing feet to boisterous applause that virtually lifted the roof of the enormous theatre. When he came off stage, he received more clapping from the stage hands and other privileged voyeurs. As he made his way to the dressing room I called out to him, "Fantastic, Jimmy!" and got a big wink in return.'

Cagney regretted not being able to explore his Irish roots while here. 'In my spare time I did a bit of sightseeing,' he told reporters at Shannon before leaving for the US where he was due to have meetings about his next movie, *The Gallant Hours.* 'I know my dad was a second generation Irishman from County Leitrim and ran an Irish bar in New York, and my grandmother on my mother's side was also from Leitrim. The family's name was O'Caigne. Maybe I'll be able to come back someday and explore that area.

'What with the weather so miserable I was only able to catch glimpses of the Irish countryside through auto windows. The shooting schedule was so rigid too that it left little time for properly looking up my family roots. As I say, hopefully next time.

'Let me say too that working at the Royal was a real thrill for me, particularly reprising the "Yankee Doodle Dandy" number. It brought back happy memories of 1942 and the movie. The theatre certainly lived up to its reputation for putting on spectacular shows and I felt honoured to be part of it all. The performers were all very pleasant to me, and what lovely and charming girls are the Royalettes. I can tell you that I was very busy too signing autographs, which was a real pleasure. I'll always remember Dublin and the Theatre Royal with great fondness.'

Earlier in the year, the smooth-voiced Welsh crooner Donald Peers, who had played the Royal in the 1930s before hitting the big time, was back in Hawkins Street performing before a new generation of swooning fans. Peers had a string of hits in Ireland, mainly due to his highly popular BBC radio show when listeners would sit alongside their large sets from beginning to end. His fan base was mainly made up of women but he appealed to both sexes.

Peers did not disappoint when he walked out on stage and did as many his songs as he could fit in, including 'A Strawberry Moon in a Blueberry Sky,' 'I'll String Along with You,' 'The Last Mile Home,' 'Powder Your Face with Sunshine,' 'A Rose in a Garden of Weeds' and his theme song, 'In a Shady Nook By a Babbling Brook.' Sadly, Peers is largely forgotten today but in the 1940s and 1950s there were fewer bigger stars than this likeable former housepainter.

Diana Dors, the sultry English movie star, did a week following Peers, but box office returns were somewhat disappointing. It seemed that the ultra-conservative Ireland of the 1950s was not quite ready for blonde bombshells such as Dors turning up live on home stages, whatever about seeing them on cinema screens. She sang several songs and told anecdotes of movie stars she had worked with and famous people she had met.

If Diana Dors was billed by her publicity people as Britain's answer to Marilyn Monroe which effectively she was, the London pop star Terry Dene was advertised somewhat ambiguously across the Irish Sea as 'Britain's Elvis Presley.' He played the Royal shortly before James Cagney's appearance and his programme included his UK Top 20s hits, his version of the Marty Robbins' song, 'A White Sports Coat,' which was a cover version of the Sal Mineo original, and another Marty Robbins' tune, 'Start Movin.' The show got mixed reviews.

Ruby Murray, who had a remarkable five singles in the Top 20 charts in March 1955

The final panto at the Royal was *Old King Cole* for the 1958-1959 season. It starred the Belfast singer Ruby Murray and the English comic Vic Oliver as the main support. Many of Oliver's jokes fell flat and seemed to be geared mainly for English audiences. Billy Kelly, the stage manager, remembered Oliver not so much for his humour, or lack of it, but for his heavy gambling habit. 'He backed horses in the hundreds,' said Kelly. 'Before each show he would ask me what my fancy was. During his act I would send out for the result and after it, he and I would hold a post mortem if he lost, which was often. But Ruby Murray? Now she was something else.'

Ruby had five singles in the Top 20 at the same time in March 1955, an extraordinary feat that was only beaten in the 1980s with the emergence of Madonna. She included all five in her programme – 'Happy Days and Lonely Nights,' 'Let Me Go Lover,' If Anyone Finds This, I Love You,' 'Heartbeat' and 'Softly, Softly.'

Another popular Irish singer, Bridie Gallagher, billed as 'The Girl from Donegal,' topped the bill in the last week of October 1959 but it was the chief support, Billy Fury, the Liverpool rock 'n' roller, who made the headlines. Fury's manager was the impresario Larry Parnes, a very successful promoter who also looked after Tommy Steele and Marty Wilde.

Parnes, however, was never able in later years to live down the fact that he twice turned down the Beatles. During auditions in Liverpool in 1959 for a new act he passed on the band, known as the Silver Beetles and led by John Lennon. A year later, he rejected them as a backing band for one of his singers, Johnny Gentle, on a Scottish tour. 'I'm looking for a band with a bit of musical talent,' he told a journalist at the time. 'These guys haven't any.' Inside four years the Beatles, now nicknamed 'The Fab Four,' had conquered America and became international stars.

The music journalist Bruce Eder remembered: 'Fury's mix of rough-hewn good looks and unassuming masculinity, coupled with an underlying vulnerability, all presented with a good voice and some serious musical talent, helped turn Fury into a major rock and roll star in short order.' Others have suggested that Fury's rapid rise to prominence was due to his 'Elvis Presley-influenced, hip-swivelling, and at times highly suggestive stage act.'

The *New Musical Express* noted that his antics were drawing much press criticism and he had been asked to tone down his act. The British Watchdog Committee was also concerned about his 'squirming' antics which they called 'totally objectionable' and that he would have to 'cut it out.' Fury and Parnes refused. 'The show must go on,' Parnes proclaimed somewhat defiantly.

Billy Fury, 'blacked out' at the Royal, seen here in discussion with his manager Larry Parnes

Phil Donohoe, who was theatre manager at the time, recalled in an interview with the *Sunday Press* in 1962: 'We knew in advance of this objectionable part of Billy's act but he arrived at 2.00 on the Sunday afternoon and as he was due to go on stage at 3.00, we had no chance to run through his show. However, implementing our "clean material" policy, we told him to leave out anything which we would consider objectionable and he nodded.

'That afternoon he was perfect and the same for the evening show. Monday was the same but on the Tuesday he started moving around the stage in what we considered an indecent manner. We warned him that if it happened again he would be blacked out. He was fine on the Wednesday but on the Thursday he did it again and when I warned him, I was sure that would be the end of it.

'But on the Friday he repeated it again and we just brought down the curtain on him, and fired him there and then. It's a funny thing but during all the time we met and warned him, he never said one thing to me, just nodded. For a while, I thought he couldn't speak, only sing.'

Frankie Vaughan, the Liverpool-born crooner, topped the Christmas show which opened in early December. Warmly received, he had by now developed his stylish stage act with trademarks such as a top hat and cane, a particularly athletic side kick and his famous theme song, 'Give Me the Moonlight.'

A singer with no less than 80 hit singles during his career, Vaughan, who was voted Showbusiness Personality of the Year in Britain in 1956, gave Royal audiences the songs they wanted to hear such as 'Kisses Sweeter Than Wine,' 'Happy Days and Lonely Nights,' 'Garden of Eden,' 'Green Door,' 'The Old Piano Rolls Blues,' the Guy Mitchell hit 'Look at That Girl' and naturally 'Give Me the Moonlight.'

Vaughan would also be one of the very few entertainers who turned down a Hollywood career. In an interview with the author in the 1980s at the Top Hat ballroom in Dun Laoghaire, he said: 'I had made several movies in England before going to Hollywood in 1961, two years after I played the Theatre Royal, to make *Let's Make Love* which starred Marilyn Monroe and the French actor Yves Montand.

'But I was completely disillusioned with the place. Afterwards I returned to England and continued my successful career on the stage and in concert. I enjoyed that much better than filming. Mention of the Royal brings back memories too. They had a great company with a lot of wonderful performers. Sadly I hear it's no more. A great pity.'

The Royal, or rather the fourth incarnation, celebrated its quartercentury in September 1960 with a big show. This is how the *Evening Mail* reported the opening night: 'Tuneful songs, rounds of quickfire humour and colourful dance routines form part of *Royal Jubilee*, the 25th birthday celebration show at the Hawkins Street venue this week – a show that should earn praise as perhaps the best production the famous theatre has put on since its opening.

· 'Last night's packed audience laughed loud and long at the antics and the comical sayings from the comedians, and sat back contentedly as the singers brought out all that is best in the make-up of · show business. The comedy is in the capable hands of Cecil Sheridan, Danny Cummins, Frank Howerd, Cecil Nash, Mickser Reid and the ever popular Jack Cruise, all first class entertainers who have provided many rounds of mirth for Royal fans over the years.

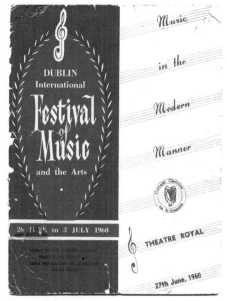

Programme for June 1960

'Popular Peggy Dell comes back this week too to provide that special kind of singing beside her piano – a style that singles her out as one of the best female entertainers the Irish show world has had in recent years. Another who makes an impressive appearance is crooner Frankie Blowers, whose scene Feathers and Fans, with attractive May Devitt and the Royalettes, is easily the most colourful and tuneful during the 90 minutes of the show's duration.

'Adding to the brightness of the show are the Comerford troupe of Irish dancers in a brilliant routine, Sean Mooney, Willie Brady and the talented and versatile Harmonichords with some catchy tunes. Special notes of praise must be awarded to Alice Dalgarno, Babs de Monte, Pauline Forbes, Jimmy Campbell and his orchestra and organist Tommy Dando for first-class performances which prove they are in the top flight of Irish show business.'

The uncredited reviewer, possibly Ernie Murray, a scriptwriter who worked in the editorial department of the *Mail*, concluded his review: 'The show is a delightful presentation of talent at its best and the management are to be congratulated on arranging an ace revue.

It was quite clearly worth all the worry and strain in getting all the stars together.' The reviewer noted that the movie was *They Got Me Covered*, a comedy starring Bob Hope who, of course, had played the Royal on two visits in the 1950s.

A huge birthday cake with 25 candles was presented to Louis Elliman at a reception in the lounge following the show. After giving gifts to members of the staff with 25 years of service to the theatre, 'Mr Louis' in a brief speech thanked artistes past and present who had made the Royal so successful and enjoyable over the years. 'In conclusion,' he said, 'let us hope that the Royal will still be here in another 25 years, providing first-class entertainment.' Sadly, the theatre would be pulled down in less than two years.

'You know, my son Jimmy Junior got his stage break on that show,' recalled Jimmy Campbell in later years. 'Being the Royal's 25th anniversary I was looking for a good gimmick. I realised that Jimmy was a dead ringer for me. He could whistle the same as me too. So to fool the audience I dressed him up in an old dress suit of mine, fixed him up with a false moustache and put him on in front of the orchestra. Nobody spotted it until I came on the stage myself. They roared the place down. It was a wonderful moment for me, I can tell you.'

When Elvis Presley was honorably discharged from the US Army as a sergeant in March 1960 after serving two years in Germany, there was a rush by promoters all over the world to sign him for tours. The most celebrated popular music phenomenon of his era, Presley had originally burst on the entertainment scene in January 1956 when he recorded his first album for RCA in their Nashville studios and he would have a succession of hits. Now, free from army duties, he was back where he left off- and a bigger attraction than ever.

Stories were circulating that he would do a short British tour culminating in several shows at the London Palladium. Elliman contacted Presley's manager Colonel Tom Parker, a former carnival barker, in Los Angeles and suggested playing the Theatre Royal whenever they were free. Louis estimated that a week with Elvis would pack the place.

'We would be interested in having Elvis, **if his** busy schedule permitted, Colonel,' said Elliman. 'What are your terms?'

'£10,000,' said Parker, removing the eight-inch Cuban cigar from between his clenched teeth. 'It's good value.'

'I'm afraid £10,000 a week would be beyond our budget, Colonel. We'd never justify that at the box office.'

'You've got me wrong, bud,' Parker exploded. 'Not £10,000 a week, £10,000 a performance!'

End of conversation. Negotiations also broke down for British appearances, unquestionably because of Parker's huge financial demands. Presley never did perform outside America in any event, with more than enough concert, movie and recording commitments to keep him busy at home.

In February 1961 a young Dublin comedian named Dave Allen made his Royal debut on a show called *Spring in the Air* and audiences liked his casual style of humour. A son of the managing editor of *The Irish Times*, Allen had made his first television appearance two years earlier on the BBC talent show *New Faces*, but by the time he came to Dublin he was still something on an unknown.

The author was working for the *Evening Mail* as show business correspondent at the time and wrote: 'A talented artiste, Allen seemed to be able to conjure laughs as easily as a magician can draw coloured silks from a hat. His jokes ranged from his wife's cooking to an engine driver at rest.'

It would be several years before Allen would perfect his lasting image on TV as he sat on a high bar stool facing his audience, smoking and occasionally sipping from a glass of what he always allowed people to assume was whiskey but in fact was merely ginger ale with ice. Allen, the first of the 'alternative' comedians so popular today, would often remember the Royal in Irish interviews.

'It was the Theatre Royal which gave me my first real break with home audiences,' he once told the *Irish Independent.*

Russ Conway, a hugely popular English pianist, played the Royal in June for a week and did very good business. Possessing a likeable personality almost to the point of shyness, Conway had spent the mid-1950s providing backing on EMI's Columbia record label for artistes on their roster, including Gracie Fields and Joan Regan, but by the time he came to Hawkins Street he was an established performer with several chart successes to his name. With a minimum of chat, he went into 'Side Saddle' and 'Roulette,' both self-penned,

Interestingly, Conway had one thing in common with Dave Allen. Both lost part of the fingers of their left hand. Questioned by an *Irish Press* reporter, Conway explained that it happened while using a bread slicer. Allen would give several versions of how his occurred, and became part of his act. They included: (a) putting the hand in his brother Joe's mouth when they were children and John biting it off, (b) self-inflicted to avoid National Service and (c) attacked and bitten by 'something evil' in a dark and haunted house. The most plausible reason was that he caught the hand in a machine cog while visiting his father in *The Irish Times.*

The husband and wife duo of Nina and Frederik were a popular Dutch singing act with their own series on British television, *Nina and Frederik at Home,* and albums in the charts when they played the Royal in September. Their repertoire consisted of a blend of folk music, calypsos and standards including 'Jamaica Farewell,' 'Mary's Boy Child,' 'Come Back Liza,' 'Little Donkey,' 'Listen to the Ocean' and their major hit, 'There's a Hole in the Bucket.'

Christmas Revels which opened in early December turned out to be the last festive show at the Royal. It was headlined by comedian Jack Cruise and starred the full company including the Dublin soprano Patricia Cahill. It was not Patricia's first time on the Royal but she remembers it well.

'My first appearance in public was on the Royal several years earlier, when I was 17,' she recalled. 'I had just left school and went with my mother for an audition as they were looking for singers and musicians and so on. I already had a job lined up in the ESB in Fleet Street but I thought it might be exciting to go for the audition and see how it worked out.

'How well I recall it. It was a big adventure. I sang 'The Fairy Tree,' my favourite song, and while the manager Phil Donohoe said it was lovely, it wouldn't be suitable for the theatre. He suggested I sing a well-known song called 'And This Is My

Singer Patricia Cahill and two friends

Beloved' from the show *Kismet*. I didn't know it at all so he asked me to come back in a week's time. I went off and bought the sheet music in Mays of Stephen's Green. I struggled with the song but eventually learned it off. When I went back for the second audition a week later I sang the song and Phil liked it. I was in the show.

'Funnily enough, I sang "The Fairy Tree" during the week and the audience loved it, so sometimes theatre managers don't really know what audiences want. I had many different plans in life but here I was getting a chance to sing in the famous Theatre Royal and I took it with both hands and I've been singing all over ever since. The Theatre Royal changed my life.

'I've sung at the London Palladium and the Royal Albert Hall and in the US as well as on BBC, ITV and RTÉ television but that first real break on the Royal was my biggest thrill. It was a magnificent theatre, a spectacular theatre. I'll always be grateful for getting the chance to sing there. I've always felt that there was no place like the Royal and the real tragedy was that it was pulled down. A shame.'

Now living in Marbella in southern Spain, Patricia is happily still performing all over the world including the US where she is billed as the 'Irish Nightingale'. She was delighted to hear from this writer and sent me some lovely photographs. Patricia is also busy recording albums. 'I'm not always in top form but I certainly do try to keep well,' she said. 'For day-to-day living it is essential to stay in good form. My diet is eating a bit of everything and not too much of anything – and lots of fresh air.'

Local artistes filled the Royal bills when *Christmas Revels* finished at the end of January. The next major visiting act was the popular English singer Adam Faith for one night in February. Faith would give up his singing career towards the end of the 1960s and became an actor, eventually moving into management and part owner of a television station, both of which made him a millionaire. He also became an established financial journalist with a national newspaper in the UK.

Pat Connell's Dixielanders on the Royal stage in June 1960

Back in February 1962, however, he was a major star on the pop scene. Here is how this writer reviewed the Royal show for the *Evening Mail*: 'The screams were too much for the fair-haired young man on the stage. He held up his hand and there was comparative silence. When he finished his first song, "What Do You Want?", the place went wild.

'The fair-haired young man was Terence Nelhams, alias Adam Faith and the place was the Theatre Royal in Dublin last night where his performance sent the many rioting, screaming teenagers into paroxysms of adoration. Adams jumped, waltzed, hopped and twisted around the stage as his fans screamed his every move, and when he bent down to kiss the heads of two girls in the front row, the Royal erupted. His. voice came through well but he often had the greatest difficulty in making himself heard amidst the crescendo of screams, applause and stamping which greeted every second or third bar.'

By now Louis Elliman was finding it hard to bring in international artistes, many of which were demanding excessively high salaries for their performances. Money was becoming increasingly scarce as well and the Royal management had to be careful in that respect. Overheads too were constantly rising.

Television was also providing strong competition when people could see all the top acts on the small screen in the comfort of their home, or at least going down to the local pub. Variety was also dying a slow death, with London theatres feeling the slump. What did not help either was a five-week strike in May/June, which also applied to the Gaiety and the Olympia, over a pay demand instructed by the unions.

Property values were also rising, especially for anything in the city centre. When Elliman talked to the Rank accountants in London, they advised him to close down the theatre and that they were going to sell out. It would be the end of a glorious, memorable era, and the climax to an iconic theatre. The final production would be fittingly called *Royale Finale*, beginning on Sunday 24 June 1962 and ending the following Saturday evening.

'It would end an era of only 26 years and nine months,' noted the historian Philip B. Ryan. 'But whereas the previous Theatre Royals had been rebuilt and loved by Dubliners for their own distinctive qualities, none more so than the last Royal which had helped to keep their spirits up during the dark, deprived days of the Emergency. Now the entire block was to be the site of high rise concrete and glass offices. The Royal, the Regal, Ostinelli's and the Kosmo bar in the comer were to disappear and be replaced by a monstrosity called Hawkins House.'

There was to be no reprieve for the Royal. The Rank Organisation had made the final irrevocable decision. On Louis Elliman's instructions, invitations went out to past performers, in whichever part of the world they were, to appear for one last time on a spectacular show on the final night.

It read: Dear ..... For the closing of the Theatre Royal, we are presenting a special show for the final night, on Saturday, 30 June 1962 at 8.00 pm and as you have been associated with the theatre for a great number of years, we would like to invite you to fill a star spot in this final performance. We would appreciate it if you would let us know as soon as possible if you will be able to accept this invitation. The rehearsals for this show will be on Saturday morning, the 30th instant. Kindest regards, yours sincerely, Phil Donohoe, Manager, Theatre Royal.

15

The Final Curtain

The gold-tasselled curtain came down on the Royal stage, followed by the heavy safety curtain covered with advertisements so familiar to regulars, on the evening of Saturday 30 June 1962 at 10.40. It was the last show but to the artistes on stage it was as important as if it had been opening night. They were nervous and they were anxious. Was everything in place? Were the sequences in the correct order? Even though they knew that the stage manager Billy Kelly would have made sure that all was well, behind it all there was worry and a great sadness.

Earlier in the evening, the final movie was *The Hands of Orlac*, a British-French horror production about a pianist who gets a hand transplant from a strange doctor, and finds he has the impulse to kill. The cast included Christopher Lee, Mel Ferrer, Donald Wolfit and Donald Pleasance.

'The last variety show of all at the Theatre Royal was far from being the greatest,' said the *Evening Herald*, 'but it was throat-catching and heart-tugging as a host of familiar performers trooped onto the stage, briefly did their spot and then bid farewell to Jimmy Campbell and the orchestra, and the vast audience.

'Peggy Dell sang "A Little Sprig of Shamrock" which she first sang 26 years ago when vocalist with the Roy Fox Orchestra in Britain in the 1930s, while Sean Mooney sang "Lili Marlene" which brought

THEATRE ROYAL, DUBLIN
SATURDAY, 30th JUNE, 1962, at 8 p.m.
"ROYALE FINALE"

1.	"PROLOGUE"	Jimmy Campbell and the Theatre Royal Orchestra.
2.	"SHOW BUSINESS" ...	Frankie Blowers, Peggy Dell, Royalettes, Jimmy Campbell Singers.
3.	"TREBLE TROUBLE" ...	Cecil Sheridan, Mickser Reid, John Molloy, Derry O'Donovan.
4.	"MUSICAL COCKTAIL." ...	Jimmy Campbell Singers.
5.	"A ROYAL OCCASION " ...	Cecil Sheridan and John Molloy.
6.	ENSEMBLE	Alice Dalgarno, Babs de Monte, Royalettes, Cora Cadwell Dancers and the Jimmy Campbell Singers.

INTERVAL:

"ROYAL CABARET"
OUR GUESTS :

Frankie Blowers	Edmund Browne	Jack Cruise
Paddy Crosbie	Danny Cummins	Ursula Doyle
Val Fitzpatrick	Pauline Forbes	Vernon Hayden
Frank Howard	Josef Locke	Sean Mooney
Jimmy O'Dea	Harry O'Donovan	Noel Purcell
Milo O'Shea		

Mickser Reid   Cecil Sheridan
Choreography and Design : Alice Dalgarno and Babs De Monte
The Jimmy Campbell Singers :
Kay Condron   Denis Claxton   Claire Kelleher   Bill Golding   Dolores Murphy
The Royalettes
JIMMY CAMPBELL and the THEATRE ROYAL ORCHESTRA
TOMMY DANDO

Programme for the final night, 30 June 1962

back memories of the 1940s. Danny Cummins bounced like a ball and danced almost as nimble as Fred Astaire.

'Noel Purcell impersonated a park attendant – another act that stirred the memory. Cecil Sheridan composed a song specially for the occasion while Jack Cruise and Pauline Forbes appeared as a pair of ever-shy newly weds.

'The Royalettes with Alice Dalgarno and Babs de Monte danced as if it were a first night before a long run and Josef Locke sang "Goodbye" from *The White Horse Inn*. There were Frankie Blowers singing "Brother Can You Spare a Dime" and being cheered to the rafters, Val Fitzpatrick with his guitar, comics Frankie Howard and Milo O'Shea, John Molloy "feeding" funny men Cecil Sheridan and Mickser Reid while the Jimmy Campbell singers consisted of Kay Condron, Denis Claxton, Clare Kelleher, Bill Golding and Dolores Murphy.

'Then there were tenor Edmund Browne, the Cora Cadwell troupe of young Irish dancers, versatile Derry O'Donovan and Tommy Dando playing the organ. Also Jimmy O'Dea, coming on stage from the Gaiety as himself and not as his character Biddy Mulligan, the Pride of the Coombe. O'Dea told us that the Royal would have closed two years earlier were it not for the intervention of Louis Elliman.'

Jimmy gave a touching valediction from the centre of the stage. 'I was asked to close the Empire Theatre in Belfast, and now I'm asked to close the Royal,' he told the audience, his voice choking with emotion and sadness in his eyes. 'I hope this won't become a habit, although I'm told that 160 variety theatres have closed in Britain. It was said that this was a wonderful theatre but too big. Bob Hope called it 'a magnificent garage.'

'This has been a great place where a great many people came to see a few give them entertainment. Louis Elliman kept it going for the past two years under great difficulties. Some of the Royal people are coming over to what is now my home, the Gaiety, but we are all sad to see the end of this great theatre. I suppose all theatre springs from Greek drama but when I talked to one of the ushers tonight about the closing, the word he used wasn't Greek. It might have come from *Lady Chatterley's Lover...'*

The full significance of the occasion came when Phil Donohoe, the theatre manager, introduced some of the people audiences never see – the stage manager, the chief electrician, the wardrobe mistress, the scene painter, the man who makes the props. Nor was the front-of-house staff forgotten. There were the chief usher, the girl in the pay-box, the girl who sells the sweets.

The Royal audience on the theatre's final night

Then, on a crowded stage with the audience pressing right up to grasp the hands of the performers, Jimmy Campbell announced the last song that would ever be heard in the Royal. The orchestra struck up the anthem of the entertainment world 'There's No Business Like Show Business' followed by 'Auld Lang Syne', with everybody joining in. The gold-tinselled curtain rose and fell half a dozen times and finally the heavy safety curtain descended for the last time. The audience filed out and there was a little rock 'n' roll in Hawkins Street. The famous Theatre Royal was finally dead.

There was a small party after the show, with more than a few tears shed. Louis Elliman, the driving force behind the Royal for 26 years, gave the final order: 'Let there be a fitting wake. Let the staff and the artistes drink the bars dry.'

Noel Purcell, who had first appeared on the Royal stage in 1939, said: 'I'm going to miss this old theatre terribly, believe me. There's never been anything quite like the Royal and there never will be either. But there you go – another mad move by developers out to make a buck. I ask you, where will it all end? God only knows.'

Babs de Monte, the principal dancer and choreographer with the Royalettes, commented: 'The closing of this beautiful theatre is a terrible, terrible disaster and it has not quite sunk in yet. A city, any city, needs a variety stage and now they are taking the Royal away from us. Without variety, a city is dead.'

Comedian Jack Cruise said: 'It might have been better had there been a sudden death, like the Cork Opera House or the Abbey. Always there was the hope that the patient would be revived but it was not to be. The patient has passed out. It's a shame to think it's all coming down. Sadly, now it is time to pack up and go.'

The orchestra leader, Jimmy Campbell, not looking anything like his cheery self of the past, commented: 'The closing of this famous theatre is the saddest thing I can recall in my entire career in the entertainment business going back to when I was 18 at the old Scala

Cinema in South Shiels. It's supposed to be all in the name of progress. I wonder if that should be greed?'

Everybody found it quite hard to believe that the Royal days were finally over. 'A lovely theatre struck down in the prime of life,' lamented Danny Hyland, an electrician at the Royal for 40 years. 'I'm now looking forward to a few weeks holidays and then – I will just trust in God for a new job.'

Billy Kelly, the stage manager, lamented: 'What a great shame that this famous theatre is having to close. A sad night indeed, but I do feel that it could have been given a longer life had it been better supported. Yes, we had full houses particularly on Sunday nights, and Fridays and Saturdays too, but some of the weekday houses were not full. But there you go. Whichever way you look at it, it's the end of the Theatre Royal.'

'It was a fond farewell that thousands paid to Dublin's Theatre Royal last night,' said the *Sunday Review*. 'But for the artistes, and the last full house to which they played, it was a sad parting. Nevertheless, the motto of show biz, that the show must go on, was maintained until the very last curtain call.

'Then, artistes, staff and friends of this famous old theatre joined a private party to have a farewell drink to an old friend, and a toast to the future, before they left to go their separate ways. The Royal's next door neighbour, the Regal Cinema, also closed last night, bringing to an end more than a century of the entertainment business in Hawkins Street.'

A separate news report from the *Evening Herald* review read: 'The final curtain descended amid the cheers of a nostalgic, emotional audience on a theatre which had become as much a part of Dublin life as Nelson's Pillar. There was something awfully final about the dimming of the lights, the closing of the great glass doors, the taking from its peg in the cloakroom the last solitary hat. This was the end.'

Jimmy Campbell, in bow-tie, Cecil Sheridan, centre with cap, and Mickser Reid, bottom right, with staff members outside the stage door on closing night of 30 June 1962

John Collins, the prop artist, took the *Herald* reporter on a last sentimental journey to his workshop where he painted palaces, castles, barns, streets, cars, planes and landscapes for many of the theatre's shows. 'It's really sad and depressing that we won't see any of this again,' he said, his voice choking with emotion. 'But there you go. You live with the good times and you live with the bad times. That's life, I suppose.'

With the closure of the Royal, an historic bar licence also ended. It was created by the Letters Patent of Queen Victoria and issued in 1900 for the convenience of the Lord Lieutenant and of army officers to enable them to entertain their friends and, more often than not, the ladies of the chorus after the show. At the time there were only about five such licences in existence, including the Gaiety in Dublin and Covent Garden Opera House in London, now known as the Royal Opera House.

With the final demolition squads ready to arrive inside a week, a three-day auction of 1,400 lots was conducted by the Dublin firm of Battersbys for the sale of equipment, fittings, foyer cards, posters and other items of memorabilia. The seats in the parterre had been unscrewed from their mounts and stacked in heaps. The stage was stripped bare of the massive curtains and painted backdrops, and for all the world the doomed theatre, looking desolate and forlorn, had the appearance as though a bomb had hit it.

The top sale was for the old Compton organ, in front of which had sat the legendary Tommy Dando for over ten years and installed originally when the 'new' Royal opened in September 1935 at a cost of £24,000. Suggested opening bids of £1,000 and £500 were not forthcoming and bidding eventually opened at £200, with a final offer of £400 made by a representative of a Belfast organ company, with the buyer saying the organ would be used 'for spare parts'.

Josef Locke, the Derry tenor and a popular performer with Royal followers, was there too, wandering between several pianos lined up for inspection on the stage and strumming the keys while, appropriately enough, humming his hit song 'Goodbye' from the show, *The White Horse Inn*. Among the pianos was the baby grand from the room of the orchestra leader Jimmy Campbell and which went for £95. Another grand piano from the orchestra pit fetched £130.

Locke said he had just bought 300 seats at 27 shillings each and, while declining to say what exactly he would do with them, commented: 'Let's just say for the moment they are a good investment.'

The wrecking ball was brought in shortly after the auction and the famous old theatre, an iconic building and part of the folk memory of the city, was just a heap of rubble inside three short weeks. One of the workers on the site was Mickser Reid, the diminutive comic who had brought such laughter to audiences over the years. He was wearing a black beret, grey jumper, his black trousers rolled up almost to his knees, and rubber boots.

Pulling on his Woodbine cigarette, he told an *Evening Herald* reporter: 'It's funny, y'know. I was on the old stage here so many times it almost became my home, and here I am back as the tea boy. They were great days on the Royal, I can tell you, and we had our laughs. I'm certainly going to miss the crack and the many friendships I made, friendships that will last forever. Maybe someday I'll sit down and write the Theatre Royal story and tell about all the famous stars, home and international, who trod its boards. Now that would be a story, eh?'

Mickser Reid, left, and Cecil Sheridan were always good for a laugh

Sadly, Mickser never got around to telling that story. He passed away in September 1968 and there was a large attendance at his funeral. 'Mickser Reid left here yesterday, and we won't see him, or anyone quite like him, ever again,' wrote Adrian MacLoughlin in the *Evening Press.*

'It's hard to define a 'character' but it is almost impossible to define the almost unique bond of affection that existed between this funny, bouncy little man and his native city. Almost as impossible to define Mickser's personal stage touch, his poignant appeal as a clown. Mickser Reid knew how to make the kids' sides ache and he knew how to make their parents feel like kids again.

'He belonged to the tinselled fairyland that usually only comes once a year, with the turkey and the plum pudding and the sequined cards and the goodwill. He was as legendary as Santa Claus. When the bulldozers moved in to tear down the mighty Theatre Royal and give the old city a heart plant it didn't want, Mickser was a silent figure from the old days, working as a nipper on site. One more change in a clown's adaptable life.'

Some of the artistes moved to the Gaiety including the Royalettes. Louis Elliman was re-located to new offices around the corner in

Poolbeg Street where he would sustain the business of Odeon Ireland and run the affairs of 15 cinemas. What caused the Royal's closure? 'We never lost money but we saw the red light at the end of 1960,' Elliman said in an interview.

'Had we carried on, we would have been in trouble. As it was, the return on investment was not high enough. Some stars were costing us up to £2,500 for a week. Apart from that, too, we just couldn't get enough worthwhile films towards the end. Yes, we had a few good ones such as *The Magnificent Seven,* but generally we had to make do with lesser ones. Even for those closing weeks we couldn't get a film to remember, unlike earlier years when we had many good ones.'

There were also several factors to be brought into consideration for the cause of the closure. The building was ripe for developers as it was in a prime location in the centre of the city and would attract a very good price at a time when property values were rising sharply. Nor did the arrival of Telefís Éireann and its novelty value help the situation. In addition, the population of Dublin was changing, with families moving out of town to housing estates.

Another important factor was that the entertainment scene was changing fast. It was much the same in Britain. Many of the big theatres there were feeling the squeeze and from the late 1950s, one after the other closed their doors. In Ireland there was another phenomenon at the time, the booming showband scene which was attracting not only the young but the young-at-heart to ballrooms in Dublin and around the country.

There was talk of Telefís Éireann taking over the Royal and using it for studio space but it never happened and the studios would move out to suburban Donnybrook and be called RTÉ. Inside a few short years a grey 12-storey office block would stand in place of the grand old theatre. Hawkins House is today the headquarters of the Department of Health.

Hawkins House, built on the site of the Royal in 1962, now the Department of Health

Designed by the English architect Sir Thomas Bennett, Hawkins House has for a long time now been the subject of controversy and has been called everything from 'the ugliest building in Dublin,' 'an eyesore,' and 'a monstrosity,' to 'a piece of sub-standard lego architecture' and in the eyes of one letter writer to a Dublin newspaper, 'a bloody hideous yoke.'

Voted by environmentalists in 1998 as 'the worst building in Dublin,' discussions were opened by the Fianna Fáil/Progressive Democrats government following mounting pressure to finally pull it down and rebuild it to modern standards as the 2000s came in, but nothing came of it. However in July 2016 the Office of Public Works announced that Hawkins House would be demolished and replaced with an 'environmentally sustainable new office quarter.'

Looking back to over half a century, Frank McDonald, environmental correspondent of *The Irish Times*, said: 'Some people said that television had killed off the Theatre Royal but this could not have been true as Telefís Éireann was only a few months old at the time.'

One of the old Royal troupers not conned by this nonsense was the comedian Cecil Sheridan. He saw all too clearly why J. Arthur Rank was planning to destroy Dublin's last great variety theatre. In his dressing room on the night of the last show, he said: 'No, it's not television that's done it. It was a matter of how much money you can make out of a square foot of property. Greed, greed, greed.'

'If only the Royal had survived, it would have made a most splendid venue for rock concerts. But the grisly business of maximising the site got underway and the building was obliterated. Not only did we lose the Royal but the site was defaced by Hawkins House, 122,000 square feet of office space encased in a formless slab block with a curtain-walled biscuit tin on either side.

'It's easily the most monstrous pile of architectural rubbish ever built in Dublin. Not surprisingly, when faced with the finished product, those who had held out such high hopes for the architect were sheepishly silent. Not only was the building a horror show but it ruined several vistas, notably the view of Trinity College from the top of Dawson Street. Personally I'm convinced that one of the reasons we have such a poor health service is that it's run by this sick building.'

Louis Elliman, the one-time apprentice chemist in his father's pharmacy in South Richmond Street who had brought the world's top entertainment to Dublin, died in 1965 at the age of 59. Elliman had kept the theatre open during the dark days of World War II when he had to depend on local talent, and very successfully too.

Micheál MacLiammóir, the actor who knew the Royal stage very well, said at the impresario's funeral: 'Louis was very good to us all, and is to be remembered in terms of brotherhood. He had the theatre in his blood and he was a friend to us all.' MacLiammóir's partner Hilton Edwards, describing Elliman as Ireland's Mr Show Business, said: 'I have known Louis for 25 years and this city is all the poorer without him.' Some 50 years on, Eddie Byrne's daughter Susan says: 'Louis Elliman and the family really kept the whole thing going. They were a huge part of the Theatre Royal. There is no doubt about that.'

All that is left of the old Theatre Royal today are the memories. Then again, in many ways, the Royal still stands, but is it a mirage? Maybe the ghosts of the great entertainers are still passing through, and climbing those familiar stairs to the dressing rooms. Who knows? It was Cecil Sheridan who described the Royal as 'a theatre with a big heart, a big capacity and big audiences.' That could well stand as its epitaph.

Select Bibliography

Books

Andrews, Eamonn. *This Is My Life.* Macdonald, London, 1963.

Andrews, Eamonn and Grainne. *For Ever and Ever.* Grafton Books, London, 1989.

Balfe, Brendan. *Radio Man*, Gill and Macmillan. Dublin, 2007.

Brennan, Steve and O'Neill, Bernadette. *Emeralds in Tinseltown,* Appletree Press. Belfast, 2007.

Broderick, Marian. *Wild Irish Women*, O'Brien Press. Dublin, 2012.

Carty, Ciaran. *Intimacy with Strangers.* Lilliput Press. Dublin, 2013.

Doonican, Val. *The Special Years*, Elm Tree Books, London, 1980.

Keenan, Jim. *Dublin Cinemas*, Picture House Publications, Dublin, 2005.

McBride, Stephaine, Flynn, Roddy. *Here's Looking at You, Kid.* Wolfhound Press, Dublin, 1996.

McDonald, Frank. *The Destruction of Dublin.* Gill and Macmillan, Dublin, 1985.

Molloy, J Fitzgerald. *The Life and Adventures of Peg Woffington,* Hurst and Blackett, London, 1884.

Purcell, Deidre. *Follow Me Down to Dublin*, Hodder Headline Ireland, Dublin, 2007.

Ryan, Philip B. *Jimmy O'Dea, The Pride of the Coombe*, Poolbeg Press, Dublin, 1990.

Ryan, Philip B. *Noel Purcell, a Biography*, Poolbeg Press, Dublin, 1992.

Ryan, Philip B. *The Lost Theatres of Dublin*, Badger Press, Wiltshire, 1998.

Taub, Michael, *Jack Doyle, The Gorgeous Gael*, Lilliput Press, Dublin, 2007

Warren, Doug. *James Cagney, The Authorised Biography*, Robson Books, London, 1983.

Newspapers and Periodicals

Irish Press

Evening Press

Sunday Press

Select Bibliography

Evening Herald

Evening Mail

Sunday Independent

Irish Independent

Irish Times

Sunday Review

Evening Post

Freeman's Journal

Dramatic Argus

Daily Mirror

Guardian

New York Times

Sunday Times

Index

Index